Technology and Toil
in Nineteenth Century Britain

Documents Edited by
Maxine Berg

CSE Books
55 Mount Pleasant
London WC1X 0AE

Humanities Press Inc.
Atlantic Highlands,
New Jersey 07716

Technology and Toil in Nineteenth Century Britain, a CSE
book, was first published by CSE Books , 55 Mount
Pleasant, London WC1X 0AE in January 1979.
And in the USA by Humanities Press Inc., Atlantic
Highlands, New Jersey 07716.

British Library Cataloguing in Publication Data
Berg, Maxine
   Technology and toil in nineteenth century Britain
   338' .0941 HC 255

  ISBN Hb 0 906336 02 3
      Pb 0 906336 03 1

Co-ordinating Editor Tim Putnam
Designed by An Dekker, 232 Mare Street, London E8
Typeset by Calverts North Star Press (TU) Ltd., 55 Mount
Pleasant, London WC1
Printed by A. Wheaton & Co. Ltd., Exeter

For my grandfather, Emil Berg who came from Sweden to Canada in 1911 to work on the land and in the towns as farm-hand, homesteader, miner, navvy, and carpenter.

Table of Illustrations

A Guide to this Book

Technology and Toil draws together over fifty accounts of the organization of work in nineteenth century Britain. Each of the selections has its own interest, and is separately introduced so as to be directly accessible to the reader. The collection as a whole is organised to aid an evaluation of the general analyses of work and technology in industrialization left by Babbage, Ure, Owen and Marx. The Introduction outlines the major features of these analyses and indicates how the documents selected exemplify or qualify them. The Introduction also offers a re-interpretation of the complex structure of the labour process as it developed in Britain during the nineteenth century, making the book a self-contained reader for the study of British industrialization.

The arrangement of the documents into three broad periods corresponds with the phases outlined in the Introduction, and chapters within each major section focus on the essential themes of division of labour, skill and capitalist management; the response to machinery in agriculture, the trades and women's work; automatic machinery *versus* skill hierarchies; mechanization and the trades; tradesmen, heavy industry and the new technology; the emergence of general labour; and the sweating system and working women. Other themes, such as the history of particular industries or of women's position in work in different periods, may be easily followed through the book from the short document titles. Full titles and sources of all the selections are listed separately, by author, for further reference, and the Introduction is followed by a number of suggestions for further reading. The original spellings and styles of the sources have been followed.

This book is one of a series of studies initiated by the Conference of Socialist Economists, with the aim of breaking down the separation between social and technical analyses of the labour process. General issues are surveyed in *The Labour Process and Class Strategies*, ed. Guttmann and Putnam, Stage 1, London, 1976. Studies of particular industries include *A Workers Enquiry Into the Motor Industry*, Institute of Workers Control Motors Group, CSE Books, 1979.

Tim Putnam
Co-ordinating Editor

Contents

Part II: Mid-Victorian Capitalism 105

Chapter 3. Automation and Skill Hierarchies 107

Chapter 4. Mechanization and the Trades 127

Part III: Climacteric or Resolution? 167

Chapter 5. Tradesmen, Heavy Industry and the New Technology 169

Chapter 6. General Labour 207

Chapter 7. The Sweating System and Working Women 225

Preface

The theme of this edition of documents is work and technical change in nineteenth century British industry. The collection has two purposes. The first is to draw attention to the specific details of production processes and work. An understanding of the changes that have taken place in the techniques of production must be based on knowledge of the kinds of combinations of physical labour, skill, time, machines and management at work within any industrial process. Secondly, these documents suggest some of the possibilities which existed for capitalists to increase their domination over these processes, and those for workers to resist encroachments on their own arenas of control. Finally, this collection shows how the technical transformations in British industrialization were seen by workers, capitalists, intellectuals and popular journalists. It shows how they used these perceptions to support their analyses of the changing division of labour, the introduction of machinery, the speed-up of work and the redefinition and displacement of skill. This consciousness of the immediate social implications of the new technologies also influenced the measures taken by workers to deal with their situations in the work place.

The collection of these documents grew out of discussions on the labour process started by a planning committee of the Conference of Socialist Economists in early 1976. These discussions generated interest in the historical development of the capitalist labour process, and in the workplace struggles of capitalists and workers. It was suggested then that a collection of documents illustrating struggles around the labour process in nineteenth century Britain would contribute to our understanding of Marx's own formulations on the transition between the phase of manufacture and that of modern industry.

Discussions on the conference committee soon led some of us to start a separate labour process historians' group. This group came together to reconsider a historiography which had hitherto given little close consideration to relations between conditions of work and class consciousness. Partly this was the result of the healthy attempts of social historians to look more broadly at the formation of class consciousness in culture, political organization and ideology. For their part, economic historians had long restricted themselves to the bleak terrain of technology and capitalist management. The consequence of this split in the interests of social and economic historians was a critical gap in history. Historians had given little consideration to the role of labour and workplace resistance within production processes. Production processes themselves, as a result, were perceived as static and purely objective factors. Economic historians observed the manifestations of technical progress. Social historians examined their implications for the standard of living and social-cultural circumstances of the working class. There was little awareness of the struggle deep at the very technical foundations of economy and society. To remedy this the historians' group engaged in a wide-ranging discussion of factors which historically had impinged on the work place and the discipline of labour. The topics raised included the state and education, the organisation of social knowledge, the location of industry and the changing definitions of skill, the sexual division of labour and the machine.

On the inspiration of both these discussions and my own research, I later collected together the historical documents presented here. This collection is now addressed to all those interested in history as a plea for the integration of economic and social history. It is also addressed to those who, in studying the social sciences as well as trade union and management strategies, have so recently rediscovered the labour process.

The collection demonstrates that a perception of many of the problems of the labour process has long been with us. The task of the historian and social scientist is to define the contextual framework for these nineteenth century commentaries on issues which also seem so immediate to us today. They should not be regarded, however as precursors to Marx, Taylor, Ford or more recent observers. They relate instead to the intellectual contexts, class forces and levels of economic development particular to a time and place. These historical conditions must direct the meaning we give to the views expressed in the collection. Limitations of space, however, have prevented the inclusion of documents relating to many of the important and widely ranging aspects of economic and social change which ultimately affect the organization of work and forms of workers' resistance, such as the internationalization of capital, the state, forms of social planning and ideology. The collection is not, therefore, illustrative of aspects of the 'labour process' writ large, but rather of technical and social change particular to the work place. The reader will find recent literature emphasizing this contextual framework.[1]

I would like to thank Robin Murray, Tim Putnam and Robbie Guttman for the interest they showed in this project in its formative stages. I benefited greatly from the discussion in the labour process historians' group meetings and would like to thank those who participated regularly and those who came to speak to us. Three of us in that group also wrote a general conference paper on 'The Labour Process in History'. I am especially grateful to Mike Sonenscher and Keith McClelland for many stimulating discussions during the time we wrote this conference paper and afterwards. I have drawn on sections of this paper in writing the introduction to this collection.

I would also like to thank Barbara Taylor for contributing 'The Well Paid Artizan and the Half Starved Labourer', 'The Reply of the Journeyman Bookbinders', 'The Women's Page' and 'To the Straw Bonnet Makers'; Jon Archer for 'An Address to the Labourers on the Subject of Destroying Machinery'; and 'Plain Sense and Reason'; Jonathan Zeitlin for Paul de Rousier's *The Labour Question in Great Britain*, and Sir Eric Roll for permission to reprint selections from chapter two of his *An Early Experiment in Industrial Engineering*. Tim Putnam, An Dekker, and Jane Kenrick provided helpful editorial advice, and Mark Robertson came to my rescue and read the proofs which arrived at a time when I was under the heavy pressure of a new teaching job.

Maxine Berg,
September 1978.

Introduction

The history of work organization and of technical change during the period of Britain's industrialization and consolidation involves both the subordination of labour to capital and labour's constant resistance to this process. Marx's analysis of the 'labour process' has captured more effectively than any other the immense range of forms of capitalist subordination and of working class struggle which lie at the basis of any change in technology and work organization. In analyzing the stages of development of the labour process during industrialization, Marx distinguished phases of co-operation, manufacture, and machinofacture (or modern industry), on the basis of the domination of particular types of technology and forms of control over labour.

In addition to describing the technical and social characteristics of each of these phases, Marx explained transformations in the labour process by reference to wider economic pressures. The basic dynamic of capitalism was the drive to increase surplus value, and changes in the labour process were connected with a shift in the dominant form of the extraction of surplus value from 'absolute' to 'relative'. Absolute surplus value was increased by coercing the workforce to produce more with the same techniques by working harder for longer hours, or by employing a larger workforce. Relative surplus value could be increased only by gains in productivity, through the introduction of new methods of working and machinery, the application of science and technology, a mobile labour force based on a reserve army of labour, and large-scale production. Marx considered the production of relative surplus value to be the most revolutionary and complete form of the production of surplus value, as it involved the development of methods for reducing necessary labour time relative to surplus labour time, and increased the turnover time of capital by exploiting machinery to raise the pace of production. Further, the workers' own surplus product could now become embodied in machinery which controlled the conditions of work.

The transition from the phase of manufacture to that of modern industry was bound up, for Marx, with a shift in the dominant mode of raising surplus value. But the connection should not be understood in a simple chronological form, identifying manufacture with the raising of absolute surplus value and modern industry with the raising of relative surplus value. For in modern industry ways would be sought for raising both relative and absolute surplus value. A labour process controlled by machinery could be both more productive *and* more intense, but the greater, and potentially limitless, possibilities were for the generation of relative surplus value, not absolute, which was limited by human endurance. Modern industry was thus to be distinguished from manufacture not in a temporal framework but by its characteristic technology and means for controlling the production process. As the CSE Brighton Labour Process Group state:

> In manufacture (a) each worker or group of workers still has some degree of control over the content, speed, intensity, rhythm etc. of work. And (b) the integration, the balancing or harmonizing of the collective work is still empirical. It is still worked out on the basis of observation of actual work rather than calculated beforehand on the basis of knowledge of the machine function.[2]

Under modern industry, in contrast, production is collective, large-scale and machine based:

> . . .capital can appropriate to itself all the functions of specification, organization and control, and perform them independently of labour. It can, therefore, impose its objectives on the labour process and so that labour, even when it is brought into association with the conditions of labour, does so in an antagonistic relation. Labour serves the machine and not the machine labour.[3]

Marx, in setting out manufacture and modern industry as phases of the capitalist labour process was using a broad sweep of history to illustrate the immanent tendencies of the capitalist mode of production. The phases delineated by Marx formed a part of his model of capitalist development. The phases of manufacture and modern industry were abstractions, and were not, therefore, meant to sum up any particular historical period.

The historian's difficulties in ascribing Marx's phases to any period of economic development are, therefore, understandable. Even if we concentrate on Britain's model industrialization, it is obvious that the characteristics Marx ascribed to any one phase only emerged historically over a very long time, and that several of the characteristics of older phases remained intact, merely adapting themselves to new economic and technical contexts. It may legitimately be argued that several of the characteristics of modern industry came to dominate the British economy by the late nineteenth century. But it must also be recognized that the process of division of labour, definition of skills and the breakdown of skill continued to characterize industry throughout the nineteenth century. Skill, moreover, dominated not just discussion of the division of labour, but also of the machine and of science. Neither can the introduction of the machine be considered outside the questions of effective management, both of labour and of the works which had long been the traditional means of raising absolute surplus value. Control of the production process was sought through order, precision and measurement. The scientific technique and the machine were introduced not just for the effect they had on productivity, but because they embodied these features of control.

Marx's model of the capitalist labour process can help us to understand the real economic and social development of modern Britain. But as with all models, it is an explanatory device which Marx illustrated by historical example, and applied to the explanation of historical situations. It is not meant to be a description of any particular history. The historian seeking empirical examples of the characteristics of modern industry can make the obvious point that in the British economy at least these developed unevenly and cannot strictly be said to have been widespread until late in the nineteenth century—that is, long after Marx set them down in *Capital*. But in pointing this out the historian has not said anything about Marx's concept of modern industry. In order to do so, he must also stress that the tendencies of mechanization and scientific control, and also the consciousness of their implications were there from early in the century. Though techniques in many industries were still traditional, labour intensive, and small in scale in the mid-Victorian British economy, the tendencies and future face of production were widely apparent. Vital elements of the economy had been transformed. It was these that set the pace, determined the markets for, and rationalized the organization for the whole. Marx was abstracting from these, the tendencies of capitalism, to create his model of modern industry. Certainly, in reality continuing symbiotic relations between old and new techniques provided a cushion for the novelty, adaptation or death of production processes. Whatever the result, the context was always one of struggle. In the work place, change or even lack of change meant interaction with a labouring class with its limits, its claims, and its own bids for the control of the personal and working lives of its members.

These documents illustrate the conscious reflection of the intellectual, journalist, industrialist or worker on several of the technical and organizational changes affecting the character of work processes in the nineteenth century. They illustrate the economic implications of technical or organizational change for cutting production costs or raising profits. But beyond this they illustrate the ultimate economic implications for labour—the effect on employment, skill and control, and workers' struggles to retain, reclaim or make new demands on these domains. The documents, arranged chronologically, emphasize the continuing importance throughout the nineteenth century of theories of mechanization, skill, speed, the length of the work day, and shopfloor management over a range of industries during Britain's industrial revolution. The documents have been chosen on the basis that they are not widely available to the general reader. Selections from obvious contemporary sources such as Ricardo's chapter on machinery, Engels' *Condition of the Working Class in England* and Marx's *Capital* are not therefore included. A bibliography of more common material is included on page 19.

Workshop, Factory and Industrialization

The first factories appeared in the context of a thriving market-orientated industrial sector which grew up rapidly in the seventeenth and eighteenth centuries. Printmaking, ironware, tobacco growing, linen and woollen manufacture, lace and stocking manufacture were all thriving country industries. Most grew up outside the context of the urban craft structure. They were based in the first instance on projects and patents, but soon acquired their own impetus.[4] The work processes of these industries also acquired their own distinct form. The celebrated woollen manufacture of West Yorkshire was based not only on the domestic unit but on large-scale workshops.[5] These workshops became the pioneering factories. As such they constituted exercise in the organization of labour rather than any change in actual mechanical processes. The jenny shops, hand-loom weaving sheds, glass and paper factories, early machine works and foundries were all premised on the division of labour, standardization and the employment of as much unskilled labour as possible. These fundamental organizing principles of the factory became widely established in the last years of the eighteenth century, not only in textiles, but in other key areas of industry.[6] By the 1790s when the Soho Foundry of Boulton and Watt was reorganized, its owners created formal structures based on the breakdown of each productive process into a long series of minor operations. This reorganization was recorded in their records at the time with a detail depicting management consciousness of gains to be made from the intensive application of job specification and order in the works (see page 27).[7] Order, job specification and division of labour had, by the end of the eighteenth century, been combined to the extent of creating assembly-line production. Samuel Bentham first applied this combination to the manufacture of ships' biscuits for the Navy, and his techniques were soon extended to the private sector in the machine shops of Nasmyth and Maudslay.[8] Techniques and principles of organization, discipline, order and factory arrangement were developed to a high degree in state production. The royal factories in Russia organized by Samuel Bentham, the Spanish royal textile works, the French royal glassworks, the Prussian armaments and the Woolwich Arsenal were all able to impose strict labour discipline and experiment with new forms of organization.[9]

The emergence of the factory, though based on the breakdown of skills and the division of labour, would not have been possible without an existing foundation of engineering, metalworking and metal-extracting skills. The metals in demand for building materials and for the machinery of the new factories were dependent on traditional mining skills and the newer skill and effort tasks of the puddler. The early Industrial Revolution appeared, therefore, to be a double-edged process. On the one hand skilled labour was displaced through factory organization and mechanization. On the other hand there were greater demands for both labour and skills in order to create the capital goods needed by the factory system. In time, however, these skills too were displaced. The all round crafts of the millwright and Cornish engineer disappeared, and were replaced by new, more highly specialized workers.[10] A new engineering and capital goods industry had grown up in the wake of the factory system. This industry soon acquired a large and specialized work force and its own product market based on home and international trade. The immediate result of the creation of this new capital goods sector was conflict with final goods producers such as textile and metal goods manufacturers. This conflict was on the surface one over trade, that is the question of whether a still scarce supply of capital goods should be sold to home or to foreign manufacturers. At a deeper level it was a conflict over the ownership and control of engineering skills, for the mobility not just of the capital goods produced, but of the producers themselves, that is, the engineering workers was restricted. These issues of skill and the capital goods sector were vividly depicted in the Export of Machinery and Emigration of Artisans Debates in 1824 and 1841 (see page 36,40).

The control and cheapening of the production process through the division of labour and the breakdown of skills affected factory, workshop and individual craft. The basis of this was theorized by the early 1830s by Charles Babbage who applied the Smithian principle of the division of labour to the microscopic analysis of workshop practice. His analysis generated far-reaching plans for cheapening the individual parts of any production process and precisely measuring the time and energy expended in all operations involved (see page 41).

The discipline and division of labour which had provided the rationale for the first factories also provided the basis for the mechanization that soon overturned the traditional tools and techniques of workshop and factory. Mechanized factories placed new demands on the labour market. Early factory recruits were not drawn from the original craft workers, but from landless agricultural labourers and domestic servants, and a large number of women and children.[11] These cheap sources of labour were indispensable for the first steps of mechanization. Country mills such as those of the Gregs, Ashworth, Drinkwater and Dales drew on indentured child, vagrant and family labour. These entrepreneurs made attempts to stabilize labour turnover through long contracts, and to discipline labour through autocratic mill communities.[12] These techniques of labour management were publicized by Robert Owen who developed them into a combined system of philanthropy and labour discipline (see page 62).[13] This consciousness of techniques for managing labour went with views on the management of the production process in general. Good order, accounting and measurement attracted the attention of George Dodd when he visited a copper and lead factory in London, and was the foundation of James Montgomery's advice on the makings of a successful cotton mill (see page 58).

The initial mechanization of the factory had involved the use of higher proportions of capital to labour. But this was later complemented by the drawing in of large reserves of labour, as the factories expanded on the basis of their existing technology. The introduction of machinery was achieved by a long period of complimentary use of domestic and factory labour. This both acted to cut the costs of full mechanization, and to offset the effects of cyclical fluctuations by expanding the employment of domestic labour in periods of expansion and retrenching on this in recession. The existence of large groups of unemployed and underemployed domestic labour thereby coincided with phases of mechanization. The situation provoked extensive struggle in the early nineteenth century between the hand and mechanized branches of many industries. The struggle between artisan and factory was also transmitted into the factory as a struggle between skills and machines. By the 1830s Andrew Ure could explicitly represent the factory system and the machine as a method of disciplining labour and dispensing with particularly difficult groups of skilled workers (see page 65). The response of workers in the handicraft textile sector, the London trades, the engineering and light metal industries, and the factories was militant and widespread. Workers based their struggles simultaneously on the length of the working day, dilution of skills, falling piece rates and technological unemployment.[14] Capitalist strategies were now confronted with the prospect of formidable barriers including demands for the taxation of machinery, demands for limits on the working day, and the emergence of general trades unions enforcing apprenticeship regulations and resisting speed-up of machinery. These demands were buttressed by militant combinations, industrial sabotage, exclusive dealing and rotating strikes.[15] The pattern of resistance revealed an immense diversity in forms of workplace struggle. Each was dependent on the particular production situation, and particular social and cultural contexts.

One impressive example of this was the rising of the agricultural proletariat. The rationalization of agriculture had produced long-term social dislocation on the land. Population increase and to a lesser extent enclosure, had generated a large underemployed agricultural proletariat, its poverty and immobility intensified by the effects of an inadequate poor law policy. Agricultural workers in the southern and midland counties terrorized contemporaries with a flurry of rick burning and machine smashing. These 'Swing' rioters chose the threshing machine for their immediate culprit, for it was responsible for taking away winter employment. The riots evoked a widespread written response both from the apologists for agricultural machinery and from those violently opposed to the extension of the machine on the land (see page 73,74).[16]

This direct action in agriculture was complemented in hand weaving by a partnership between weavers and large employers (the so-called honourable masters) against the small speculator and interloper.[17] Radicals and weavers debated at length with those political economists blindly assertive of the universal benefits of machinery. In the end they forced many political economists to recognise the validity of their case, though they were unsuccessful in their demands for taxes on machinery, fixed wages enforced across the firms and shorter hours in factories (see page 78,80).[18]

In engineering and metal-working, workers reacted to capitalist strategies for dilution and deskilling by forming exclusive craft unions to prevent the entry of women, and the unskilled too demanded their place. Debates and struggles on these many-sided issues of the work place were conducted between the 1820s and 1830s[19] in the context of the movements of Owenism and Chartism. These offered not only a reversal of the established order but also alternative production arrangements. The socialist vision included plans for co-operative production, spade husbandry, the right to the land, the definition of machinery and skill as the property of the working man and alternative technologies using higher proportions of labour to capital. As national movements based on local circumstances, both Owenism and Chartism were sufficiently flexible to adapt to diverse elements of the working class. But the extent to which contemporary radicalism mounted an effective barrier to capital's advance is questionable. For in its very eclecticism it generated indecisive, equivocal and divisive attitudes to the technical transformation engulfing workers and their crafts.[20] The radical newspapers and pamphlets of the period depict these debates on machinery and skill from the context of radical strategy, the trades, women and the unskilled (see page 83-102).

Mid-Victorian Capitalism

The years between 1850 and 1870 form the classical period of British industrial capitalism. Britain's world monopoly position enabled her to consolidate her industrialization mainly by the diffusion of mechanization, new techniques and new materials to many sectors.[21] But, significantly, this consolidation coincided with the expansion of industry on the basis of the degradation of the old crafts. This involved the incursion of a new division of labour and new phases in the dilution of skills. The diffusion of mechanization was aided by key technical changes, gradually perfected and extended in application. In these decades and those to come, the development and application of steam power, gas lighting, chromium tungsten, steel and lubrication technology, along with the invention of precision machine tools and the employment of interchangeable parts, contributed to expansions in scale, speed and standardization of production.[22] Yet simultaneously pre-capitalist and early capitalist methods survived and were redeveloped. Basic manual and highly skilled labour were still integral to many production processes.[23] But if a certain number of key skills maintained their stronghold, the economy was much more significantly transformed by an enormous expansion in the scale of heavy industry, by the spread of precision, by the growth of an integral role for science in the chemical, metallurgical and agricultural industries, and by the adaptation and diffusion of mechanical techniques across industries. In these years the prospect, both anticipated and dreaded, of machines made by machines became a reality (see page 108). The wonders of machinery were perhaps nowhere so evident as in papermaking and printing (see p110,116).With the development of steam-powered printing, the highly skilled work of the compositor, though not yet superseded, already seemed doomed.

The success of the 'new' craft unions' appeal to exclusiveness in the middle of the century partly depended on the continued existence of a small number of important skills in basic industries. But divisions between the skilled and the unskilled extended far back to the first part of the nineteenth century and even earlier. The difference in the living and working conditions of the skilled and the unskilled which gave rise to the 'labour aristocracy' in the mid nineteenth century were not, therefore, anything new; they were only sharpened. Distinctions between the skilled and the unskilled were wide ones indeed, and in mid century were virtually identified with the extent of organization or unionization in a trade, and with particular areas. Distinct varieties of working-class co-operation in production processes became identified with certain job territories, types of discipline and hierarchy, and habits, ways and haunts of life (see page122). It is important to re-iterate, however, that these splits within the working class were manifest much earlier. They related as much to the character, limitations and divisions of early nineteenth-century radicalism as they did to the so-called collaboration of mid-nineteenth-century working-class movements.[24] The skilled tradesman of the early nineteenth century turned to radicalism partly in order to prevent the encroachment of unskilled men and women on his craft, just as the mid-nineteenth-century trade unionist tried among other things to secure the privileged working position of himself and his fellow skilled workers.

Divisions within the working class were manifest in many different ways across industries. The railwayman's regular secure job went with his tied cottage, his graded uniform and his dedication to the railway company.[25] In engineering a number of specialized craft unions amalgamated to form the Amalgamated Society of Engineers to fight more effectively for job control by skilled members. Issues confronted in the 1852 lockout included systematic overtime, piecework and the manning of machines by skilled or unskilled men. The loss of this particular struggle speeded the rationalization of the industry (see p155). In shipbuilding the gradual transfer of the bulk of the industry away from London to escape the high labour costs of the Thames was hastened on Clydeside at least by the availability of a culturally split population. A hierarchically split labour force was established on the basis of differences between Lowland Scots, Highland Scots and Irish workers.[27]

Innovations and mechanization were spreading rapidly in the woodworking, building and metal trades. In woodworking, long, drawn-out struggles against mechanical saw mills reached back to the 1830s (see page 129).[28] In the metal trades and brickmaking, capitalist measures for violating traditional skill boundaries and introducing machinery provoked bitter and violent protest. In the Sheffield trades, workers imposed strict control on apprenticeship and output, made effective by work-oriented resistance, such as 'rattenings', the cutting of bellows, the appropriation of tools, or the destruction of work. The file strike of 1866 was in part provoked by the introduction of machine cutting and grinding and of steam hammers. After the Sheffield Outrages the unions were defeated, and the grinding machines installed (see p134,144).[29] In brickmaking, the crucial changes in work organization and job control occurred at about the same time and with similar results. Workers attempted to maintain a strict job hierarchy based on skill and fought the use of too many apprentices or non-union men. The introduction of mechanical means for replacing the moulder's skill was yet another provocation to the violence of the Manchester outrages (see page 132).[30] The miner's labour, affected only indirectly by mechanization, was marked by the expansion of the labour force and not its displacement. Strict hierarchies in the production process complemented the massive expansion in the scale of the industry (see page 159,164).[31]

The extension of machinery and the dilution of skill had its own special economic context. In the eighteenth and early nineteenth centuries Britain's international economic position had been based on textile exports. But now her trade sector reached increasingly into the export of railway materials and capital goods complemented by the growing sophistication of mercantile, commercial and financial capital markets. The demands not only of home but of foreign markets led to a great expansion in the scale of industry which had the effect too of enormously increasing labour requirements. The employment of more labour was combined with a mounting intensity of labour achieved through the diffusion of speed-up and piece work. Because of this massive increase in the scale of production, the employment of more labour and the inducement to greater intensity of labour went on step by step with mechanization and the dilution of skills.

These shifts in the economic structure of the country and the organization of the labour process were, however, met in turn by important developments in working-class organization. These included 'new model' unions, the movement for amalgamation of many craft unions, and renewed interest in co-operative production. Still, the exclusive character of these unions was divisive, generating inter-union and inter-class rivalry, such as the antagonism between the shipyard helpers and the skilled platers of North East England in 1872.[32] Urban unskilled labourers, their numbers growing rapidly, and still by and large unorganized, had become the new enabling factor of the rapid expansion of heavy industry in coal, iron and engineering and in the equally important consumer and retail trades. The mid-Victorian economy cannot be encapsulated by pat references to the transition from manufacture to modern industry. Important as technical transformation was to this economy, its even more significant characterization was expansion in every way. More labour, working harder, longer and at greater speed built the very foundations and created the possibilities for the greater and greater scale of production on which all technical change was in the first place predicated.[33]

Climacteric or Resolution?

Britain's development after 1870 is usually compared by historians not to her own past, but to that of other industrializing nations, notably Germany and America. Since Britain's initial industrialization had had no rivals, it sets its own standards of achievement. But now Germany and America, industrializing late, created new patterns and left Britain in a shadow. German capital, backed by the state, moved rapidly into the chemical and electrical industries, making selective use of a tecnically trained workforce and scientific research. The American high-wage, labour-scarce economy developed and applied labour-saving automatic machines such as the draper loom, ring spinning and mechanical reaping.[34] The Great Depression (1873-96) revealed in Britain a fundamental lack of high-yield outlets for new investments. Here the economy continued to be based to a large extent on the old industrial spheres. The strategy of British industry was to shift investment to shipbuilding and other home enterprises of relatively low expected yields, in order to maintain the same quantity of sales abroad at lower, but still profitable, prices. The new light industries—sewing machine, cycle and electrical—deploying the highest levels of technical and scientific expertise were left to establish their strongholds in other industrial nations.[35]

Whatever Britain's overall comparative performance,[36] her own industries were marked by rapid and striking changes in basic work organization and industrial techniques. Last ditch hand processes in boot- and shoemaking, shipbuilding and typesetting were mechanized. In shipbuilding the transfer from wood to iron shipbuilding had the effect actually of increasing the number of specialized crafts in the industry. The resulting endless demarcation disputes were one cause of repeated efforts to mechanize shipbuilding where possible (see p175,179).[37] In the engineering trades the centre lathe was replaced by the turret and capstan lathe and a new screw-cutting machine was introduced. High-speed tool steels and the development of standardization and interchangeable parts were technical strategies designed to allow industries to escape the grip of militant and highly skilled workers.

Capitalists either integrated these technical changes with, or developed more extensively the possibilities of bigger plant size and the vertical or horizontal integration of labour. These contributed to further increases in speed and productivity and these changes were, in turn, accompanied by new management strategies—further specialization and the splitting up of various trades into further new occupations. Other strategies included the development of uninterrupted flow techniques, mass production in the manufacture of paper and in the light industries, feed and speed systems, and the premium bond wage incentive system.[38]

The desire of management to gain control over all the functions of the production process was met by rising working-class militancy. Craft unions fought the attempts of management to deprive machine tool operators of the power to determine speeds and cutting angles, and did prevent to a great extent the intrusion of 'feed and speed' men. They also fought for their apprenticeship-journeymen ratios, and the standard rate. In ring spinning the spinners' unions struggled over picce rates and manning skill, and this long prevented the profitable introduction of ring spinning techniques.[39] Outright opposition to machinery continued in Britain among the rank and file in the cutlery trades, the forge workers, file-making labourers, pattern makers, silk workers and farriers, and in the striking and deep-seated hostility of typesetters to the introduction of the lynotype. Hostility towards machinery was complemented by other long practised labour tactics to 'brake' the rate of exploitation, including ca'canny, or go slow (especially in the building trades), the enforcement of machine manning and apprenticeship rules, and restrictions on output, (especially in the boot and shoe, coal mining and typesetting industries).[40]

Perhaps the greatest new barrier, created in part by capitalist strategies to reduce skills, was the organization of the unskilled. The 'new unions' were created in the 1880s to organize the mass of the working class in Britain by waging struggles based upon class solidarity rather than craft exclusiveness. In 1889 the English dockworkers struck and won. The victory of the dockers brought widespread organization among the gas workers, labourers on Tyneside in engineering and shipbuilding, the Birmingham metal trades and the South Wales tinplate industry. At the same time this new unionism which, in fact, was significant for only a few years, gave impetus to a new phase of mechanization in the dockyards and gasworks. Following on from the organization of the unskilled came that of the 'semi-skilled' as in the Miners' Federation (see p 206-7).[41] If, however, these developments brought about changes of great importance within the working class— among them the blurring of distinctions between the more and the less skilled—the process of unionization was also used by capital to separate the respectable working class from unfit casual labour. The middle classes welcomed the unionization of the unskilled that took place in the dockyards as a way of bringing greater regularity and discipline to the lives of the poor.[42]

Technical and managerial innovation was especially rapid and sharply resisted in the metal-working and engineering industries, where skilled workers watched the degradation of their craftsmanship by the introduction of boy labour and machinery (see p186,201). They reacted with attempts to impose machine manning rules and to reduce the length of the working day. The result was the Eight Hours Movement and the Engineering Trades Lockout in 1897-8.[43]

The context for these struggles was not just one of struggle with labour for control. It was the desire to rationalize production during and after the Great Depression. Though there was little systematic application of scientific management in Britain at the time, several of the techniques of what was later to be called scientific management were adapted and applied, including the premium bond wage system.[44] Mechanization went ahead in industries which had previously escaped. Shoemaking was one. This industry, developed on the basis of outwork in the villages around Northampton from early in the century had known continuous and largely successful struggle against the introduction of the sewing machine. Mechanization and the use of women's labour in factories at length proceeded. But there was still hostility to the factory system in Northamptonshire villages and indoor working was not general until the 1890s (see page 171).[45]

Mechanization had also come to the sweated domestic industries in tailoring and shoemaking. It was the lot of the sewing machine both to bring relief from much dreary and tedious labour, but at the same time to create the possibilities for the extension of home work, based on a market for rented machines (see page 227). Home work and small sweated workshops continued to grow in London, especially in the ready-made cheap clothing industry. It expanded on the basis of the peculiar characteristics of the East London labour market and on the basis of the contradictory effects of state control on factories and workshops.[46] The sexual division of labour increased though women's employment was also rising. Women were increasingly forced into the unskilled low wage, sweated sectors of the economy, and the men's trades they did take over were already degraded (see page 236). New unionism left 31 per cent, or 4.1 million workers, in trade unions, but despite this the nineteenth century left a legacy of even wider wage differences between skilled and unskilled workers, and an economy increasingly subordinate to the dictates of mechanization, the division of labour and to measures for both increasing the intensity and the productivity of labour.[47]

Techniques for extending the control of capital over every possible movement and function in the work place cannot be easily assigned to particular historical periods. They were rather adapted to the situation of each industry, sector and region, and the most suitable combination was developed to the highest pitch. This helps to explain the continuity of forms of workers' resistance and their grievances. Resistance to the dilution of skills and to the introduction of machinery did not succeed each other, but rather existed in combination from the eighteenth century to the twentieth. The picture across all of industry over the course of the nineteenth century indicates the persistence of these themes of work place resistance despite the multiple transformations in the techniques and organization of work.

Notes

1. For this type of broad based discussion of the labour process see: London Labour Process Group, 'The Crisis of Social Capital: Money, State and Labour Process', CSE Conference Paper, 1976; Brighton

15

Labour Process Group, 'The Capitalist Labour Process', *Capital and Class*, No. 1, Spring 1977; Harry Braverman, *Labour and Monopoly Capitalism*, London, 1974; André Gorz, *The Division of Labour. The Labour Process and Class Struggle in Modern Capitalism*, Atlantic Highlands, N. J., 1976.

2. Brighton Labour Process Group, Conference Paper, 1976, p. 16.

3. *Ibid.*, p. 14.

4. Joan Thirsk ed., *The Agrarian History of England and Wales*, Cambridge, 1967; Charles Webster, *The Great Instauration*, London, 1975; Sidney Pollard, 'Industrialization and the European Economies', *Economic History Review*, 1973.

5. D. Defoe, *A Tour through the Whole Island of England*, Letter No. 8, Harmondsworth, 1971.

6. Jennifer Tann, *The Development of the Factory*, London, 1970, pp. 3-7. Also see Stephen Marglin, 'What do Bosses Do?', in André Gorz, *The Division of Labour*, pp. 28-41.

7. Eric Roll, *An Early Experiment in Industrial Organization, being a History of Boulton and Watt*, London, 1930, ch. 2.

8. W. H. G. Armytage, *A Social History of Engineering*, London, 1970.

9. See Peter Mathias, 'Skills and the Diffusion of Innovation from Britain in the Eighteenth Century', *Trans. Royal Historical Society*, xxv, 1975; J. R. Harris, 'Steam Power in the Eighteenth Century', *History*, 1969; E. H. Robinson, 'The Early Diffusion of Steam Power', *Journal of Economic History*, Vol. 34 (1-2), 1974.

10. *The Life of Sir William Fairbairn*, ed. W. Pole, 1877, p. 47; D. B. Barton, *Cornish Beam Engines*, Truro, 1966; Sidney Pollard, *The Genesis of Modern Management*, Harmondsworth, 1965, pp. 152-155.

11. Edwards and Jones Lloyd, 'Smelser and the Cotton Factory Family: a Reassessment', in *Textile History and Economic History*, ed. N. Harte and K. Ponting, Manchester, 1973.

12. S. D. Chapman, *The Early Factory Masters*, 1967; Sidney Pollard, *The Genesis of Modern Management*, ch. 5; and Rheinhard Bendix, *Work and Authority in Industry*, 2nd ed. Berkely, 1965, ch. 2.

13. A. J. Robertson, 'Robert Owen: Cotton Spinner New Lanark', in Pollard and Salt eds., *Robert Owen Prophet of the Poor*, London, 1971.

14. See Maxine Berg, 'The Machinery Question', D.Phil Thesis, Oxford, 1976. ch. 8; and Maxine Berg, 'Mills of the Millennium: Machinery and Labour during the Industrial Revolution', (forthcoming).

15. See G. D. H. Cole, *Attempts at General Union: A Study in Trade Union History*, London, 1953. On the grievances and resistance of the tailors see I. Prothero and T. Porsinnen, 'The London Tailors'

Strike of 1834', *International Review of Social History*, February, 1976. On the Cotton textile unions and strategy see H. A. Turner, *Trade Union Growth, Structure and Policy*, London, 1962, pp. 70-105.

16. See E. J. T. Collins, 'Harvest Technology and Labour Supply in Britain, 1790-1870', *Economic History Review*, 1969; E. J. Hobsbawm and G. Rudé, *Captain Swing*, London, 1968.

17. See E. P. Thompson, *The Making of the English Working Class*, Harmondsworth, 1968, ch. 9; D. Blythall, *The Handloom Weavers*, Cambridge, 1969.

18. See M. Berg, 'The Machinery Question', ch. 8.

19. Dorothy Thompson, 'Women and Nineteenth Century Radical Politics', in *The Rights and Wrongs of Women*, ed. A. Oakley and J. Mitchell, Harmondsworth, 1976.

20. See M. Berg, 'Mills of the Millennium'.

21. For general histories of this period see E. J. Hobsbawm, *The Age of Capital 1848-1875*, London, 1975, and reviews of this book by David Landes ('The Ubiquitous Bourgeoisie', *Times Literary Supplement*, June 4, 1976) and Gareth Stedman Jones ('Society and Politics at the Beginning of the World Economy', *Cambridge Journal of Economics*, No. 1, 1978). Also see David Landes, *The Unbound Prometheus*, Cambridge, 1969, ch. 5.

22. David Landes, *The Unbound Prometheus*, ch. 5.

23. See S. Alexander, 'Women's Work in Nineteenth-Century London, in *Rights and Wrongs of Women*, ed. A. Oakley and J. Mitchell, for some examples of the growth of sweated industries in London. Raphael Samuel's 'Workshop of the World', *History Workshop 3*, reminds us that there were still artisans in mid- and late-nineteenth-century Britain.

24. This highly contentious subject has been recently debated by John Foster, *Class Struggle and the Industrial Revolution*, London, 1974; John Foster, 'Imperialism and the Aristocracy of Labour', in J. Skelley ed., *The General Strike 1926*, London, 1976; J. Musson and J. Foster, 'Class Struggle and the Labour Aristocracy', *Social History*, October 1976; G. Stedman Jones, 'Class Struggle and the Industrial Revolution', *New Left Review*, No. 90, (Spring 1975); and R. Q. Gray, 'The Labour Aristocracy in Edinburgh', *International Review of Social History*, 1973.

25. Frank McKenna, 'Victorian Railway Workers', *History Workshop I*.

26. J. B. Jeffreys, *The Story of the Engineers*, London, 1945, ch. 2; Keith Burgess, 'Technological change and the 1852 Lockout in the British Engineering Industry', *International Review of Social History*, XIV, 1969.

27. John Foster, 'Capitalism and the Scottish Nation', *The Red Paper on Scotland*, Edinburgh, 1974.

28. See R. Samuel, 'The Workshop of the World', for interesting information on changes in woodworkers' techniques, pp. 36-7.

29. Sidney Pollard, *A History of Labour in Sheffield, 1850-1939*, Liverpool, 1971, pp. 127-8.

30. R. N. Price, 'Violence in the Manchester Brickworking Trade', *Past and Present*, 66, February 1975, pp. 120-124.

31. A. J. Taylor, 'Labour Productivity and Technological Innovation in the British Coal Industry', *Economic History Review*, Vol. XIV, 1961; A. Slaven, 'Earnings and Productivity in the Scottish Coal Mining Industry during the Nineteenth Century', in P. L. Payne ed., *Studies in Scottish Business History*, 1967; R. Samuel, 'The Workshop of the World', p. 21.

32. I owe this example to Keith McClelland.

33. It is instructive to examine the introduction to the 1861 census. Striking increases in employment in key basic and now standardized consumer industries indicate the scale of overall growth.

34. H. J. Habbakuk, *American and British Technology in the Nineteenth Century*, Cambridge, 1962; and S. B. Saul ed., *Technological Change: The US and Britain in the Nineteenth Century*, London, 1970.

35. See David Landes, *The Unbound Prometheus*, ch. 5; A. L. Levine, *Industrial Retardation in Britain 1880-1914*, London, 1967.

36. For the debate on the backwardness of the late-nineteenth-century British economy, see D. McCloskey ed., *Essays on a Mature Economy*, London, 1972; D. C. Coleman, 'Gentlemen and Players', *Economic History Review*, 1973; D. McCloskey, 'Did Victorian Britain Fail?', *Economic History Review*, 1970; and Roderick Floud, *The British Machine Tool Industry 1850-1914*, Cambridge, 1976.

37. P. L. Robertson, 'Demarcation Disputes in the British Shipbuilding Industry', *International Review of Social History*, 20, (2), 1975.

38. See A. L. Levine, *Industrial Retardation in Britain 1880-1914*, London, 1967, p. 67; and D. Landes, *The Unbound Prometheus*, Cambridge, 1969.

39. Lars Sandberg, 'Rings and Mules in British and American Textiles', in R. Floud, *Essays in Quantitative Economic History*, October, 1974.

40. A. L. Levine, *Industrial Retardation*, p. 79.

41. E. J. Hobsbawm, 'Trends in the British Labour Movement since 1850', and 'General Labour Unions in Britain 1889-1914', *Labouring Men*, New York, 1963.

42. G. Stedman Jones, *Outcast London*, Oxford, 1971, ch. 17.

43. J. B. Jeffreys, *The Story of the Engineers*, 1943.
44. A. L. Levine, *Industrial Retardation*.
45. Roy Church, 'Labour Supply and Innovation in 1800-1860: The Boot and Shoe Industry', *Business History*, 1970.
46. G. Stedman Jones, *Outcast London*, ch. 4; and J. A. Schmiechen, 'State Reform and the Local Economy: an Aspect of Industrialization in late Victorian and Edwardian London', *Economic History Review*, 28 (3), 1975.
47. Sidney Pollard, *The Development of the British Economy 1914 to 1967*, London, 1969, ch. 1.

Bibliography

W. H. G. Armytage, *A Social History of Engineering*, London, 1970.

R. Bendix, *Work and Authority in Industry*, (1956), Berkely, 1965.

M. Bienefield, *Working Hours in British Industry: An Economic History*, London, 1972.

H. Braverman, *Labour and Monopoly Capital*, New York, 1974.

The Brighton Group, 'The Capitalist Labour Process', *Capital and Class*, I, 1977.

Geoff Brown, *Sabotage*, Nottingham, 1977.

John Burnett, *Useful Toil*, Harmondsworth, 1977.

R. Church, 'Labour Supply and Innovation: the Boot- and Shoe Industry', *Business History*, 1970.

E. J. T. Collins, 'Harvest Technology and Labour Supply in Britain, 1790-1870', *Economic History Review*, 1969.

Conference of Socialist Economists, ed., *The Labour Process and Class Strategies*, CSE Pamphlet No. 1, London, Stage 1, 1976.

Conference of Socialist Economists, ed., *On the Political Economy of Women*, CSE Pamphlet No. 2, Stage 1, London, 1976.

J. P. D. Dunbabbin, *Rural Discontent*, London, 1974.

Edwards and Jones Lloyd, 'Smelser and the Cotton Factory Family: a Reassessment', in *Textile History and Economic History*, ed. N. Harte and K. Ponting, Manchester, 1973.

John Foster, *Class Struggle and the Industrial Revolution*, London, 1974.

John Foster, 'Imperialism and the Aristocracy of Labour', in J. Skelley, ed., *The General Strike 1926*, London, 1976.

John Foster and J. Musson, 'Class Struggle and the Labour Aristocracy', *Social History*, October, 1976.

Andrew Friedman, *Industry and Labour*, London, 1977.

André Gorz, ed., *The Division of Labour*, Brighton, 1976.

Ian Gough, 'Productive and Unproductive Labour in Marx', *New Left Review*, 76, Nov/Dec 1972.

R. Q. Gray, *The Labour Aristocracy in Edinburgh*, Oxford, 1976.

S. Gideon, *Mechanization Takes Command*, N.Y.

H. Gutman, *Work, Culture and Society in Industrializing America*, Oxford, 1978.

J. R. Harris, 'Skills, Coal and British Industry in the 18th Century', *History*, Vol. 61, No. 202, June, 1976.

H. J. Habakkuk, *American and British Technology in the Nineteenth Century: the Search for Labour Saving Inventions*, Cambridge, 1962.

D. Hay, P. Linebaugh and E. P. Thompson ed., *Albion's Fatal Tree*, London, 1975.

E. J. Hobsbawm, *The Age of Capital, 1848-1875*, London, 1975.

E. J. Hobsbawm and G. Rudé, *Captain Swing*, London 1968.

E. J. Hobsbawm, *Industry and Empire*, Harmondsworth, 1968.

E. J. Hobsbawm, *Labouring Men*, London, 1964.

A. Klima, 'The Role of Rural Domestic Industry in Bohemia in the 18th Century', *Economic History Review*, 1974.

David Landes, *The Unbound Prometheus*, Cambridge, 1969.

A. L. Levine, *Industrial Retardation in Britain, 1880-1914*, London, 1967.

M. Levy-Leboyer, 'Le Patronat Francais a-t-il été Malthusien? *Le Mouvement Social*, 1974.

Karl Marx, *Capital*, Vol. I—chapter 7, 'The Labour Process and the Process of Producing Surplus Value', chapter 9, 'The Working Day', chapter 13, 'Co-operation', chapter 14, 'Division of Labour and Manufactures', chapter 15, 'Machinery and Modern Industry', chapter 16, 'Absolute and Relative Surplus Value'; New chapter 6 in Marx Library edition of *Capital* Penguin, 1976.

Neil McKendrick, 'Josiah Wedgewood and Factory Discipline', *Historical Journal*, 4, 1961.

Seymour Melman, *Decision Making and Productivity*, Oxford, 1958.

Ivy Pinchbeck, *Women Workers and the Industrial Revolution 1750-1850*, Frank Cass, 1969.

Sidney Pollard, *The Genesis of Modern Management*, (1965), Harmondsworth, 1968.

Sidney Pollard, *A History of Labour in Sheffield, 1850-1939*, Liverpool, 1971.

Sidney Pollard, 'Industrialization and the European Economies', *Economic History Review*, 1973.

David Ricardo, *On the Principles of Political Economy and Taxation*, chapter 31 'On Machinery', 1821.

N. Rosenberg, *Perspectives on Technology*, Cambridge, 1976.

R. Samuel, ed., *Miners, Quarrymen and Saltworkers*, London, 1977.

R. Samuel, ed., *Village Life and Labour*, London, 1975.

R. Samuel, 'The Workshop of the World', *History Workshop* No. 3, 1977.

S. B. Saul, ed., *Technological Change: the US and Britain in the 19th Century*, London, 1970.

J. Schmiechen, 'State Reform and the Local Economy: An Aspect of Industrialization in Late Victorian and Edwardian London', *Economic History Review*, 28 (3), August, 1975.

J. Scott and L. Tilly, 'Women's Work and the Family in 19th Century Europe', *Comparative Studies in History and Society*, Winter, 1975.

P. Stearns and D. Walkowitz, ed., *Workers in the Industrial Revolution*, New Brunswick, N.J., 1974.

G. Stedman Jones, 'Class Struggle and the Industrial Revolution', essay review of John Foster's book of this title, *New Left Review*, No. 90, March/April, 1975.

M. Stewart and L. Hunter, *The Needle is Threaded*, London, 1964.

Jennifer Tann, *The Development of the Factory*, London 1972.

Joan Thirsk, *The Agrarian History of England and Wales*, Cambridge, 1967.

Joan Thirsk, *Economic Policy and Projects, The Rise of a Consumer Society*, Oxford, 1978.

E. P. Thompson, *The Making of the English Working Class*, (1963), Harmondsworth, 1968.

E. P. Thompson, 'Time, Work Discipline and the Industrial Revolution', *Past and Present*, No. 38, 1967.

H. A. Turner, *Trade Union Growth, Structure and Policy*, London, 1962.

Charles Webster, *The Great Instauration*, London, 1975.

Part I
Workshop, Factory
and Industrialization

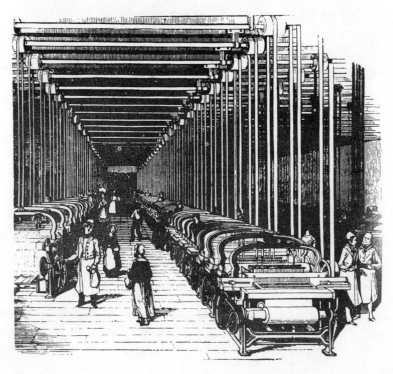

Chapter One

Division of Labour, Skill and Capitalist Management

The early phases of industrialization in Britain were characterized both by the differentiation of the old crafts through the division of labour, and by the development of new, highly sophisticated skills. Marx chose to characterize the division of labour within the context of workshop production and hand technology as the defining feature of the phase of manufacture. Yet the development and manufacture of the very machines which allowed for the extension of the division of labour on an unprecedented scale actually required highly specialized, sophisticated and skilled labour.

In building the steam engines which provided a major basis for the industrial revolution Boulton and Watt discovered the limitations of the precision skills and discipline of the workmen they employed. They instituted a systematic division of labour within their Soho plant, dictated as much by the need for highly specialized skills as by the problems they encountered in controlling the pre-industrial craftsmen they had gathered from various trades. The Soho workmen produced by this process were not craftsmen being denuded of their skills. They were possessed rather of a new skill, and were strongly conscious of this.

The debates on the Export of Machinery in the early nineteenth century reflect the challenge of this new skill of machine-making. For artisans claimed rights of control over the mobility between industries and geographical areas of the crucial specialized skills embodied in their own persons. Capitalist manufacturing interests, recognizing the value of such skilled labour, tried to claim their own proprietary rights to the machine-making skills which could not be separated from the person of the machine-maker, by restricting the rights of movement of skilled workmen.

Another aspect of early industrial innovation was the attempt to reduce the skill levels required by individual operations. At the same time efforts were made to organize production rationally by planning scale and layout, by carefully accounting for input costs, and by promoting increases in labour productivity. The most revolutionary method for rationalizing production was the application of machinery both to jobs previously simplified by means of the division of labour,

I.I.– C

and even to jobs requiring the indispensable skilled labourer.

The antagonistic process of creating new industrial skills, while attempting to reduce the significance of these skills through the division of labour and the introduction of machinery were evident together in the British economy from the mid eighteenth century to the mid nineteenth century. Marx abstracted from only one side of this process, that is, the reduction of skill, in setting out the conditions for his phases of manufacture and the origins of modern industry. The evidence of strategies to reduce and control skills was indeed clearly abundant. Boulton's and Watt's programme for the division of labour certainly contained a strong element of discipline and control. But it was Babbage who produced the greatest contemporary analysis of the extensive capitalist gains to be made through an elaborated division of labour reaching as far even as the division of mental labour.

Some of the earliest application of mechanization, steam power and innovation in layout and organization took place in government controlled workshops, such as the arsenals, dockyards and navy yards. One such example was the manufacture of ships' blocks, to which was applied some of Brunel's and Maudslay's earliest engineering machinery and Samuel Bentham's early development of assembly-line techniques.

Innovations in organization and technology were to have their most startling impact in the early nineteenth century. The changes in organization and technique which Marx analyzed into 'manufactures' and 'modern industry' respectively were actually integrated processes. The conscious organization, precise measurement, standardization and attempts to raise labour productivity which Owen, Dodd and Montgomery (p 40,58,62) all highlighted as significant aspects of the factory system, were also essential to the orderly and efficient running of the new machines. In the context of the factory system, the machines, as Ure so nakedly expressed (page 65) could place the control of production unutterably in the hands of the capitalist. For the machine could simply displace the indomitable skilled workman, and then set the pace for all its unskilled human appendages.

1 An Early Experiment in Industrial Organization: Boulton and Watt 1775-1805   Eric Roll, 1930

This is the only secondary text in this collection on the history of technology and work. However, what is reprinted here, from chapter two of the book, simply describes the contents of a number of Boulton and Watt manuscripts. Eric Roll, influenced as he was at the time of writing this book by the volume of writing then appearing on Taylorism and other aspects of scientific management, is impressed by the similarities he finds between scientific management and the systematic organization of one of Britain's first large-scale factories. He draws attention to documents of 1799-1801 indicating extreme division of labour, conscious reduction of skill requirements, and strategy on scale, layout, and speeds of machinery. Another reason, however, for the strict organization and standardization of processes, was the need to create the types of skills needed to build such large-scale machinery as the steam engine.

What distinguishes Soho from all other factories of the time—and there were at the beginning of the new century many industrial enterprises which could be called factories—was the fact that these lists were the result of a definite systematic and preconceived plan of what the Soho Engine Manufactory should be.

A number of documents are in existence which show that the methods of planning and works designing were by no means different from those stipulated to-day by Industrial Works Designers, Scientific Managers, or Efficiency Engineers. The limitations were only those imposed by the degree of technical knowledge or rather by the degree of its application. 'More can be attributed to the quiet, pervasive influence of the engineers who rose to executive positions in industry,' writes a foremost authority on this new modern science, in discussing the new spirit in American industry in the present century, and this factor will certainly have to be included when we come to discuss later the probable incentives for this 'new spirit' at Soho in 1800.

The basic document in the series mentioned deals with the layout proper and is entitled 'Arrangement of the Engine Manufactory, Soho,

December, 1801.' The memorandum consists of two parts. The first gives a list of the shops, mostly already in existence, but partly still to be erected, together with their machinery, the operations performed in each and, most important of all, their relative situation and communications. The second part contains a list of all the machines required in the production process already in use at Soho, together with their respective uses.

The first part of this document evidently served as the basis for all the arrangements that were made later. In the first column it enumerates ten different shops, designated from A to K, by which letters they were afterwards referred to. These shops were:

A. The drilling shop, or rather the heavy drilling shop in which the boring and drilling of such heavy articles as condensers, air and hot and cold water pumps, steam pipes, &c., was done. A large and a small drill were used in this shop, and it was provided with a hearth, a convenience for holding grinding and mending tools, and other minor appliances.

B. The heavy turning shop, provided with the great lathe and a second special lathe for turning piston rods, in addition to the usual conveniences. Worthy of mention, among these, is a 'tackle for lifting heavy weights into lathe.' This shop was used for all turning work, such as for pistons, cylinder lids, gudgeons, shafts, piston rods, rotative wheels, &c.

C. The heavy fitting shop, which, in addition to the usual benches and grinding stone, was to have a lapping machine and a small drill. Here the heavier articles were fitted, such as plumber blocks, pistons, glands, &c.

D. The nozzle shop, used exclusively for the fitting of nozzles.

E. A general fitting shop which was intended to be provided with a separate drill, and, apart from the usual conveniences, with a 'small portable furnace for heating pins' as well as with 'a crane for lifting heavy weights.' Here, steam cases, inner and outer bottoms and pipes were fitted and the fitting of air pumps was completed.

F. This was a special shop for the fitting of parallel motions and working gears and governors, and had two lathes as well as another smaller lathe for turning pins.

G. This was the next and was called the light fitting shop. Here all the lighter parts—safety, throttle and stop pipes, &c., were fitted.

H. Was the pattern-makers' shop and had the usual benches, grind stone, and a lathe.

I. Was the casters' shop, and for this no particulars are given.

K. The last on the list was the smiths' shop, and was stated to contain a hearth and a vice-bench.

It seems that some of the machinery considered necessary and enumerated in this list had not yet been set up. At any rate the second part dealing with machinery mentions the following as already in use: A large and a small drill, both vertical and with gear control and sliding;

the large turning lathe with both 'centres' and 'chucks', also special lathes for piston rods, nozzles, parallel motions, a lathe in the light fitting shop, one other small lathe, and the pattern-makers' lathe. A lapping machine used for 'lapping all brasses and plummer blocks, &c.', and, lastly, there was installed a steam case drill in the fitting shed.

As far as the technical side of the machinery is concerned, it is of interest to note that both 'centre-lathe working' and 'face-lathe working' were used. The latter method is, of course, the most widely used to-day, and has given rise to a very great increase in the application of automatic and semi-automatic machines. There is no evidence to show which of the two methods was more extensively employed at Soho; but we know, at any rate, that they both were available.

Soho also did not depart from old practice in the use of hand tools by the turners. The most important factor diminishing the degree of skill required at the present time of the turners is the almost complete disappearance of the hand tool. From the references in the lists of machinery to 'conveniences for holding tools' and 'tool cupboards', it is obvious that hand tools were still largely in use at Soho. The now usual special grinding and cutting department did not exist, and each bench was provided with a grindstone. It is usually supposed that, as regards the provision of new tools, the almost universal practice in the early days of the nineteenth century was for workmen not only to bear the expense of repairs, but also that of new tools. In this respect the following provision for borers—it was probably applied generally— shows Soho in advance of the time: 'Current repairs of tools and grinding them to be borne by the borer and new tools to be provided at our expense.'

The most surprising advance, however, is the fact that the list of machines contains, together with statements of their present speeds, proposed new speeds which were evidently calculated to serve as standards. Generally, the proposed speed showed an increase over the existing speed. The small drill was to be speeded up from 50 revolutions per minute to 75; the pattern-makers' lathe was to have a speed of between 200 and 300 revolutions per minute, and for most other machines three or four standard speeds were established, such as for the parallel motion lathe which, from a speed of 65 revolutions per minute, was to run at 18, 50, 70 and 100 per minute. 'Forty or even thirty years ago,' remarks a recent writer, 'the turner would have to decide for himself what "speed" and "feed" he required: to-day, tables are worked out for nearly all machines. . . ' According to this statement, Soho would correspond more nearly to what is described as the practice of 'to-day' than to that of thirty or forty years ago. Speculation on the reasons for the introduction of such methods are very interesting; but they will be deferred for the moment until more of them have been discussed.

So far, the most exceptional qualities of this new plan of Soho lay in the fact that a list of all required shops had been drawn up, the machinery to be included, and the operations to be performed in each explicitly stated, and definite specialized uses assigned to each machine and their speed standardized. A more remarkable sign of 'modernity,' however, is to be found in the fourth column of the Memorandum dealing with the arrangement of the shops which is entitled: 'Relative Situation and Communications', for this, although in primitive form, definitely shows that the persons responsible for the design had a very clear idea of what is now termed 'routing'.

The first two shops are for drilling and turning respectively. The next three are for fitting in general. These five shops are concerned, on the one hand, with the production of the engine proper, that is, its power generating parts, and on the other hand, with those parts producing the rotative motion; and they form, therefore, the centre of the whole plant, with the drilling shop a centre within it.

The actual positions are given as follows: The drilling shop, where boring in general and drilling of the heavy parts took place, was to have direct communication with the heavy turning shop on the one hand, and with the three fitting shops on the other—'the principal heavy articles being carried from hence to those shops.' Again, this central shop, A, was to be directly accessible from the yard 'for the convenience of bringing in the goods.' The heavy turning shop, B, too, was to be entered from the yard and was to have direct communication with A, and C, the heavy fitting shop. It was also to be near the original power. This provision for the shop in which the principal lathes were situated can be easily understood; for if it had been at a great distance from the source of power, much inconvenience would have been experienced in the transmission. The heavy fitting shop, C, was to be contiguous both to the drilling machine and the two large lathes. D, the nozzle shop, needed direct communication with the drilling shop only; while the position of E, the fitting shed for steam cases and air pumps, depended on whether it was provided with a separate drill or not. In the former case its communications were of less importance, but in the latter it was necessary that it should have easy access to the drilling shop where the steam case panels could be drilled.

The position of the next five shops is not so clearly stated, and was obviously considered less important. The parallel motion shop was to be on the ground floor preferably; but, most of the articles worked in it being portable, it was not imperative that it should be contiguous to the drilling machine. The shop was to be provided with three lathes, and the communications with the engine were, therefore, important. It was not necessary that the light fitting shop should be on the ground floor or immediately accessible to the great turning lathe and the great drill as the articles to be fitted in it were also portable. The position of the pattern-makers' shop was not material, except in so far as the convenience of transmitting power for turning the lathe was concerned; while the situation of the last two, the casters' and smiths' shops, is stated to be immaterial.

Unfortunately, the earliest plan of Soho in existence dates from nearly half a century later than the Memorandum outlined above. It is, therefore, impossible to compare the arrangement of the shops on the actual site with the positions here stipulated. According to these, there would be a more or less radial arrangement of the workshops: A would occupy a central position. Communicating with it and each other would be, on the one side, shops B and C and on the other, shop D. The position of E, which depended on the installation of another drilling machine, is not certain. According to the machinery list it was proposed to install a steam case drill in the fitting shed, and if that was done, the latter would not necessarily have had any direct communication with A. Shop F was probably at some distance from the first five, although not too far from the engine house. Shop G was on a second floor, the lathe in it being referred to as 'lathe in upper fitting shop'. The other three shops would be more or less separate buildings.

From this we gain some idea of the layout of the Soho factory, and we can also see the considerations that dictated it. A certain sequence of production processes was definitely contemplated as the basis of the layout. Some castings would be brought from the yard into shop, A, to be bored and drilled, and others into the heavy turning shop. The two would also have to be communicating; for most castings would have to be turned first and drilled afterwards. From these two shops the articles would then go to their respective fitting shops. One was reserved for heavy articles—pistons, plumber blocks, rotative wheels and shafts, and the other for steam cases, air pumps, inner and outer bottoms, that is, those articles which would probably demand less alterations in the fitting. Here also the fitting together of most of the articles already finished would be completed. Lastly, there was a special shop in which the all-important nozzle was fitted. Two special fitting shops were in existence—one for the parallel motions and working gears and one in which all the smaller and lighter articles, mainly boiler furniture such as injection cocks, steam gauges, reverse valves, &c., were fitted.

Two other papers approach the same matter from a different angle. The first of these, with the same date as that already discussed, is entitled 'Specification of the Fitting of Engine Materials and the Shops where it is to be done. December 3, 1801.' This gives in one column a complete list of all the constituent parts of the steam engine, with their subdivisions, and sets out in very great detail all the operations to be performed on each article in their proper sequence. In the second column, the shops and the machines on which each particular job is to be done are stated. This paper provides a complete list of all the production processes and fixes a definite standard regulation on the part of the management, thus relieving the workmen of the larger part of their independence and individual responsibility.

The details of jobs are remarkable. The cylinder heads the list and the other articles follow in practically the same order in which they are dealt with in the shops. First, all the articles belonging to the cylinder—pistons, piston rods, steam cases; then the several pumps—air, hot and cold water, followed by the nozzles and the various gudgeons. The rotative motion or crank is next dealt with, together with the connecting rod and, lastly, the condenser. A very detailed list of boiler furniture follows; and the rest is made up of such additional articles as fly-wheel, governor, parallel motion and working gear. The last two items are: General Fitting and Labour, the latter including the weighing, blacking, and packing of goods. For each article or part thereof, the operations are given in their temporal sequence and are, therefore, of considerable technico-historical interest. From our point of view their main importance lies in the fact that at Soho the production processes had, for each particular article, already been broken up into a long series of various minor operations, showing thus a very high degree of the application of division of labour to factory routine.

The statement that division of labour and subdivision of jobs had been developed to a high degree, is borne out by the last paper in this series which is of a somewhat earlier date than the one preceding. Entitled 'Arrangement of Workmen and Distribution of Work at Soho Foundry, September 14, 1801', it gives a detailed list of the jobs assigned to each workman or small group of workmen. The total number of work-people enumerated on this list is forty-one men and seven boys; but a note at the end informs us that, to make up that complement, eight men and four boys were required. There can be no doubt that this list was intended to supply a fixed standard job for each worker. The first item states that Wells, two assistant men and one lad were 'to be employed constantly in fitting nozzles.' The word 'constantly', though not explicitly repeated in the following entries, applied, no doubt, to them all. We are thus afforded an interesting view of the classes of skill into which machine production in the early engineering industry had divided the workers.

The first important group are the fitters. In this class, which to-day still preserves the old generic name, the new industrial revolution, as it is sometimes called, has brought an important change. To-day there exist a large number of 'fitters' whose degree of skill is by no means equal. Whilst the engine erector proper still remains a highly-skilled craftsman whose efficiency will be measured by his experience and personal touch, the skill of the others is certainly lower than that required forty or fifty years ago. The great advance in the quality of the castings and the superiority of the work performed on them in the subsequent stages of production, such as turning, boring and drilling, owing to the introduction of improved machinery, have minimized the adjustments to which they have to be subjected by the fitter; further, where these are necessary, they are no longer done by hand. Planing and milling machines are used extensively. Automatic machinery with its mass production has divided the fitters into a number of classes, each performing a small job that has become almost as much one of routine as that of the other semi-skilled workers.

In the early days of the nineteenth century the fitter was still a very highly-skilled craftsman, with an experience acquired only after many years of apprenticeship and work as an assistant. Soho formed no exception. All filing and chipping was still done by hand, and the fitter had to combine manual skill with a certain degree of empirical technical knowledge demanded by the undeveloped state of both the product and the machinery which produced it. In one way, however, the beginnings of modern practice can be seen. Fitting did not remain a general unregulated job. A subdivision had already taken place, and the varieties of fitting work were strictly systematised. To each fitter or group of fitters only one article or group of similar articles was assigned. The nozzles, which demanded a very high degree of skill were, as we have seen, dealt with separately. Similarly all the different valves were fitted by one man and two assistants; and the following are some of the other groups of engine parts fitted separately: parallel motions; governors and throttle valves; working gears; steam cases; the various pumps and so on.

The grouping of these parts was done in the same logical way in which they appeared on the Memoranda previously discussed. The basis was technological and the articles which each group of workmen (consisting, sometimes, of a foreman with several assistants, sometimes, of only one or two men with one boy) was asked to work, were all more or less of a similar type. The principle of division of labour had in this way obtained a strong foothold in the engineering industry—the least suited to an early introduction of it—and it is undoubtedly the desire to increase each man's efficiency in the performance of a particular job, though probably decreasing his general skill, which accounts for it.

The next important class is that of the turners. They, too, had long been general workmen of whom a high degree of skill was expected. Most of the boring work also was usually done by them on an ordinary lathe. To-day greater subdivisions have been introduced, and with the improvements in lathes, such as the automatic lathe, 'the province of the turner has been lessened more and more . . . The natural result is that he has ceased to be the all-round workman that he used to be.' At Soho, although he was a skilled craftsman, the turner was by no means the general workman taken as typical even of the later part of the last century. We find that a number of different classes had been set up and that different work was assigned to each. So the turning, drawfiling and finishing of pistons and air-pump rods was to be done by William Buxton and John Mincham, while John Allport and John Hunt were detailed for the turning of the heavier parts—cylinders, pistons, rotative shafts, etc. Another man and his assistant did the turning of smaller parts, such as gudgeons for engines below 16 horse-power; but here a certain mixing of functions seems to have existed, for they were also to fit the 'Sun and Planet' wheels and certain other parts.

Boring was done by two other men specially employed for this job, and the large and small drills were worked by Samuel Eales and Francis Evans respectively.

———

Now, after this detailed study of the four papers dealing with the layout of shops and machinery, routing of processes and division of work, some general idea can, perhaps be formed of the organization of production at Soho and the principles underlying these plans. The first thing to note is the fact that plans were drawn up at all; and the methods of planning adopted can, without any exaggeration, be described as scientific. In essence they follow the steps laid down as scientifically correct by modern theories. What is the main principle of this new science? For the best and shortest definition of it we must look to the economist rather than to the professional expert. 'Scientific Management', writes Marshall, 'is in the main a method of redistributing and reorganizing the functions and the mutual relations of the personnel of a great business, with the purpose of increasing aggregate efficiency by narrowing the range of responsibility of its employees and bringing careful studies to bear on the instructions given in regard to the simplest manual operations.'

This simple, yet fundamental, definition is certainly applicable to the Soho firm. One authority quoted before describes the scientific method as mainly consisting of the analysis of the problems into their elements, the collection of elaborate statistical data concerning these problems and the drawing of inferences from the records so collected. It is exactly in this way that Matthew Robinson Boulton and James Watt, jr., proceeded once they had reached the decision to extend and reorganize the existing plant. For some time previous to the drawing up of the plans, elaborate statistical records had been kept and these continued for some years after the establishment of the new *regime*. From the tables showing the value of goods sent out from Soho, together with the proportions of those made outside for the years 1791 to 1794, it is clear that some thought had been bestowed on the problem of estimating the prospective production. Details of the technical side of processes were also recorded. One of these, a 'Specification of articles bored, under the large drill for ye purpose of fixing a ratio for ye firm,' gives such items as the number, diameter, length and thickness of all bored parts for the various sizes of engines.

Thus, after some idea of the desired productive capacity of the plant had been reached, the problem of organizing the production processes was tackled from the technical point of view. The requirements in the way of machinery were ascertained, together with the shops in which it was to be housed, and the men who would be required to work it. In deciding the situation of the shops and the sequence of processes the state of development of engineering was the determining factor. Already, in 1779, Watt had written and printed for private circulation a small booklet entitled 'Directions for erecting and working the newly invented steam engines by Boulton & Watt.' It was intended to be used by clients of the firm and, above all, by their engine erectors; and it deals at great length with every step in the erection of an engine. By 1800 the booklet was to some extent out of date; but it undoubtedly helped considerably in the drawing up of the order of operations to be performed at Soho.

How does the layout compare with what is now considered the 'optimum'? It is usual to contrast the modern 'flow-of-work' structure with the old workshop structure. In the latter the arrangement is on the basis of shops in each of which only one particular operation is performed, e.g. drilling, boring, turning, or fitting. Historically this system arose as a result of manual production being superseded by the new machine technique which shifted the centre of interest from the whole product to a part process. Shops became separated in space. The new industrial revolution, however, established the doctrine of cheaper production through mass production. This could only be achieved through the avoidance of wasteful intervals (one of the causes of which is the retrograde movement of articles necessitated by the shop structure) in which the raw material would be brought from the stores into the first shop where it would travel to and fro between the various benches, and so on through the different shops, causing lack of work in one place and congestion in another.

The shop structure is by modern authorities considered a 'historical rather than a logical category'. It forms 'a transition between handicraft production and modern mass production'. The writer here quoted qualifies himself, however, by admitting that the workshop structure may be quite a good system provided the situation of the workshops follows the sequence of the production processes. This would be similar, to some extent, to the flow of work structure according to which there is only one gigantic shop in which the benches follow each other in space in the same order as the operations in time. The compromise between the two systems corresponds actually to the method employed at Soho. It is evident from the arrangement that this easy flow of the castings from one shop to the next was kept in mind. As far as the technical achievements of the time permitted, this was the best plan that could have been adopted. It was suited both to the size of the demand which, though considerable for the time, was certainly not large enough to call for mass production, as well as to the degree to which the application of machinery had been carried. In this respect there can be no doubt that all that the time could offer was adopted; and that amounted to considerably more than was customary. It brought with it an extension in the division and specialisation of labour, and, although manual work still remained in use for finer operations, it can, nevertheless, be stated that Soho was a scientifically planned factory, manufacturing steam engines by machines driven in their turn by steam power.

Today the adoption of scientific methods in the designing of plant is expected to lead to the all-round employment of the same methods: in solving problems of wage payment, book-keeping, costing, &c.; and since a high degree of scientific planning is claimed for Soho, further proof for this contention will be forthcoming in the discussion of those records that deal with the other factors mentioned.

2 Address on the Export of Machinery
Manchester Chamber of Commerce, 1826

Restrictive laws on the mobility of artisans and machines were first imposed in the 1770s. These were steadily extended in the first part of the nineteenth century, and were the subject of extensive debate. The laws against emigration were finally repealed in 1825 along with the Combination Laws. Restrictions of the export of machinery, however, continued until 1844. Issues of dispute centred on the definition and control over skill, the role of workmen and capitalists in invention, the definition of tools and machinery in relation to artisan skill, and the pivotal role of the capital goods sector. This document indicates the views of leading Lancashire textile manufacturers. They are calling here for further protection of their own interests by limiting the export of British machinery. They fear that the free access of foreign industrialists to British-made machines will lead to such improvements in foreign textile industries that they will pose a threat to British markets. To buttress their case, they argue that Britain's general industrial superiority rests on the advances she has made in her capital goods sector. This source of all other industrial progress should not, therefore, be made freely available to others.

Machinery cannot be classed either with raw produce or with manufactures. It differs essentially in character from both these great objects of commerce, and should be dealt with, in the arrangement of our general polity, according to its peculiar and distinctive properties. It consists of the concentrated mechanical skill of the country, embodied in a form by which we are enabled to produce our manufactures at a much less price than we could otherwise do.

The advocates for exportation alledge—

1st.—That we cannot prevent clandestine exportation.

2ndly.—That if we could prevent it, other countries would, by the aid of drawings and of emigrant English mechanics, make equally good machinery for themselves.—And

3rdly.—That we are witholding from our machine-makers, a branch of trade which they are entitled to enjoy, and from the country at large, the advantage which would follow from its existence.

To these allegations it may be answered—

1st.—That complicated and indistinct as the existing Laws are, regarding the exportation of machinery, there can be no doubt that they have materially checked, though they have not altogether prevented, the exportation of the machinery used in our principal manufactures.

2ndly.—To the second assumption—viz: that other nations would make machinery equal to ours, it is sufficient to reply, that they have never yet done it—that they are far behind us at present—and that while they are following in our steps, we may hope still to keep the lead, by our further progress in mechanical improvement.—And

3rdly.—That our machine-makers and mechanics are unable to supply the actual demand which already exists for their labour, for the use of our own manufactures, and that the interests of a particular class are never to be put in competition with the general welfare. As the exportation of machinery has not hitherto been allowed, no injury will be done to anyone by continuing the prohibiton.—To withhold a boon may be unjust, when no one would suffer from its concession—but to confer a bounty on one class, to the detriment of the whole, is partiality and favouritism—not substantial justice.

It is gratuitously assumed, that if an Export trade in machinery were allowed, it would be permanent.—The probability is great that it would not.—If, as is asserted, our rivals would soon make machinery equal to ours if we continue to withhold our own from them, this latent power would be called into successful exercise, much more rapidly, when an unrestrained export gave them free access to all our best machines.—The greater the first apparent success of the measure, the more speedy would be its decay. The power to use good machinery to advantage, implies and requires a power to keep it in perfect repair—but, as high a degree of mechanical skill is necessary *for repairing as for making anew.* —Why then should we presume that they would permanently continue to buy their new machines from us, and employ themselves only in repairs? Why, when they are eager to possess Machines that they may produce *manufactures* independently of us, should they not seek to become independent of us for their supply of *machinery* also?

The improvements in our machinery having been effected, by slow degrees and at great expense, by the reiterated and combined efforts of many individuals, we should, by exporting it, put our rivals, in a short time, and comparatively, at a small cost, in possession of what has, with us, been the result of so much ingenuity and perseverance.

Our machine-makers, who generally are not the authors of our mechanical inventions, but persons employed to put together the laborious and successful exertions of others, would for a time be almost exclusively exmployed in supplying foreign spinners and manufacturers with machinery of the newest and best construction, while we should be obliged to work on with our old machines, without being able, from the want of hands, to repair them, but at enormous expense. Our rivals would thus acquire, through our means, and at our cost, advantages which we ourselves have never enjoyed; and we should at the same time, be depriving ourselves of the power of entering fairly into compeition with them.

3 On the Evils of the Law Prohibiting the Export of Machinery
Manchester Committee of Machine Makers, 1841

The debates on the export of machinery continued into the 1840s when the restrictions on the free export of machinery were repealed. The answer to the case made (above) by the textile master for further restriction, was provided by the machine makers in their own agitation to have the laws repealed. They argued that England could expand her own small but crucial capital goods sector into the capital goods industry for the world. She ought to make the most of her ample markets for capital and highly skilled labour, as well as her resources of coal and iron, by making engineering her staple industry.

We come now to *The Advantages to be gained from the abolition of the Law*. These will partly have appeared from previous considerations, and will multiply upon us in proportion as we extend our reflections. The great and inevitable effect of the removal of the present restrictions will be, to make England the centre of mechanical inventions, and of their applications for the world. The strength and spirit of its trade will be seen when suffered to grapple with unfettered hands, with all the supposed advantages of other climes. Its internal resources will multiply with the sphere of its operation, and it will still be upon the advance of other countries in the march of civilization and moral worth. The character of the inhabitants of this island, its constitution, and its climate, are admirably adapted to ensure its ascendancy in proportion to the freedom of its trade. The skill and assiduity of our artizans are well known, and give us in point of labour an advantage over all other countries. The condition of society amongst us, renders it all but innate in the inhabitants of this isle. It is impossible that any Nation, without the greatest natural revolution, which it is absurd to anticipate, could rival us in a steady working population. It is this which has given this country its pre-eminence, and will so still more, in proportion as it receives encouragement from the extension of its commerce and manufactures. There is an extraordinary facility in an English workman, in making himself master of a Machine, simplifying and improving its working parts, keeping it in excellent condition, and turning it to the best account. This peculiarity in our national character, is stimulated by the certainty of meeting with its reward, and the prospect and ambition of rising in the world. How many splendid examples might be cited of our workmen raising themselves to enviable distinction and honourably-acquired wealth, by their own native energies? How many living instances have we, of men who have emancipated themselves from the trammels of inauspicious birth and neglected education, and taken their station in that class of society, where superior intelligence and moral worth are patented qualifications for admiration and esteem? The great mass of Continental workmen have no honourable pride or enterprise of this kind. Their ambition flows in other channels. In vain should we inquire amongst them for a Smeaton, a Watt, an Arkwright, a Peel, or a Telford. We should hear of a Massena, a Murat, and other chiefs, who have acquired for themselves a vain glorious renown, not as the benefactors, but as the destroyers of mankind.

In addition to the steady perseverance and active intelligence of its artizans, England possesses capital far more ample than any other Nation; she also abounds in cheap and inexhaustible Mines of Coal, Iron, and other Metals: the source of far greater riches to her than ever issued from the Mines of Golconda, or Peru, without which it would be next to impossible to carry out our great mechanical improvements, and to find profitable employment for which it is surely our duty as well as our interest to raising of the *Ore to the finished Machine.* Should we not foster and encourage such a trade, by every means in our power, instead of, as heretofore, paralyzing its onward march by legislative restriction and prohibition?

The erasure of this Law from the Statute book, will secure to our manufacturers, the advantage which they have hitherto so pre-eminently enjoyed, of being the first successfully to introduce and perfect New Machines and Inventions, and which, if they can maintain, will give them a decided advantage over the rest of the world. For if, by its removal, this country becomes the Mart for Machinery for the world, we hold out a premium for the Inventors of other countries, to make this their home, by offering to them the largest and most profitable market for their inventions; and where, from the skill of our artizans, and the great advancement of the mechanical arts, their crude ideas are most likely to be perfected and brought into profitable operation. And though the mechanical skill of this country has never been surpassed, we must not suppose that we have monopolized the inventive genius of our race, and that we have nothing to learn or fear from the ingenuity and experience of other nations.

———

The time cannot be far distant, when, in addition to the present markets, there will be New Continents of vast and unknown extent, as well as the numerous Islands of Polynesia, where civilization and inquiry have begun to dawn; and who will seek to avail themselves of the power of Machines, to effect local improvements in their country, as well as for the purposes of trade. Who are to become their Machine Makers? Are they to get them as other Nations have done, by offering a high premium to the smuggler? Or shall we force them to resort to Foreign Machine-makers, and deprive ourselves of so profitable a branch of trade? The question not being, whether our Machinery, with all its improvements shall go abroad, but whether we will quietly concede the trade to other Nations, and not secure to ourselves the legitimate profits of our own Inventions.

4 Block Machinery
George Dodd, 1867

George Dodd, the well-known popular journalist of industry here describes one of the most influential innovations of the first years of the
nineteenth century. The use of steam power and ordered 'assembly line'
production achieved one of its first successes in the manufacture of
ships' blocks. Brunel's designs and Maudslay's machines encapsulated
the principles which were to become important in technical change and
the organization of work much later in the century.

Block Machinery, A ship's *block*, or *tackle-block*, with its *shell, sheaves*,
and other parts, being a curious curved mass of wood, it occurred to the
elder Brunel, about the beginning of the present century that it ought
to be within the power of steam-worked machinery to fashion these
articles. Accordingly, by a due exercise of his remarkable ingenuity, he
devised the exquisite machinery which began to work in 1808. The
block passes through several beautiful machines in succession:—(1), A
straight cross-cutting saw cuts up elm to the proper lengths; (2), a
circular cross-cutting saw similarly prepares smaller pieces; (3), a reciprocating ripping saw cuts these pieces to the proximate length and
breadth of the block; (4), a circular ripping saw does the same thing for
smaller sizes; (5), a boring machine makes the perforations for the
sheave-holes; (6), a mortising machine cuts out the hollow cavity in the
block; (7), a corner saw cuts off the angles of the block diagonally, but
without rounding them; (8), a shaping machine gives the general
curvatures to the exterior; (9), a grooving machine makes the scores or
grooves which are to take the ropes; (10), a converting machine cuts off
and roughly shapes the slices of lignum vitae to make the sheaves; (11),
a coaking engine forms the cavity at the centre of the sheave, to receive
the bush and pins; (12), a drilling machine perfects this cavity; (13), a
facing lathe gives the exterior form to the sheave. The putting together
of the shell, the sheave, and the pin is hand-work. Messrs. Maudslay
made two complete sets of Brunel's machines—one for Portsmouth
dockyard, and one for Chatham. Brunel received £20,000 in six years
for his services in this matter; but it was estimated that the Government
saved much more than this amount in the first two years. Brunel's
block machinery undoubtedly established the principle of employing
steam-worked machines instead of hand-tools in fashioning wood for
carpentry etc.

5 On the Economy of Machinery and Manufactures
Charles Babbage, 1835

This extremely popular study of the principles of organization in factories and workshops (the first edition of 1833 sold 3,000 copies within a few months) was a far-seeing analysis of industry in terms of computer technology. Babbage spent most of his life attempting to devise a working computer. His singular study of the principles of manufacturing was the result of his observations in travels in the Midlands, the North of England and France, but many of his more striking insights seem derived from his preoccupation with the principles of the computer. The sections of his book here reprinted indicate his thoughts on time and motion studies and his ideas on the concept of manufacture. They also show his development of the analysis of the division of labour into the 'Babbage principle' that dividing the craft means cheapening the individual parts of a process. Another section indicates how he applied this notion to the division of mental labour. The final section shows his ideas on some sophisticated schemes for piece rates and workers' participation. Babbage wrote from the standpoint of the employers' interest, and was very much opposed to trade unions.

On the Method of Observing Manufactories

(160.) Having now reviewed the *mechanical* principles which regulate the successful application of mechanical science to great establishments for the production of manufactured goods, it remains for us to suggest a few inquiries, and to offer a few observations, to those whom an enlightened curiosity may lead to examine the factories of this or of other countries.

The remark,—that *it is important to commit to writing all information as soon as possible after it is received, especially when numbers are concerned,*—applies to almost all inquiries. It is frequently impossible to do this at the time of visiting an establishment, although not the slightest jealousy may exist; the mere act of writing information as it is communicated orally, is a great interruption to the examination of machinery. In such cases, therefore, it is advisable to have prepared beforehand the questions to be asked, and to leave blanks for the answers, which may be quickly inserted, as, in a multitude of cases, they are merely numbers. Those who have not tried this plan will be surprised at the quantity of information which may, through its means, be acquired, even by a short examination. Each manufacture requires its own list of questions, which will be better drawn up after the first visit. The following outline, which is very generally applicable, may suffice for an illustration; and to save time, it may be convenient to have it printed; and to bind up, in the form of a pocket book, a hundred copies of the skeleton forms for processes, with about twenty of the general enquiries.

GENERAL INQUIRIES
Outlines of a Description of any of the Mechanical Arts ought to contain Information on the following points.

Brief sketch of its history, particularly the date of its invention, and of its introduction into England.

Short reference to the previous states through which the material employed has passed; the places whence it is procured; the price of a given quantity.

(The various processes must now be described successively according to the plan which will be given in §161; after which the following information should be given.)

Are various kinds of the same article made in one establishment, or at different ones, and are there differences in the processes?

To what defects are the goods liable?

What substitutes or adulterations are used?

What waste is allowed by the master?

What tests are there of the goodness of the manufactured articles?

The weight of a given quantity, or number, and a comparison with that of the raw material?

The wholesale price at the manufactory? £ s. d. per

The usual retail price? £ s. d.

Who provide tools? Master, or men? Who repair tools? Master or men?

What is the expense of the machinery?

What is the annual wear and tear, and what its duration?

Is there any particular trade for making it? Where?

Is it made and repaired at the manufactory?

In any manufactory visited, state the number (   ) of processes; and of the persons employed in each process; and the quantity of manufactured produce.

What quantity is made annually in Great Britain?

Is the capital invested in manufactories large or small?

Mention the principal seats of this manufacture in England; and if it flourishes abroad, the places where it is established.

The duty, excise, or bounty, if any, should be stated, and any alterations in past years; and also the amount exported or imported for a series of years.

Whether the same article, but of superior, equal, or inferior make, is imported?

Does the manufacturer export, or sell, to a middleman, who supplies the merchant?

To what countries is it chiefly sent?—and in what goods are the returns made?

(161) Each process requires a separate skeleton, and the following outline will be sufficient for many different manufactories:—

Process(   ) Manufacture (   )
Place (   ) Name (   )
        date   183

The mode of executing it, with sketches of the tools or machine if necessary.

The number of persons necessary to attend the machine.

Are the operatives men, (   ) women, (   ) or children? (   ) If mixed, what are the proportions? ?

What is the pay of each? (s.   d.) (s.   d.) (s.   d.) per

What number (   ) of hours do they work per day?

Is it usual, or necessary, to work night and day without stopping?

Is the labour performed by piece or by day-work?

Who provide tools? Master, or men? Who repair tools? Master, or men?

What degree of skill is required, and how many years' (   ) apprenticeship?

The number of times (   ) the operation is repeated per day or per hour?

The number of failures (   ) in a thousand?

Whether the workmen or the master loses by the broken or damaged articles?

What is done with them?

If the same process is repeated several times, state the diminution or increase of measure, and the loss, if any, at each repetition.

(162.) In this skeleton, the answers to the questions are in some cases printed, as 'Who repair the tools?—*Masters, Men;*' in order that the proper answer may be underlined with a pencil. In filling up the answers which require numbers, some care should be taken: for instance, if the observer stands with his watch in his hand before a person heading a pin, the workman will almost certainly increase his speed, and the estimate will be too large. A much better average will result from inquiring what quantity is considered a fair day's work. When this cannot be ascertained, the number of operations performed in a given time may frequently be counted when the workman is quite unconscious that any person is observing him. Thus the sound made by the motion of a loom may enable the observer to count the number of strokes per minute, even though he is outside the building in which it is contained. It frequently happens, that in a series of answers to such questions, there are some which, although given directly, may also be deduced by a short calculation from others that are given or known; and advantage should always be taken of these verifications, in order to confirm the accuracy of the statements; or, in case they are discordant, to correct the apparent anomalies. In putting lists of questions into the hands of a person undertaking to give information upon any subject, it is in some cases desirable to have an estimate of the soundness of his judgement. The questions can frequently be so shaped, that some of them may indirectly depend on others; and one or two may be inserted whose answers can be obtained by other methods: nor is this process without its advantages in enabling us to determine the value of our own judgement. The habit of forming an estimate of the magnitude of any object or the frequency of any occurrence, immediately previous to our applying to it measure or number, tends materially to fix the attention and to improve the judgment.

Distinction between Making and Manufacturing

(163.) The *economical principles* which regulate the application of machinery, and which govern the interior of all our great factories, are quite as essential to the prosperity of a great commercial country, as are those mechanical principles, the operation of which has been illustrated in the preceding section.

(164.) A considerable difference exists between the terms *making* and *manufacturing*. The former refers to the production of *a small*, the latter to that of *a very large number of individuals*; and the difference is well illustrated in the evidence, given before the Committee of the House of Commons, on the Export of Tools and Machinery. On that occasion Mr. Maudslay stated, that he had been applied to by the Navy Board to make iron tanks for ships, and that he was rather unwilling to do so, as he considered it to be out of his line of business; however, he undertook to make one as a trial. The holes for the rivets were punched by hand-punching with presses, and the 1680 holes which each tank required cost seven shillings. The Navy Board, who required a large number, proposed that he should supply forty tanks a week for many months. The magnitude of the order made it worth his while to commence *manufacture*, and to make tools for the express business. Mr. Maudslay therefore offered, if the Board would give him an order for two thousand tanks, to supply them at the rate of eighty per week. The order was given: he made tools, by which the expense of punching the rivet-holes of each tank was reduced from seven shillings to ninepence; he supplied ninety-eight tanks a week for six months, and the price charged for each was reduced from seventeen pounds to fifteen.

(165.) If, therefore, the *maker* of an article wish to become a *manufacturer*, in the more extended sense of the term, he must attend to other principles besides those mechanical ones on which the successful execution of his work depends; and he must carefully arrange the whole system of his factory in such a manner, that the article he sells to the public may be produced at as small a cost as possible. Should he not be actuated at first by motives so remote, he will, in every highly civilized country, be compelled, by the powerful stimulus of competition, to attend to the principles of the domestic economy of manufactures. At every reduction in price of the commodity he makes, he will be driven to seek compensation in a saving of expense in some of the processes; and his ingenuity will be sharpened in this inquiry by the hope of being able in his turn to undersell his rivals. The benefit of the improvements thus engendered is, for a short time, confined to those from whose ingenuity they derive their origin; but when a sufficient experience has proved their value, they become generally adopted, until in their turn they are superseded by other more economical methods.

On the Division of Labour

(217.) Perhaps the most important principle on which the economy of a manufacture depends, is the *division of labour* amongst the persons who perform the work. The first application of this principle must have been made in a very early stage of society; for it must soon have been apparent, that a larger number of comforts and conveniences could be acquired by each individual, if one man restricted his occupation to the art of making bows, another to that of building houses, a third boats, and so on. This division of labour into trades was not, however, the result of an opinion that the general riches of the community would be increased by such an arrangement; but it must have arisen from the circumstance of each individual so employed discovering that he himself could thus make a greater profit of his labour than by pursuing more varied occupations. Society must have made considerable advances before this principle could have been carried into the workshop; for it is only in countries which have attained a high degree of civilization, and in articles in which there is a great competion amongst the producers, that the most perfect system of the division of labour is to be observed. The various principles on which the advantages of this system depend, have been much the subject of discussion amongst writers on Political Economy; but the relative importance of their influence does not appear, in all cases, to have been estimated with sufficient precision. It is my intention, in the first instance, to state shortly those principles, and then to point out what appears to me to have been omitted by those who have previously treated the subject.

(218.) 1. *Of the time required for learning.*—It will readily be admitted, that the portion of time occupied in the acquisition of any art will depend on the difficulty of its execution; and that the greater the number of distinct processes, the longer will be the time which the apprentice must employ in acquiring it. Five or seven years have been adopted, in a great many trades, as the time considered requisite for a lad to acquire a sufficient knowledge of his art, and to enable him to repay by his labour, during the latter portion of his time, the expense incurred by his master at its commencement. If, however, instead of learning *all* the different processes for making a needle, for instance, his attention be confined to one operation, the portion of time consumed unprofitably at the commencement of his apprenticeship will be small, and all the rest of it will be beneficial to his master: and, consequently, if there be any competition amongst the masters, the apprentice will be able to make better terms, and diminish the period of his servitude. Again, the facility of acquiring skill in a single process, and the early period of life at which it can be made a source of profit, will induce a greater number of parents to bring up their children to it; and from this circumstance also, the number of workmen being increased, the wages will soon fall.

(219.) 2. *Of waste of materials in learning.*—A certain quantity of material will, in all cases, be consumed unprofitably, or spoiled by every person who learns an art; and as he applies himself to each new process, he will waste some of the raw material, or of the partly manufactured commodity. But if each man commit this waste in acquiring successively every process, the quantity of waste will be much greater than if each person confine his attention to one process; in this view of the subject, therefore, the division of labour will diminish the price of production.

(220.) 3. Another advantage resulting from the division of labour is, *the saving of that portion of time which is always lost in changing from one occupation to another.* —When the human hand, or the human head has been for some time occupied in any kind of work, it cannot instantly change its employment with full effect. The muscles of the limbs employed have acquired a flexibility during their exertion, and those not in action a stiffness during rest, which renders every change slow and unequal in the commencement. Long habit also produces in the muscles exercised a capacity for enduring fatigue to a much greater degree than they could support under other circumstances. A similar result seems to take place in any change of mental exertion; the attention bestowed on the new subject not being so perfect at first as it becomes after some exercise.

(221.) 4. *Change of Tools.*—The employment of different tools in the successive processes is another cause of the loss of time in changing from one operation to another. If these tools are simple, and the change is not frequent, the loss of time is not considerable; but in many processes of the arts the tools are of great delicacy, requiring accurate adjustment every time they are used; and in many cases the time employed in adjusting bears a large proportion to that employed in using the tool. The sliding-rest, the dividing and the drilling-engine, are of this kind; and hence, in manufactories of sufficient extent, it is found to be good economy to keep one machine constantly employed in one kind of work: one lathe, for example, having a screw motion to its sliding-rest along the whole length of its bed, is kept constantly making cylinders; another, having a motion for equalizing the velocity of the work at the point at which it passes the tool, is kept for facing surfaces; whilst a third is constantly employed in cutting wheels.

(222.) 5. *Skill acquired by frequent repetition of the same process.* —The constant repetition of the same process necessarily produces in the workman a degree of excellence and rapidity in his particular department, which is never possessed by a person who is obliged to execute many different processes. This rapidity is still further increased from the circumstance that most of the operations in factories, where the division of labour is carried to a considerable extent, are paid for as piece-work. It is difficult to estimate in number the effect of this cause upon production. In nail-making, Adam Smith has stated, that it is almost three to one, for, he observes, that a smith accustomed to make nails, but whose whole business has not been that of a nailer, can make only from eight hundred to a thousand per day; whilst a lad who had never exercised any other trade, can make upwards of two thousand three hundred a day.

(223.) In different trades, the economy of production arising from the last-mentioned cause will necessarily be different. The case of nail-making, is, perhaps, rather an extreme one. It must, however be observed, that, in one sense, this is not a permanent source of advantage; for, though it acts at the commencement of an establishment, yet every month adds to the skill of the workmen; and at the end of three or four years they will not be very far behind those who have never practised any other branch of their art. Upon an occasion when a large issue of bank-notes was required, a clerk at the Bank of England signed his name, consisting of seven letters, including the initial of his Christian name, five thousand three hundred times during eleven working hours, besides arranging the notes he had signed in parcels of fifty each.

(224.) 6. *The division of labour suggests the contrivance of tools and machinery to execute its processes.*—When each process, by which any article is produced, is the sole occupation of one individual, his whole attention being devoted to a very limited and simple operation, improvements in the form of his tools, or in the mode of using them are much more likely to occur to his mind, then if it were distracted by a greater variety of circumstances. Such an improvement in the tool is generally the first step towards a machine. If a piece of metal is to be cut in a lathe, for example, there is one particular angle at which the cutting-tool must be held to insure the cleanest cut; and it is quite natural that the idea of fixing the tool at that angle should present itself to an intelligent workman. The necessity of moving the tool slowly, and in the direction parallel to itself, would suggest the use of a screw, and thus arises the sliding-rest. It was probably the idea of mounting a chisel in a frame, to prevent its cutting too deeply, which gave rise to the common carpenter's plane. In cases where a blow from a hammer is employed, experience teaches the proper force required. The transition from the hammer held in the hand to one mounted upon an axis, and lifted regularly to a certain height by some mechanical contrivance, requires perhaps a greater degree of invention than those just instanced; yet it is not difficult to perceive, that, if the hammer always falls from the same height, its effect must always be the same.

(225.) When each process has been reduced to the use of some simple tool, the union of all these tools, actuated by one moving power, constitutes a machine. In contriving tools and simplifying processes, the operative workmen are, perhaps, most successful; but it requires far other habits to combine into one machine these scattered arts. A previous education as a workman in a peculiar trade, is undoubtedly a valuable preliminary; but in order to make such combinations with any reasonable expectation of success, an extensive knowledge of machinery, and the power of making mechanical drawings, are essentially requisite. These accomplishments are now much more common than they were formally; and their absence was, perhaps, one of the causes of the multitude of failures in the early history of many of our manufactures.

(226.) Such are the principles usually assigned as the causes of the advantage resulting from the division of labour. As in the view I have taken of the question, the most important and influential cause has been altogether unnoticed, I shall re-state those principles in the words of Adam Smith: 'The great increase in the quantity of work, which, in consequence of the division of labour, the same number of people are capable of performing, is owing to three different circumstances: first, to the increase of dexterity in every particular workman; secondly, to the saving of time, which is commonly lost in passing from one species of work to another; and, lastly, to the invention of a great number of machines which facilitate and abridge labour, and enable one man to do the work of many.' Now, although all these are important causes, and each has its influence on the result; yet it appears to me, that any explanation of the cheapness of manufactured articles, as consequent upon the division of labour, would be imcomplete if the following principle were omitted to be stated.

That the master manufacturer, by dividing the work to be executed into different processes, each requiring different degrees of skill or of force, can purchase exactly that precise quantity of both which is necessary for each process; whereas, if the whole work were executed by one workman, that person must possess sufficient skill to perform the most difficult, and sufficient strength to execute the most laborious, of the operations into which the art is divided.

(241.) We have already mentioned what may, perhaps, appear paradoxical to some of our readers,—that the division of labour can be applied with equal success to mental as to mechanical operations, and that it ensures in both the same economy of time. A short account of its practical application, in the most extensive series of calculations ever executed, will offer an interesting illustration of this fact, whilst at the same time it will afford an occasion for shewing that the arrangements which ought to regulate the interior economy of a manufactory, are founded on principles of deeper root than may have been supposed, and are capable of being usefully employed in preparing the road to some of the sublimest investigations of the human mind.

(242.) In the midst of that excitement which accompanied the Revolution of France and the succeeding wars, the ambition of the nation, unexhausted by its fatal passion for military renown, was at the same time directed to some of the nobler and more permanent triumphs which mark the era of a people's greatness,—and which receive the applause of posterity long after their conquests have been wrested from them, or even when their existence as a nation may be told only by the page of history. Amongst their enterprises of science, the French government was desirous of producing a series of mathematical tables, to facilitate the application of the decimal system which they had so recently adopted. They directed, therefore, their mathematicians to construct such tables, on the most extensive scale. Their most distinguished philosophers, responding fully to the call of their country, invented new methods for this laborious task; and a work, completely answering the large demands of the government, was produced in a remarkably short period of time.

——————

(244.) The ancient methods of computing tables were altogether inapplicable to such a proceeding. M. Prony, therefore, wishing to avail himself of all the talent of his country in devising new methods, formed the first section of those who were to take part in this enterprise out of five or six of the most eminent mathematicians in France.

First Section.—The duty of this first section was to investigate, amongst the various analytical expressions which could be found for the same function, that which was most readily adapted to simple numerical calculation by many individuals employed at the same time. This section had little or nothing to do with the actual numerical work. When its labours were concluded, the formulae on the use of which it had decided, were delivered to the second section.

Second Section.—This section consisted of seven or eight persons of considerable acquaintance with mathematics; and their duty was to convert into numbers the formulae put into their hands by the first section,—an operation of great labour; and then to deliver out these formulae to the members of the third section, and receive from them the finished calculations. The members of this second section had certain means of verifying the calculations without the necessity of repeating, or even of examining, the whole of the work done by the third section.

Third Section.—The members of this section, whose number varied from sixty to eighty, received certain numbers from the second section, and, using nothing more than simple addition and subtraction, they returned to that section the tables in a finished state. It is remarkable that nine-tenths of this class had no knowledge of arithmetic beyond the two first rules which they were thus called upon to exercise, and that these persons were usually found more correct in their calculations, than those who possessed a more extensive knowledge of the subject.

(245.) When it is stated that the tables thus computed occupy seventeen large folio volumes, some idea may perhaps be formed of the labour. From that part executed by the third class, which may almost be termed mechanical, requiring the least knowledge and by far the greatest exertions, the first class were entirely exempt. Such labour can always be purchased at an easy rate. The duties of the second class, although requiring considerable skill in arithmetical operations, were yet in some measure relieved by the higher interest naturally felt in those more difficult operations. The exertions of the first class are not likely to require, upon another occasion, so much skill and labour as they did upon the first attempt to introduce such a method; but when the completion of a calculating-engine shall have produced a substitute for the whole of the third section of computers, the attention of analysts will naturally be directed to simplifying its application, by a new discussion of the methods of converting analytical formulae into numbers.

(246.) The proceeding of M. Prony, in this celebrated system of calculation, much resembles that of a skilful person about to construct a cotton or silk-mill, or any similar establishment. Having, by his own genius, or through the aid of his friends, found that some improved machinery may be successfully applied to his pursuit, he makes drawings of his plans of the machinery, and may himself be considered as constituting the first section. He next requires the assistance of operative engineers capable of executing the machinery he has designed, some of whom should understand the nature of the processes to be carried on; and these constitute his second section. When a sufficient number of machines have been made, a multitude of other persons, possessed of a lower degree of skill, must be employed in using them; these form the third section: but their work, and the just performance of the machines, must be still superintended by the second class.

———

(305.) A most erroneous and unfortunate opinion prevails amongst workmen in many manufacturing countries, that their own interest and that of their employers are at variance. The consequences are,—that valuable machinery is sometimes neglected, and even privately injured,—that new improvements, introduced by the masters, do not receive a fair trial,—and that the talents and observations of the workmen are not directed to the improvement of the processes in which they are employed. This error is, perhaps, most prevalent where the establishment of manufactories has been of recent origin, and where the number of persons employed in them is not very large: thus, in some of the Prussian provinces on the Rhine it prevails to a much greater extent than in Lancashire. Perhaps its diminished prevalence in our own manufacturing districts, arises partly from the superior information spread amongst the workmen; and partly from the frequent examples of persons, who by good conduct and an attention to the interests of their employers for a series of years, have become foremen, or who have ultimately been admitted into advantageous partnerships. Convinced as I am, from my own observation, that the prosperity and success of the master manufacturer is essential to the welfare of the workman, I am yet compelled to admit that this connection is, in many cases, too remote to be always understood by the latter: and whilst it is perfectly true that workmen, as a class, derive advantage from the prosperity of their employers, I do not think that each individual partakes of that advantage exactly in proportion to the extent to which he contributes to it; nor do I perceive that the resulting advantage is as immediate as it might become under a different system.

(306.) It would be of great importance, if, in every large establishment the mode of payment could be so arranged, that every person employed should derive advantage from the success of the whole: and that the profits of each individual should advance, as the factory itself produced profit, without the necessity of making any change in the wages. This is by no means easy to effect, particularly amongst that class whose daily labour procures for them their daily food. The system which has long been pursued in working the Cornish mines, although not exactly fulfilling these conditions, yet possesses advantages which make it worthy of attention, as having nearly approached towards them, and as tending to render fully effective the faculties of all who are engaged in it. I am the more strongly induced to place before the reader a short sketch of this system, because its similarity to that which I shall afterwards recommend for trial, will perhaps remove some objections to the latter, and may also furnish some valuable hints for conducting any experiment which might be undertaken.

(307.) In the mines of Cornwall, almost the whole of the operations, both above and below ground, are contracted for. The manner of making the contract is nearly as follows. At the end of every two months, the work which it is proposed to carry on during the next period is marked out. It is of three kinds. 1. *Tutwork*, which consists in sinking shafts, driving levels, and making excavations: this is paid for by the fathom in depth, or in length, or by the cubic fathom. 2. *Tribute*, which is payment for raising and dressing the ore, by means of a certain part of its value when rendered merchantable. It is this mode of payment which produces such admirable effects. The miners, who are to be paid in proportion to the richness of the vein, and the quantity of metal extracted from it, naturally become quick-sighted in the discovery of ore, and in estimating its value; and it is their interest to avail themselves of every improvement that can bring it more cheaply to market. 3. *Dressing*. The 'Tributors', who dig and dress the ore, can seldom afford to dress the coarser parts of what they raise, at their contract price; this portion, therefore, is again let out to other persons, who agree to dress it at an advanced price.

(308.) I shall now present the outline of a system which appears to me to be pregnant with the most important results, both to the class of workmen and to the country at large; and which, if acted upon, would, in my opinion, permanently raise the working classes, and greatly extend the manufacturing system.

The general principles on which the proposed system is founded, are—

1st. *That a considerable part of the wages received by each person employed should depend on the profits made by the establishment; and,*

2nd. *That every person connected with it should derive more advantage from applying any improvement he might discover, to the factory in which he is employed, than he could by any other course.*

(309.) It would be difficult to prevail on the large capitalist to enter upon any system, which would change the division of the profits arising from the employment of his capital in setting skill and labour in action; any alteration, therefore, must be expected from the small capitalist, or from the higher class of workmen, who combine the two characters; and to these latter classes, whose welfare will be first affected, the change is most important. I shall therefore first point out the course to be pursued in making the experiment; and then, taking a particular branch of trade as an illustration, I shall examine the merits and defects of the proposed system as applied to it.

BUTTON .MAKING. STAMPING.PRESSING AND PUNCHING.

(310.) Let us suppose, in some large manufacturing town, ten or twelve of the most intelligent and skilful workmen to unite, whose character for sobriety and steadiness are good, and are well known among their own class. Such persons will each possess some small portion of capital; and let them join with one or two others who have raised themselves into the class of small master manufacturers, and, therefore possess rather a larger portion of capital. Let these persons, after well considering the subject, agree to establish a manufactory of fire-irons and fenders; and let us suppose that each of the ten workmen can command forty pounds, and each of the small capitalists possesses two hundred pounds: thus they have a capital of 800*l*. with which to commence business; and, for the sake of simplifying, let us further suppose the labour of each of these twelve persons to be worth two pounds a week. One portion of their capital will be expended in procuring the tools necessary for their trade, which we shall take at 100*l*., and this must be considered as their fixed capital. The remaining 400*l*. must be employed as circulating capital, in purchasing the iron with which their articles are made, in paying the rent of their workshops, and in supporting themselves and their families until some portion of it is replaced by the sale of the goods produced.

(311.) Now the first question to be settled is, what proportion of the profit should be allowed for the use of capital, and what for skill and labour? It does not seem possible to decide this question by any abstract reasoning: if the capital supplied by each partner is equal, all difficulty will be removed; if otherwise, the proportion must be left to find its level, and will be discovered by experience; and it is probable that it will not fluctuate much. Let us suppose it to be agreed that the capital of 800*l*. shall receive the wages of one workman. At the end of each week every workman is to receive one pound as wages, and one pound is to be divided amonst the owners of the capital. After a few weeks the returns will begin to come in; and they will soon become nearly uniform. Accurate accounts should be kept of every expense and of all the sales; and at the end of each week the profit should be divided. A certain portion should be laid aside as a reserved fund, another portion for repair of the tools, and the remainder being divided into thirteen parts, one of these parts would be divided amongst the capitalist and one belong to each workman. Thus each man would, in ordinary circumstances, make up his usual wages of two pounds weekly. If the factory went on prosperously, the wages of the men would increase; if the sales fell off they would be diminished. It is important that every person employed in the establishment, whatever might be the amount paid for his services, whether he act as labourer or porter, as the clerk who keeps the accounts, or as book-keeper employed for a few hours once a week to superintend them, should receive one half of what his service is worth in fixed salary, the other part varying with the success of the undertaking.

(312.) In such a factory, of course, division of labour would be introduced; some of the workmen would be constantly employed in forging the fire-irons, others in polishing them, others in piercing and forming the fenders. It would be essential that the time occupied in each process, and also its expense, should be well ascertained; information which would soon be obtained very precisely. Now, if a workman should find a mode of shortening any of the processes, he would confer a benefit on the whole party, even if they received but a small part of the resulting profit. For the promotion of such discoveries, it would be desirable that those who make them should either receive some reward, to be determined after a sufficient trial by a committee assembling periodically; or if they be of high importance, that the discoverer should receive one-half, or two-thirds, of the profit resulting from them during the next year, or some other determinate period, as might be found expedient. As the advantages of such improvements would be clear gain to the factory, it is obvious that such a share might be allowed to the inventor, that it would be for his interest rather to give the benefit of them to his partners, than to dispose of them in any other way.

(313.) The result of such arrangements in a factory would be,

1. That every person engaged in it would have a *direct* interest in its prosperity; since the effect of any success, or falling off, would almost

immediately produce a corresponding change in his own weekly receipts.

2. Every person concerned in the factory would have an immediate interest in preventing any waste or mismanagement in all the departments.

3. The talents of all connected with it would be strongly directed to its improvement in every department.

4. None but workmen of high character and qualifications could obtain admission into such establishments; because when any additional hands were required, it would be the common interest of all to admit only the most respectable and skilful; and it would be far less easy to impose upon a dozen factory workmen than upon the single proprietor of a factory.

5. When any circumstance produced a glut in the market, more skill would be directed to diminishing the cost of production; and a portion of the time of the men might then be occupied in a repairing and improving their tools, for which a reserved fund would pay, thus checking present, and at the same time facilitating future production.

6. Another advantage, of no small importance, would be the total removal of all real or imaginary causes for combinations. The workmen and the capitalist would so shade into each other, — would so *evidently* have a common interest, and their difficulties and distresses would be mutually so well understood, that, instead of combining to oppress one another, the only combination which could exist would be a most powerful union *between* both parties to overcome their common difficulties.

(314.) One of the difficulties attending such a system is, that capitalists would at first fear to embark in it, imagining that the workmen would receive too large a share of the profits: and it is quite true that the workmen would have a larger share than at present: but, at the same time, it is presumed the effect of the whole system would be, that the total profits of the establishment being much increased, the smaller proportion allowed to capital under this system would yet be greater in actual amount, than that which results to it from the larger share in the system now existing.

(315.) It is possible that the present laws relating to partnerships might interfere with factories so conducted. If this interference could be obviated by confining their purchases under the proposed system to ready money, it would be desirable to consider what changes in the law would be necessary to its existence:— and this furnishes another reason for entering into the question of limited partnerships.

(316.) A difficulty would occur also in discharging workmen who behaved ill, or who were not competent to their work; this would arise from their having a certain interest in the reserved fund, and, perhaps, from their possessing a certain portion of the capital employed; but without entering into detail, it may be observed, that such cases might be determined on by meetings of the whole establishment; and that if the policy of the laws favoured such establishments, it would scarcely be more difficult to enforce just regulations, than it now is to enforce some which are unjust, by means of combinations either amongst the masters or the men.

(317.) Some approach to this system is already practised in several trades: the mode of conducting the Cornish mines has already been alluded to; the payment to the crew of whaling ships is governed by this principle; the profits arising from fishing with nets on the south coast of England are thus divided: one-half the produce belongs to the owner of the boat and net; the other half is divided in equal portions between the persons using it, who are also bound to assist in repairing the net when injured.

6 A Day at a Copper and Lead Factory
George Dodd, 1843

This extract is taken from one of Dodd's popular collections on British industry. This book focussed on factories in London, and describes a wide array of activities from pianoforte manufacture to the gasworks, where certain factory principles had been applied. The selection here, from his essay on a copper and lead factory, shows concern for 'systematic arrangement', and an early application of the overhead assembly track.

The various trades, therefore, of 'copper-smiths,' 'brass-founders,' 'engine-makers,' 'lead-manufacturers,' 'back and vat makers,' and several others, are all combined by this firm.

Under these circumstances, a detailed account of all the operations would be wholly beyond our range in this article: we shall therefore only give a general description of the factory and its internal economy, together with the operations of the copper, lead, and mixed-metal manufacture.

On proceeding from Holborn to Farringdon Market, through the narrow crooked thoroughfare of Shoe Lane, we come to an open warehouse, on the outside of which are generally cranes, and porters employed in loading waggons with various manufactured articles of lead or copper. Into this warehouse, which immediately adjoins the northern side of the market, we enter, and see around us a mixed assemblage of rolls of lead, coils of pipe, cog-wheels, parts of machinery, and other articles of metal. Before analysing the dark, the dirty, the busy, the noisy scene which the ground-floor of the factory presents, we will descend a flight of iron steps leading therefrom, and grope our way through a series of underground vaults. These vaults are used principally as storerooms for metal in the crude and the partially-manufactured state, and exhibit evidences of a very complete system of arrangement. In one department are the 'pigs of lead,' just as they were received from the smelters; in another are 'blocks' of tin, ready to be melted and worked;

in other departments are all the various pieces and parts for pumps, engines, machines, etc., either cast in the foundry on the premises, or brought from foundries in the iron-districts. Every room or vault is surrounded by shelves or drawers, every shelf is marked, and every piece of metal, even to the smallest screw or nut, deposited in its proper compartment, and registered in a book. The superintendent of this department, who conducts his operations by lamp-light, receives from the founders these multifarious pieces, and delivers them to the foremen of the works upstairs when wanted for manufacturing purposes. Many hundred tons of metal, comprising iron, copper, brass, gun-metal, tin, and lead, are here deposited.

COPPERSMITHS.

Among the mechanical arrangements for facilitating the removal of heavy goods from one part of the factory to another, we noticed an ingenious railway fixed *near the ceiling or roof*, whereby boilers, coppers, stills, engines, etc., suspended from a wheeled carriage or frame, could be easily moved along above the head of the workmen without disturbing the manufacturing arrangements beneath. This contrivance arose out of the necessity for economizing space, but we are inclined to think that it might be advantageously employed under many other circumstances in large factories.

Let us now pass upwards from the ground-floor, and glance through the upper ranges of shops. The front portion of the first floor is occupied chiefly as a warehouse for finished goods in copper, gun-metal, lead, etc. Here, too, are various offices and counting-houses, and also a room appropriated to the draughtsmen. In the fitting-up of large factories, such as sugar refineries and distilleries, there are, as may be supposed, many drawings of plans, sections, elevations, diagrams, etc., necessary not only for making a contract and showing the proposed action of the whole machinery, but as working drawings for the guidance of the workmen. The preparation of such drawings is effected in the office here alluded to, where labelled drawers are devoted to the reception of different classes of drawings.

Behind the ware-rooms and offices extends a long apartment having windows all along both sides, and benches immediately beneath them: this busily-occupied room is the 'brazier's shop'. The 'pattern-room' is another of those which exhibit the advantages of systematic arrangement in a large factory. This room is fitted up with cases, shelves, and boxes, filled with patterns in wood, clay or metal, of the various pieces required to be cast in the foundry below. Every pattern, large and small, is numbered, or ticketed, so as to be readily found when wanted. To let everything 'have its place and be in its place,' is the simple but valuable principle on which alone the operations of such establishments as these can be kept free from confusion.

––––––

The remaining workshops of the factory are occupied by millwrights, machine-makers, pump-makers, and others employed in fitting up and putting together the various pieces of metal which, after being cast and forged elsewhere, are employed for the construction of machines and other apparatus. To enumerate all these various machines would be here both impracticable and unnecessary: they are of all degrees of complexity, from a water-cock to a steam-engine, and of various kinds of metal. But we may observe that one of these workshops extends a hundred and fifty feet in length; and along the entire extent of the room, just below the ceiling, and midway between the sides, is a roller or hollow cylinder, kept in rotation by a connecting band from the steam-engine beneath: this, as a source of power, sets in motion a large number of lathes, drilling machines, screw-cutting machines, etc., placed beneath.

––––––

We will now endeavour to follow the routine of some of the processes glanced at in the preceding paragraphs; explaining, as we proceed, the nature of some of the very effective machines brought into requisition. Perhaps it may be well to speak first of the principle of checking all the accounts. Every piece of copper, brass, etc., is weighed when given by the store-keeper to the foreman-of the works; every order has a symbol attached to it, not only on the books, but also stamped on the principal pieces of metal employed; the mode in which every hour of every man's time has been employed is strictly ascertained, in connection with the symbols attached to the respective orders; the 'time' of each workman is so ascertained and recorded that an error can hardly occur; and the wages and materials are so classed as to afford ready means of reference at any subsequent time. The details of the system we of course cannot enter into; but we may remark, that a period of six or eight years is stated to have elapsed in bringing the system, by gradual stages, to the degree of completeness necessary for the complicated operations of the factory.

7 On the Theory and Practice of Cotton Spinning
James Montgomery, 1836

This early guide to factory management shows perception of the significance of precision, speed control and layout in the factory. It also gives detailed advice on personnel management, and on levels of control over men's and women's work.

Cotton Spinning Factories, like all other establishments where a large capital is invested for the purpose of manufacturing any particular kind of goods upon an extensive scale, require to be very skilfully managed in order to make them profitable, either for producing a superior quality of yarn, or turning off a large quantity in proportion to the extent of the machinery. All the different departments may be arranged in the most judicious manner, and every machine made and adjusted on the most approved principles, and yet the establishment, from the way it is managed and the mode of government which generally prevails, may be greatly deficient in respect both to the quantity and quality of its produce.

It would be advantageous for the manager of a Cotton Mill to have a thorough knowledge of the business *in all* its details, as without this he must sometimes leave much of the management of certain departments to others, and they, occupying only a subordinate situation, are likely to feel a subordinate responsibility, and hence may arise much mismanagement, attended with loss to the proprietors, and followed with reflections on the manager; and if he is not himself thoroughly acquainted with the business, he will not be able to detect the deficiencies of others, and therefore be more liable to be taken advantage of. But the manager who knows his business, can both give directions to those that are under him, as well as discern whether they are qualified for the situations they occupy, and when they fail in their duty.

It is a most essential qualification on the part of the manager, that he be expert in performing *all kinds* of calculations connected with the business; the advantages of which will be apparent in various respects. First, in regulating the *speeds* of the different machines; second, in adjusting the *draughts* of the various machines; and third, in making *changes* in the qualities of the cotton and sizes of the yarn.

In regulating the *speeds* of the various machines, particularly in the preparation department, it is important to have them so that the one shall not be overdriven, nor the other working at an underspeed. Let the carding engines be adjusted to such a speed as will suit the nature of the cotton and the quality of the yarn for which they are preparing it; the speed of the drawing frame should also be regulated to take up exactly what the carding engines bring forward, without any unnecessary loss of time on the part of either, and all the other machines should be regulated in the same manner. But it might be desirable to ascertain the most advantageous speed, at which the different machines should be driven for the various qualities of yarn. The number of carding engines that should be allowed to the drawing frame, supposing the carding engines to be two feet broad, and the heads of the drawing frame paired two by two. It might, likewise, be proper to know the number of fly frame and jenny spindles that should be allowed to the foot of finishing carding, that is to every foot in the breadth of doffing cylinders. But, perhaps, there is nothing in the whole process, regarding which there exists a greater diversity of opinion amongst managers than these particulars; in fact, it is almost impossible to find two Mills exactly alike in this respect; some managers drive their machinery at a greater speed than others; some spread the cotton heavier, others pass it quicker through the carding: there are also some carding engines with more working tops than others, which admit of the cotton being put quicker through, whilst the same effect is produced upon it, etc., It is, therefore, impossible to lay down any rule that might be taken as a standard for every Factory; because what would suit one could not be adopted in another, as their system of working might be very different in various respects.

––––––

To have the large gearing all fitted up on the most approved plan, and the machinery arranged in the manner best calculated to facilitate the progress of the work, are, doubtless, objects of the greatest importance; but when once the establishment has been filled with machinery, and all its arrangements completed, it is better to let it remain as it is, than try to improve it; and, indeed, to begin then to make alterations, would be highly objectionable, because the money expended on these alterations might far exceed all the advantages arising from the supposed improvements. To keep all the machinery in good repair, and in the best working order, cannot be too highly recommended; as without doing so, it is impossible to produce a regular and uniform good quality of yarn; and to keep machinery in good order, by regular care and attention, is much easier than to repair it after it has been allowed to go out of repair from negligence and want of care.

But if it be necessary in order to render the business a source of profit to the proprietors that the manager know how to adjust the various machines, and adapt them to suit the different kinds of cotton and qualities of yarn, and that he be properly qualified to superintend and direct the various operations through which the cotton must pass, in being manufactured into yarn; it is no less necessary that a proper mode of government should generally prevail throughout the whole establishment, and, doubtless, it requires much wisdom and consid-

First Process
The Opener

eration, to know how to act on all occasions in the government of a large establishment, where there are a number of different classes of workers employed, so as to avoid all *unnecessary* severity, and, at the same time, maintain proper authority. I do not hesitate to assert, that a Spinning Factory can never be managed more profitably, and more to the satisfaction of the proprietors, than when there exists a good feeling and a good understanding between the manager and workers. But to the manager who has an extensive charge, the duties of which he is anxious to discharge faithfully, circumstances will frequently occur, tending to agitate the mind and ruffle the temper, on which occasions it is difficult for him to act with that consideration and prudence which he himself would approve of; and it is, perhaps, much easier for one person to lay down rules for another to walk by, than to act up to them himself. But this is a very tender point to touch upon, and shall, therefore, be treated very briefly. It may, therefore, be stated, in a general way, that in governing a Spinning Factory with propriety, it would be prudent for the manager, while guarding against too much *lenity* on the one hand, to be careful to avoid too much *severity* on the other; let him be firm and decisive in all his measures, but not over-

bearing and tyrannical; not too distant and haughty, but affable and easy of access, yet not too familiar. In the giving or orders or directions, it is much better to give them in a pleasant manner, but with few words; they are then likely to be received with a good grace, and promptly obeyed. But to be frequently giving orders and laying down rules, which are never followed up, tends only to harass the mind without any good effect. If the manager be strictly just and impartial, showing no desire to favour one more than another, but always treating every person according to their merits, it generally has a good effect on the minds of those who are under him, by impressing them with the assurance that it is only by uniform attention to their business that they can secure his approbation: in a word, let the manager, at all times, maintain that dignified deportment which good sense would dictate — let him conduct himself so as to make this impression on the minds of all who are under him, viz. that while they continue to attend their work quietly and diligently, they will not be causelessly interfered with, but allowed to attend their employment in peace.

———

Such, then, are a few of those things which cause frequent disputes between the masters and operatives; they are merely stated here without saying whether they are right or wrong, or whether it is the duty of the masters to attend to them or not. But to proceed with this delicate subject. In regard to the carding and spinning master's situation, these being rather different, require somewhat different modes of government. In the spinning department there are men who have the charge of their own work, and are paid only for what they do, and responsible both for the quantity and quality of their work; they can also be made sensible of the consequences that would result from any degree of carelessness or negligence on their part; and hence it is not necessary that the spinning master should be always present. But this is not the case in the carding department, for there they are mostly women on set wages, whom it is difficult to make sensible of their responsibility, and the evils resulting from carelessness on their part; and, therefore, they require to be constantly looked over: hence, the carding master should never be out of their view, as much depends upon the proper management of the carding department for making good yarn.

8 To the Superintendents of Manufactories
Robert Owen, 1813

Robert Owen, the successful manager and textile industrialist, turned to philanthropy and socialism in later life. From 1800 to 1829 Owen was partner and manager of the New Lanark mill community. He spent these years organising the community as a model of the humane treatment, and effective disciplining, of labour. Here he explains, in a language purposely designed to convince his capitalist audience, the advantages involved in looking to the good order and good repair of labour as well as of machinery.

An Address
To the Superintendents of Manufactories and to those Individuals generally, who, by giving Employment to an aggregated Population, may easily adopt the Means to form the sentiments and Manners of such a Population.

Like you, I am a manufacturer for pecuniary profit. But having for many years acted on principles the reverse in many respects of those in which you have been instructed, and having found my procedure beneficial to others and to myself, even in a pecuniary point of view, I am anxious to explain such valuable principles, that you and those under your influence may equally partake of their advantages.

In two Essays, already published, I have developed some of these principles, and in the following pages you will find still more of them explained, with some detail of their application to practice, under the particular local circumstances in which I undertook the direction of the New Lanark Mills and Establishment.

By those details you will find, that from the commencement of my management I viewed the population, with the mechanism and every other part of the establishment, as a system composed of many parts, and which it was my duty and interest so to combine, as that every hand, as well as every spring, lever, and wheel, should effectually cooperate to produce the greatest pecuniary gain to the proprietors.

Many of you have long experienced in your manufacturing operations the advantages of substantial, well-contrived, and well-executed machinery.

Experience has also shown you the difference of the results between mechanism which is neat, clean, well arranged, and always in a high state of repair, and that which is allowed to be dirty, in disorder, without the means of preventing unnecessary friction, and which therefore becomes, and works, much out of repair.

In the first case, the whole economy and management are good; every operation proceeds with ease, order, and success. In the last, the reverse must follow, and a scene be presented of counteraction, confusion, and dissatisfaction among all the agents and instruments interested or occupied in the general process, which cannot fail to create great loss.

If then due care as to the state of your inanimate machines can produce such beneficial results, what may not be expected if you devote equal attention to your vital machines, which are far more wonderfully constructed?

When you shall acquire a right knowledge of these, of their curious mechanism, of their self-adjusting powers; when the proper main spring shall be applied to their varied movements, you will become conscious of their real value, and you will be readily induced to turn your thoughts more frequently from your inanimate to your living machines; you will discover that the latter may be easily trained and directed to procure a large increase of pecuniary gain, while you may also derive from them high and substantial gratification.

Will you then continue to expend large sums of money to procure the best devised mechanism of wood, brass, or iron; to retain it in perfect repair; to provide the best substance for the prevention of unnecessary friction, and to save it from falling into premature decay? Will you also devote years of intense application to understand the connexion of the various parts of these lifeless machines, to improve their effective powers, and to calculate with mathematical precision all their minute and combined movements? And when in these transactions you estimate time by minutes, and the money expended for the chance of increased gain by fractions, will you not afford some of your attention to consider whether a portion of your time and capital would not be more advantageously applied to improve your living machines?

From experience which cannot deceive me, I venture to assure you, that your time and money so applied, if directed by a true knowledge of the subject, would return you not five, ten, or fifteen per cent for your capital so expended, but often fifty and in many cases a hundred per cent.

I have expended much time and capital upon improvements of the living machinery; and it will soon appear that the time and money so expended in the manufactory at New Lanark, even while such improvements are in progress only, and but half their beneficial effects attained, are now producing a return exceeding fifty per cent, and will shortly create profits equal to cent per cent on the original capital expended in them.

Indeed, after experience of the beneficial effects, from due care and attention to the mechanical implements, it became easy to a reflecting mind to conclude at once, that at least equal advantages would arise from the application of similar care and attention to the living instruments. And when it was perceived that inanimate mechanism was greatly improved by being made firm and substantial; that it was the essence of economy to keep it neat, clean, regularly supplied with the best substance to prevent unnecessary friction, and, by proper provision for the purpose, to preserve it in good repair; it was natural to conclude that the more delicate, complex, living mechanism would be equally improved by being trained to strength and activity; and that it would also prove true economy to keep it neat and clean; to treat it with kindness, that its mental movements might not experience too much irritating friction; to endeavour by every means to make it more perfect; to supply it regularly with a sufficient quantity of wholesome food and other necessaries of life, that the body might be preserved in good working condition, and prevented from being out of repair, or falling prematurely to decay.

These anticipations are proved by experience to be just.

Since the general introduction of inanimate mechanism into British manufactories, man, with few exceptions, has been treated as a secondary and inferior machine; and far more attention has been given to perfect the raw materials of wood and metals than those of body and mind. Give but due reflection to the subject, and you will find that man, even as an instrument for the creation of wealth, may be still greatly improved.

But, my friends, a far more interesting and gratifying consideration remains. Adopt the means which ere long shall be rendered obvious to every understanding, and you may not only partially improve those living instruments, but learn how to impart to them such excellence as shall make them infinitely surpass those of the present and all former times.

Here then is an object which truly deserves your attention; and instead of devoting all your faculties to invent improved inanimate mechanism, let your thoughts be, at least in part, directed to discover how to combine the more excellent materials of body and mind, which, by a well-devised experiment, will be found capable of progressive improvement.

Thus seeing with the clearness of noon-day light, thus convinced with the certainty of conviction itself, let us not perpetuate the really unnecessary evils, which our present practices inflict on this large proportion of our fellow subjects. Should your pecuniary interests somewhat suffer by adopting the line of conduct now urged, many of you are so wealthy, that the expense of founding and continuing at your respective establishments the institutions necessary to improve your animate machines, would not be felt. But when you may have ocular demonstration that, instead of any pecuniary loss, a well-directed attention to form the character and increase the comforts of those who are so entirely at your mercy will essentially add to your gains, prosperity, and happiness; no reasons except those founded on ignorance of your self-interest, can in future prevent you from bestowing your chief care on the living machines which you employ; and by so doing you will prevent an accumulation of human misery, of which it is now difficult to form an adequate conception.

That you may be convinced of this most valuable truth, which due reflection will show you is founded on the evidence of unerring facts, is the sincere wish of

The Author

9 The Philosophy of Manufactures
Andrew Ure, 1835

Ure was a well-known lecturer at the Andersonian Institute (one of the first technical schools) between 1804 and 1830, and during and after that time was a scientific and technical consultant to various manufacturers. His *Philosophy of Manufactures* was a famous apologia for the factory system. The sections here reprinted indicate his fascination with self-acting machinery and automatic processes, and his view that the major feature of the factory system was to remove skilled work from the workman and to place it under the control of self-regulating machinery. He criticized Babbage's ideas on the division of labour and looked instead to the impact of self-regulating power. His book clearly indicates a fear of the militancy of skilled labour and a conscious attempt to connect technology with capitalist control of the work process.

The term *Factory*, in technology, designates the combined operation of many orders of work-people, adult and young, in tending with assiduous skill a system of productive machines continuously impelled by a central power. This definition includes such organisations as cotton-mills, flax-mills, silk-mills, woollen-mills, and certain engineering works; but it excludes those in which the mechanisms do not form a connected series, nor are dependent on one prime mover. Of the latter class, examples occur in iron-works, dye-works, soap-works, brass-foundries, etc. Some authors, indeed, have comprehended under the title *factory*, all extensive establishments wherein a number of people co-operate towards a common purpose of art; and would therefore rank breweries, distilleries, as well as the workshops of carpenters, turners, coopers, etc., under the factory system. But I conceive that this title, in its strictest sense, involves the idea of a vast automatom, composed of various mechanical and intellectual organs, acting in uninterrupted concert for the production of a common object, all of them being sub-ordinated to a self-regulating moving force. If the marshalling of human beings in systematic order for the execution of any technical enterprise were allowed to constitute a factory, this term might embrace every department of civil and military engineering; a latitude of application quite inadmissable.

In its precise acceptation, the Factory system is of recent origin, and may claim England for its birth-place. The mills for throwing silk, or making organzine, which were mounted centuries ago in several of the Italian states, and furtively transferred to this country by Sir Thomas Lombe in 1718, contained indeed certain elements of a factory, and probably suggested some hints of those grander and more complex combinations of self-acting machines, which were first embodied half a century later in our cotton manufacture by Richard Arkwright, assisted by gentlemen of Derby, well acquainted with its celebrated silk establishment.

Arkwright alone had the sagacity to discern, and the boldness to predict in glowing language, how vastly productive human industry would become, when no longer proportioned in its results to muscular effort, which is by its nature fitful and capricious, but when made to consist in the task of guiding the work of mechanical fingers and arms, regularly impelled with great velocity by some indefatigable physical power. What his judgement so clearly led him to perceive, his energy of will enabled him to realize with such rapidity and success, as would have done honour to the most influential individuals, but were truly wonderful in that obscure and indigent artisan. The main difficulty did not, to my apprehension, lie so much in the invention of a proper self-acting mechanism for drawing out and twisting cotton into a continuous thread, as in the distribution of the different members of the apparatus into one co-operative body, in impelling each organ with its appropriate delicacy and speed, and above all, in training human beings to renounce their desultory habits of work, and to identify themselves with the un-varying regularity of the complex automaton. To devise and administer a successful code of factory discipline, suited to the necessities of factory diligence, was the Herculean enterprise, the noble achievement of Arkwright. Even at the present day, when the system is perfectly organized, and its labour lightened to the utmost, it is found nearly impossible to convert persons past the age of puberty, whether drawn from rural or from handicraft occupations, into useful factory hands.

When Adam Smith wrote his immortal elements of economics, automatic machinery being hardly known, he was properly led to regard the division of labour as the grand principle of manufacturing improvement; and he showed, in the example of pin-making, how each handicraftsman, being thereby enabled to perfect himself by practice in one point, became a quicker and cheaper workman. In each branch of manufacture he saw that some parts were, on that principle, of easy execution, like the cutting of pin wires into uniform lengths, and some were comparatively difficult, like the formation and fixation of their heads; and therefore he concluded that to each a workman of appropriate value and cost was naturally assigned. This appropriation forms the very essence of the division of labour, and has been constantly made since the origin of society. The ploughman, with powerful hand and skilful eye, has been always hired at high wages to form the furrow, and the ploughboy at low wages, to lead the team. But what was in Dr. Smith's time a topic of useful illustration, cannot now be used without risk of misleading the public mind as to the right principle of manufacturing industry. In fact, the division, or rather adaptation of labour to the different talents of men, is little thought of in factory employment. On the contrary, wherever a process requires a peculiar dexterity and steadiness of hand, it is withdrawn as soon as possible from the *cunning* workman, who is prone to irregularities of many kinds, and it is placed in charge of a peculiar mechanism, so self-regulating, that a child may superintend it.

The principle of the factory system then is, to substitute mechanical science for hand skill, and the partition of a process into its essential constituents for the division or graduation of labour among artisans. On the handicraft plan, labour more or less skilled, was usually the most expensive element of production—*Materiam superabat opus*; but on the automatic plan, skilled labour gets progressively superseded, and will, eventually, be replaced by mere overlookers of machines.

By the infirmity of human nature it happens, that the more skilful the workman, the more self-willed and intractable he is apt to become, and, of course, the less fit a component of a mechanical system, in which, by occasional irregularities, he may do great damage to the whole. The grand object therefore of the modern manufacturer is, through the union of capital and science, to reduce the task of his work-people to the exercise of vigilance and dexterity,—faculties, when concentred to one process, speedily brought to perfection in the young. In the infancy of mechanical engineering, a machine-factory displayed the division of labour in manifold gradations—the file, the drill, the lathe, having each its different workmen in the order of skill: but the dexterous hands of the filer and driller are now superseded by the planing, the key-groove cutting, and the drilling-machines; and those of the iron and brass turners, by the self-acting slide-lathe. Mr. Anthony Strutt, who conducts the mechanical department of the great cotton factories of Belper and Milford, has so thoroughly departed from the old routine of the schools, that he will employ no man who has learned his craft by regular apprenticeship; but in contempt, as it were, of the division of labour principle, he sets a ploughboy to turn a shaft of perhaps several tons weight, and never has reason to repent his preference, because he infuses into the turning apparatus a precision of action, equal, if not superior, to the skill of the most experienced journeyman.

An eminent mechanician in Manchester told me, that he does not choose to make any steam-engines at present, because with his existing means, he would need to resort to the old principle of the division of labour, so fruitful of jealousies and strikes among workmen; but he intends to prosecute that branch of business whenever he has prepared suitable arrangements on the equalization of labour, or automatic plan.

It is, in fact, the constant aim and tendency of every improvement in machinery to supersede human labour altogether, or to diminish its cost, by substituting the industry of women and children for that of men; or that of ordinary labourers, for trained artisans. In most of the water-twist, or throstle cotton mills, the spinning is entirely managed by females of sixteen years and upwards. The effect of substituting the self-acting mule for the common mule, is to discharge the greater part of the men spinners, and to retain adolescents and children. The proprietor of a factory near Stockport states, in evidence to the commissioners, that by such substitution, he would save 50l. a week in wages, in consequence of dispensing with nearly forty male spinners, at about 25s. of wages each. This tendency to employ merely children with watchful eyes and nimble fingers, instead of journeymen of long experience, shows how the scholastic dogma of the division of labour into degrees of skill has been exploded by our enlightened manufacturers.

The blessings which physico-mechanical science has bestowed on society, and the means it has still in store for ameliorating the lot of mankind, have been too little dwelt upon; while, on the other hand, it has been accused of lending itself to the rich capitalist as an instrument for harassing the poor, and of exacting from the operative an accelerated rate of work. It has been said, for example, that the steam-engine now drives the power-looms with such velocity as to urge on their attendant weavers at the same rapid pace; but that the hand-weaver, not being subjected to this restless agent, can throw his shuttle and move his treddles at his convenience. There is, however, this difference in the two cases, that in the factory, every member of the loom is so adjusted, that the driving force leaves the attendant nearly nothing at all to do, certainly no muscular fatigue to sustain, while it procures for him good, unfailing wages, besides a healthy workshop *gratis*: whereas the non-factory weaver, having everything to execute by muscular exertion, finds the labour irksome, makes in consequence innumerable short pauses, separately of little account, but great when added together, earns therefore proportionally low wages, while he loses his health by poor diet and the dampness of his hovel.

The constant aim and effect of scientific improvement in manufactures are philanthropic, as they tend to relieve the workman either from niceties of adjustment which exhaust his mind and fatigue his eyes, or from painful repetition of effort which distort or wear out his frame. At every step of each manufacturing process described in this volume, the humanity of science will be manifest. New illustrations of this truth appear almost every day, of which a remarkable one has just come to my knowledge. In the woollen-cloth trade there is a process between carding and spinning the wool, called *slubbing*, which converts the spongy rolls, turned off from the cards, into a continuous length of fine porous cord. Now, though carding and spinning lie within the domain of automatic science, yet slubbing is a handicraft operation, depending on the skill of the slubber, and participating therefore in all his irregularities. If he be a steady, temperate man, he will conduct his business regularly, without needing to harass his juvenile assistants, who join together the series of card rolls, and thus feed his machine; but if he be addicted to liquor, and passionate, he has it in his power to exercise a fearful despotism over the young pieceners, in violation of the proprietor's benevolent regulations. This class of operatives, who, though inmates of factories, are not, properly speaking, factory workers, being independent of the moving power, have been the principal source of the obloquy so unsparingly cast on the cotton and other factories, in which no such capricious practices or cruelties exist. The wool slubber, when behind hand with his work, after a visit to the beer-shop, resumes his task with violence, and drives his machine at a speed beyond the power of the pieceners to accompany; and if he finds them deficient in the least point, he does not hesitate to lift up the long wooden rod from his slubbing-frame, called a billy-roller, and beat them unmercifully. I rejoice to find that science now promises to rescue this branch of the business from handicraft caprice, and to place it, like the rest, under the safeguard of automatic mechanism.

In an analysis of manufacturing industry, the general functions of machines, and the effects of their improvements, ought to be well considered. Machines are of three kinds:—

1. Machines concerned in the production of power.

2. Machines concerned in the transmission and regulation of power.

3. Machines concerned in the application of power, to modify the various forms of matter into objects of commerce.

I. Machines engaged in producing power operate by counteracting gravity, inertia, or cohesion. The steam engine, by the expansive agency of vapour, raises and depresses its ponderous piston, and thereby moves its massive beams and geering. The hydraulic wheel produces similar effects by the natural flow or fall of water from a higher to a lower level; and the windmill by the currents of the atmosphere. Blasting of rocks, in mining, exhibits elastic power overcoming cohesion.

II. The machines engaged in transmitting and regulating power are toothed wheels, fly wheels of various kinds, valve governors, shafts, and other geering of mills.

III. The machines engaged in applying power to modify the forms of matter appear, at first sight, to be so multifarious as to set systematic arrangement at defiance. An outline of their connexions and dependencies has been attempted in the next chapter.

Improvements in machinery have a three-fold bearing:—

1st. They make it possible to fabricate some articles which, but for them, could not be fabricated at all.

2nd. They enable an operative to turn out a greater quantity of work than he could before,—time, labour, and quality of work remaining constant.

3rd. They effect a substitution of labour comparatively unskilled, for that which is more skilled.

———

It is one of the most important truths resulting from the analysis of manufacturing industry, that unions are conspiracies of workmen against the interests of their own order, and never fail to end in the suicide of the body corporate which forms them; an event the more speedy, the more coercive or the better organized the union is. The very name of union makes capital restive and puts ingenuity on the alert to defeat its objects. When the stream of labour is suffered to glide on quietly within its banks, all goes well; when forcibly dammed up, it becomes unprofitably stagnant for a time, and then brings on a disastrous inundation. Were it not for unions, the vicissitudes of employment, and the substitution of automatic for hand work, would seldom be so abrupt as to distress the operative.

Chapter Two

The Response to Machinery: Agriculture, the Trades, Women's Work

The first widespread introduction of machinery and the further differentiation of the trades bringing the breakdown of the old craft customs came to the British economy in the early nineteenth century. The response of workers to inroads on their jobs and skills was eloquently expressed in many broadsides and pamphlets of the day. In some cases the resistance to machinery took the form of violent demonstrations and machine breaking. This was the case in particular amongst the agricultural labourers in the celebrated Swing Riots of 1830-31, where fires were set among the hay ricks and threshing machines were broken. The handloom weavers were also involved in violent demonstrations which included powerloom wrecking in 1826 and 1829. Both cases were but examples of the continuing resistance to machinery after the repression following the classic Luddite events of 1811-12 and 1816 which pitted croppers and shearmen of the woollen industry, stocking knitters and handloom cotton weavers against the mechanization of their trades.

The largest group to experience technological unemployment was the handloom weavers, whose trade dwindled over the course of the first half of the nineteenth century. The large numbers of the weavers, the bitterness of their poverty, and the remarkable range of political and literary tracts their experience inspired made them an example to all. Middle-class writers tried to overcome the 'irrational' resistance among farm labourers and weavers to the progress of technology, but they were soon to be answered by the working man's own political economy. Owenite and trade union newspapers such as *The Pioneer* and *United Trades Co-operative Journal*, radical political economists such as Thomas Hodgskin and William Thompson, and Chartist political leaders such as Bronterre O'Brien and William Lovett soon produced their own economic analysis of the impact of machinery, the division of labour, women's work and the trades, and the significance of skill. Opinions among workers on the strategies labour ought to take towards mechanization and the progressive division of labour could bring no universal benefits as long as the returns from technical progress went almost entirely to the capitalist class. The working class had to mount its own bids for control both of the machine and of the organization of production.

10 Address to Labourers on the Subject of Destroying Machinery
Henry Brougham, 1830

The agricultural disturbances of the early 1830s, also known as the Swing Riots included a special violence towards threshing machines. Workers resented the mechanization of their already too scarce winter employment. The scale of destruction of the threshing machine shocked middle class observers. The Society for the Diffusion of Useful Knowledge, a middle class voluntary society set up to 'educate' poor people by printing cheap tracts full of middle class homilies, responded quickly to the Swing uprisings. It commissioned a pamphlet to be distributed to farm labourers, and this was hastily written by Henry Brougham, a leading light of the society.

The following plain and simple Observations are addressed to you, on a subject which deeply concerns you all; in which your interest is as much at stake as that of the Farmer and Landlord.

You appear to have contracted a great dislike to the use of what are termed Machines, and chiefly to the use of Thrashing Machines. You have never well considered the Reason of your dislike. You merely state, that Machines are hurtful to the Labourers — that they prevent the Poor being employed. Upon these grounds you proceed to destroy them.

The word *Machine* seems to convey to your minds, some contrivance necessarily attended with mischief to the Poor; whereas, in truth, the word Machine means the same as Tool or Instrument, on all occasions has the same signification. A Thrashing Machine is a tool or instrument with which we thrash; so is a Flail, only that it is a far less useful Machine.

Now remember, Labourers, there is no difference between the case of the Labourer who breaks the Thrashing Machine of the Farmer, and that of the Labourer who destroys the tools or machines of the carpenter. The injustice is equal in both cases, although the consequences are more striking in the case of the Farmer, from the greater value of machines destroyed, and the greater injury sustained by the numerous individuals who depend upon the Farmer for a supply of Corn. When the Farmer has cut his corn and housed it, the grain must be separated from the chaff and straw; you would not, surely, desire to rub it out with your hands, though certainly that would take more Labourers. Some Machine or Instrument must be used to thrash it out. Why should not the Farmer be permitted to use the instrument which will do this work most readily and effectually — which will do it at the least cost, and enable him to send the corn to market, to be sold at the lowest price?

Your clothes, your stockings, your shirts, are all made by Machines, far more curiously contrived than the Thrashing Machines. The calico which makes your shirts, is woven by a Machine, attended only by a girl; but in consequence of the little labour required to manage it, the shirt which formerly cost seven shillings, now costs only eighteen pence.

It is undoubtedly true, that all Machinery which spares human labour, unavoidably, on its first invention and on beginning of its work, throws some persons out of the employment in which they had been engaged, and they must seek their means of support in some other way; this is the necessary consequence of the introduction into use of the most simple instrument, and of all improvements in art. But on the whole, the Public, and every individual in it, are in the end infinitely the gainers. In following the course you are now pursuing, you are driving men back to their savage state, when they lived upon acorns and roots, and had no machines nor tools at all, a great demand for labour, and very little to eat.

The Object of this Address is to point out to you, that the breaking of Machinery will not remedy the Evils of which you complain. You will soon deeply repent of your projects and your acts. You will find that Corn will rise in price, in proportion to the increase of labour bestowed in bringing it to market.

11 Letters on the Unrestrained Use of Modern Machinery
George Burges, 1831?

This writer expresses views on machinery typical of the 'tory radical' representatives of the time. The tory radicals wished for a return to a simpler peasant society, and for a 'revival' of close bonds between the great lords and the people. They attributed rural and urban poverty to capitalism and industrialism. They accordingly resisted the introduction of machinery in any form or under any circumstances. This particular tory radical tract indicates the anti-machinery sentiment in the countryside. It also proposes a tax on the threshing machine. The policy of taxing machinery in order to slow down its progress was one popular to working-class, radical and tory circles in the early nineteenth century.

Letter IV

Although it is difficult to judge to what degree of misery competition in machinery may reduce the inhabitants of Great Britain, yet some notion of it may be formed when it is known, that machinery is extensively introduced into the East Indies, superintended by British artisans, and that the rate of wages to the natives is about 2s 6d. per month, or 1d. per day. The power of machinery is the same in every place, climate and seasons have little effect on it; goods made thereby will wear the same appearance, and be appropriated to the same purposes, whether made on the healthy shores of Britain, or in the fruitful but pestilential swamps of the East or West Indies.

———

When Colquhoun wrote, about thirty-three in every hundred of the population of this country were actively employed; of these sixteen were engaged in agricultural pursuits, the rest in manufactures and in commerce. Since that time the relative numbers may have altered considerably, and the manufacturing population may have increased; the agricultural decreased. Many of the country labourers may have become weavers—from local circumstances being able to work cheaper than citizens, and have the preference; 'cheap being the order of the day.' The citizens, also from local circumstances, being unable to compete with the country people, have been and are unemployed. The application of machinery to agriculture rendering a less agricultural population necessary; and this competition must, under such circumstances, always thus affect the citizens, were *they* not rendered *surplus* by the application of machinery to *their* natural pursuits.

———

Agriculture requires able-bodied men, manufactures do not; able-bodied men can more easily become inmates of a factory than inmates of factories become labourers in the field. Our agricultural forefathers never dreamt of applying machinery to render useless and burdensome members of society any part of their community: they were all employed on the land or in the barns, in *the very barns we see now standing* they did thresh out all the corn without machinery. Those *very barns* will at this moment find the same employment for all the labourers by the canting politicians of the present day called 'surplus,' and agriculture would, as in the days of our forefathers, occasionally require the assistance of some of the manufacturing population.

———

In a case so clear as this, one would have imagined the machinery might easily have been dispensed with; but it could not, it had assisted mainly in reducing the capital employed in agriculture; had enabled the farmer to turn his crop into money as soon as harvest had ended, and, calculating on the growing crop, some farmers occupied farms larger than they could otherwise have done: others endeavouring to continue their farms, loth to lose their credit in business, continued to pay more than the *money produce* of the land would admit, wasted the capital necessary to carry their farms round; and, to meet their payments, had recourse to threshing machines. On the other hand, the landlord, seeing the crop upon the land, and knowing that the corn would be brought to market as soon as ripe, by the aid of these machines, would give the farmer more credit; that in very many cases no rent has been paid for the land, but from the growing crop, and little capital is employed. The impossibility by the flail thus to meet their payments, would have deterrred any men not mad from entering upon farms, without a sufficient capital to carry on a year, leaving the first crop untouched. But the poor and the occupier have not been the only sufferers; thousands of men who had invested their all in land, or had borrowed money on estates, were, with the decreasing value of produce, (not, that the quantity was materially lessened or the intrinsic value of it, or land,) ruined, and the estates have fallen into the hands of money lenders; or if not, after having paid repairs, other unavoidable expences, and interest to these money lenders, have little left but name, of their estates. But their day is nearly past, and the capital they have mainly assisted in taking from the land must be returned; a whole year's rent must be forthcoming from some quarter; these money lenders, will they advance it? They are the persons who have reaped the greatest profit on this great loss.

Such has been the effects of these machines, and will not they be abolished? No theories, no intense intellect, none of the political economists, no Malthusians, none of the anti-population committees, no march of mind men, opposed their progress; but the good plain sense of common minds, of men, who, feeling their effect most keenly, seeing the barns in which their fathers earned an honest living, alive with these inanimate vermin, (their bellies rebelling against all law,) stopped not, knowing the cause, till in attempting to root it out, they have brought upon their heads the penalties of the law.

They could not understand with empty bellies the industry of machinery — they well knew if industry was wealth, they possessed that disposition — they well knew it must be active or it would avail them nothing — they knew little and cared less about any other wealth than that which fills the belly — they knew that without money they could get no food — they wished not to have that money without earning it, and they were not too blind to discover, that these threshing machines were the main cause of their not earning money, and rendering their wealth in industry of no avail. They have taken the laws into their own hands — they have violated the laws of the land, which protect all property — protect machines as well as lives; and for their error they await the punishment. They should have petitioned without ceasing till the grievance was removed. The law protects machines, and while that law remains, machinery will be protected, and revived as caprice may give occasion. Modern machinery must be *restrained or abolished by law*. No tax short of total prohibition can, in many instances, be of any benefit; any tax short of that would enable monopolists to continue some in use to the incalculable mischief to society.

What tax on thrashing machines could be equivalent to their detrimental effect on the community? See their effect in figures! And where is the man, or set of men, not to be startled, to find thrashing machines causing the agricultural population a direct loss, to the full amount of the agricultural poor rate, — that thrashing machines in thrashing wheat alone, on a moderate calculation, and not to be disputed, occasion the enormous loss of £3,339,886 8s. to the inhabitants of this country?

Three Million Three Hundred and Thirty-nine Thousand Eight Hundred and Sixty-six Pounds, Eight Shillings!!! Every thrashing machine averaging sixty quarters of wheat per week, if taxed to the amount of direct loss to the community, must be taxed annually £868 8s.; and this pretty sum, Eight Hundred and Sixty-eight Pounds, Eight Shillings, is without calculating the mischief resulting from a lessened circulating medium, and the amount of capital withdrawn from the cultivation of the land through their agency. These machines cannot well be taxed. Who would propose an annual tax of £868 8s. when the gross earning of the same machine is but £234 in the year? but if taxed at all, such is the amount each ought to pay. And if the tax be levied as an equivalent to the mischief, this sum levied on every machine must be repaid the parties within the range of its pernicious operations.

Machinery Must Be Restrained

Unrestrained machinery demoralises society — substitutes idleness for industry — want for competence — immorality for virtue. It has pauperised the peasant, — pauperised the citizen. It has abstracted capital from agriculture; capital from manufactures. — It has abstracted money from circulation, and drawn it into heaps.—*It has created taxes.*—It has destroyed domestic trade, — domestic consumption, — domestic industry. It has concentrated the population, and collected the people into dense masses. Wherever it does give a scanty sustenance, it is in *crowded factories*, prejudicial to health; the nurseries of every evil; setting at defiance every endeavour to work moral improvement; where the very means used to that end, are marshalled in formidable array, dangerous to social happiness. Where *children* are employed in the room of *men*; and the heads of families, instead of leading in the paths of virtue, are starving, turned adrift, to sigh for departed happiness; and to meditate on desperate plans to restore their *cherished, but long-lost independence.*

Such is machinery: and unless restrained, will, ere long, involve this country in every horror and calamity attending the bursting of all the bonds that hold society together.

Fellow citizens! a minister of the crown represents you in parliament; as your representative, He has pledged himself to listen to your complaints. *Address yourselves to him*, and he will support the prayer of your petition. Fellow citizens, and countrymen! should opportunity offer, (and it may be soon,) as you value your existence, return not one man to parliament who will not pledge himself to the restriction or abolition of modern machinery, in all that in him lays. And should such occasion not offer, *form Anti-Machinery Societies to petition, nor let your petitions cease till you get them granted.*

Fellow- citizens! Fellow-countrymen! Fellow-sufferers! Thus have I thrown down the gauntlet in defiance of the *liberal opinions* of the day; and in the hope that men of leisure and acquirements will pursue this subject in all its bearings, I beg to subscribe myself,

Your devoted servant,
The Author.

"LET THE POOR PETITION AGAINST MACHINERY, DEPRIVED THEREBY OF DAILY BREAD. LET THE MIDDLE CLASS, FOR BY IT THEY ARE DAILY SINKING INTO POVERTY. — LET THE PHIL-ANTHROPIST, THAT HE MAY RENDER THE HUMAN RACE MORE SERVICE. —LET THE RELIGIONIST, THAT HE MAY ASSIST IN PURGING THE COMMUNITY OF THE PROLIFIC CAUSE OF IM-MORALITY; AND LET THE RICH THAT THEY MAY RETAIN THEIR POSSESSIONS."

12 Political Economy versus the Handloom Weavers
Richard Oastler and others, 1835

This pamphlet was alleged to have been written at least partly by Richard Oastler, the renowned tory radical and factory reformer. The pamphlet attacks another pamphlet by G.P. Scrope, political economist and M.P. who claimed that the handloom weavers' problems were due not to the introduction of the power loom, but to an overstocked labour market. Scrope thought the best solution for this was emigration. The reply by Oastler and others has the colourful language and the sense of righteous indignation found in many anti-machinery tracts of the time.

6 Chapel Lane
Bradford, Yorkshire.
May 11th 1835

To George Poulett Scrope, Esq., M.P.

Sir,

The Hand-Loom Worsted Weavers are greatly obliged by the reply you have given to their request that you would support their petition; for although you refuse to do so, you have candidly explained the reasons of your conduct. Your letter in this point of view, has given us all great satisfaction, because, though we cannot subscribe to your doctrines, it is *honest and candid.* and fairly lets us know what we have to expect, if "the soundest principles of Political Economy" prevail.

Many public men are not half so honest, and we venture to guess, that several who have fallen in our way, would say "Amen to every part of your doctrine, but for the base fear of being unpopular. You have not recommended us, as a certain M.P. did the Glasgow Weavers, "to find other Trades," but you tell us at once that *we must clear off*; to make way for the Machinery of the Capitalist. You, Sir, deserve better at our hands than *these*, for *you speak right out.* We shall venture without any intention to be disrespectful, to do the same.

You are opposed to all restraint of any kind of Machinery, and that because, in your opinion, its freest and most extensive use is certain to be the most beneficial to all mankind.

But Sir, it was not necessary in arguing this principle, to drive, as you do, into absurdities and *extremes,* and to set a trap in the way of the unwary Labourer, who is not up to the quirks and shifts of Logicians and Casuists like yourself — who has no time to study those subtleties which are used by you to support and elucidate "the soundest Principles of Political Economy." Is it not a bare *imposition* to tell us, we had as good *tear* what we want *from the woods and the soil with our nails,* thus assuming that a man must be an out-and-out disciple of yours, or else turn Barbarian? We *could not,* if we would, adopt your recommendation. Our barbarous forefathers might and could have done it, for they were Nature's own children—hardy and strong—but *we,* the children, or we had rather said, the Slaves of so much mis-directed "Science", are no longer an athletic race.

Our best blood is drained away by Scientific Avarice, whose prescription of long hours and short wages upon "the soundest Principles of Political Economy," we have been forced to take, till we have degenerated into *women* in Physical strength, and into *children* in Understanding. But, Sir, Barbarism in our estimation would be preferable to that sort of Civilization which you prescribe; and therefore, if yourself and other honest and well-instructed Members of Parliament and Political Economists, whose cupboards and cellars are always well stored, who *live well and lie warm,* and whose tables are never tainted with "our coarser food," will come and shew us how it is done. We are willing to return to a state of nature again, and when you have taught us to "dig with our nails" and other barbarous usages, we will freely consent that you should take all this System of *unrestrained* Machinery and Capital to the "outlying countries," and the fairer plains of Canada and Australia. This we hope is a modest request — we resign the best part of the Empire to such Scientific Gentlemen as yourself — leave us the secondary and less happy soils of the British Islands, and we have no doubt that in a few Generations, when our children have ceased to be torn from their beds at five o'clock every morning, and to be confined in the unwholesome atmosphere of these Modern Bastiles, for thirteen or fifteen hours a day, we shall recover our strength both of body and mind, and be able once more to gain the honest point of our ambition, *a fair reward for a fair day's work, and reasonable Time for the enjoyment* of Religious, Literary, and Social blessings.

13 Popular Political Economy
Thomas Hodgskin, 1827

One of the radical editors of the *Mechanics Magazine* gave this series of lectures, at the London Mechanics Institute in 1826. In the passages reprinted here, Hodgskin looks at the meaning of skill. He argues that skill becomes embodied in machines, and that workers should not seek to prevent the introduction of machinery, but rather to take over the machines, which rightly belong to them. Via this analysis, he concludes that with economic development, skills are not dispensed with. Rather, more skilled labour (embodied in machines and complex processes) displaces less skilled labour.

I do not mean to notice the various sources of what I conceive to be the error of the Economists, as to capital, though it is justly said, "to trace an error to its source is half way towards destroying it;" but the language commonly in use is so palpably wrong, leading to many mistakes, that I cannot pass it by altogether in silence. We speak, for example, in a vague manner, of a windmill grinding corn, and of steam engines doing the work of several millions of people. This gives a very incorrect view of the phenomena. It is not the instruments which grind corn, and spin cotton, but the labour of those who make, and the labour of those who use them. The co-operating labours of the millwright, for example, and the almost numberless other workmen who prepare his tools and the materials, of which the mill is fabricated, or who bring them from remote parts of the earth,—they themselves using very complicated machines for this purpose, which are prepared by the combined labour of a vast number of persons, — and in the first instance construct the mill; and then the labour of the miller, assisted also by various instruments, millstones, sieves, sacks, etc. which are made by some other labourers, profiting by the force of the wind, and the natural hardness of the stones, as compared to the hardness of corn, grinds it, sifts it, and prepares it for the use of the baker. So the united labours of the miner, the smelter, the smith, the engineer, the stoker, and of numberless other persons, and not the lifeless machines, perform whatever is done by steam engines. Formerly all spinning was done by the hand, and probably the spinner or the spinner's husband made with a knife the rude distaff and twirl, which were then the only instruments used in spinning. When spinning wheels were invented, the co-operating labours of the wheelwright and the spinner were necessary to complete the thread; but the result was the production of a much greater quantity of yarn than could before be produced by any given quantity of labour. Subsequently those who make steam engines, and set them in motion, and those who make mules and spinning frames, became the assistants of the spinner; and so much more efficacious is this knowledge-guided labour than the first rude mode of spinning, by twirling a piece of wood between the finger and thumb, and causing it to draw out the thread , as it sinks towards the earth, by its own weight, that one person can now probably spin as much thread in a given time, as four or five thousand primitive spinners. The fact is, that the enlightened skill of the different classes of workmen alluded to, comes to be substituted in the natural progress of society, for less skilful labour; and this enlightened skill produces an almost infinitely greater quantity of useful commodities, than the rude labour it has gradually displaced. By the common mode of speaking, the productive power of this skill is attributed to its visible products, the instruments, the mere owners of which, who neither make nor use them, imagine themselves to be very productive persons; particularly, if they are at the same time labourers, planning and directing the operations of those who make and use the instruments. Political Economists have probably been led by this incorrect language into their mistake; and have accordingly attributed that increased productive power, which has its source in the increased knowledge and skill of society at large, to the accumulation of fixed capital.

The great importance of relieving every natural principle from any imputation cast on it, in order to know correctly what are the causes of social misery, makes me advert to another case in which division of labour has been made the scape-goat for theorists and statesmen, and has borne the blame for the evils caused by their institutions. It is a common complaint, to adopt the language of M. Storch, among both these classes, "That it is a miserable condition to be only employed in making the eighteenth part of a pin. The workman who carries a whole trade in his single arm, may go where he pleases to exercise his industry, and find the means of existence; the maker of the eighteenth part of a pin, is only an accessory, who, separated from his comrades, has neither capacity nor independence, and is obliged to receive the law which may be dictated to him. This evil is more particularly felt in England, primarily because the regulations on this subject are there of a vexatious nature; and secondarily, because the division of labour is carried farther in that country than in any other."

But this idea of dependence arising from one man's performing only one part of a productive operation, or being an accessory to others, is common to any and every species of industry in the present state of society, as well as making pins. The phrase of "carrying a *whole trade in a single arm*" is very pretty, but in the sense here employed it is not true. It must be admitted, that a man who has learnt any one established *trade*, may be said to carry *it* in his single arm; but no one tradesman completes of himself any one commodity. A carpenter does not grow wood, nor fell timber, nor saw it into planks, nor bring it to the spot where he uses it, nor does he make his own tools or nails. A shoemaker, neither tans skins, nor curries leather, neither grows flax, nor makes threads, nor lasts, nor awls. For their tools and materials these workmen are dependent on other men, and both are only accessories in building houses or making shoes. Each labourer, let his task be what it may, only performs a part in the great work of civilized social production, and separated from his comrades, from other productive labourers, he has little or no wealth-creating power. If there be any man who completes a commodity of himself, it is the agricultural labourer, who is just as poor, wretched, and dependent as the pin-maker, - if there be any labourer who does not complete of himself the work of production, it is the merchant trading with foreign countries. He requires the assistance, in two countries, of, at least, those two classes of labourers who make the articles he exports and imports, and he requires the assistance of all those labourers who make and prepare his vehicles, and of the seamen or carriers who actually transport the goods he orders. Without the assistance of every one of these workmen, amounting, perhaps, to many hundreds, he could not possibly carry on his business. As far as division of labour is concerned, therefore, he is more dependent on other men for his revenue or support, than the man who only does the smallest and meanest part of pin making. He performs much less, in truth, than the eighteenth part of that productive operation by which he subsists, but he never has any sentiment of painful dependence, nor is he ever the object of pity and commiseration. In the same manner the landlord or the capitalist, who perhaps derives all his revenue from the labours of the pitied and despised pin-maker, is never regarded as dependent, and never feels that he is miserable and degraded. The dependence complained of and mourned over, therefore, is the dependence of poverty and slavery, and not the mutual dependence occasioned by division of labour.

This practice is one great means of adding to the productive power of the labourer, and, of course, to the sum of wealth he is capable of producing, and actually produces. It is therefore a manifest contradiction to attribute the poverty and wretchedness of the pin-maker to his labouring in conjuction with other men. Whatever it may be which makes the reward of the pin-maker so small, and his toil so excessive, it is not division of labour, for that makes his task easy, and his produce great. We are thus compelled to fix our attention on the other cause mentioned by M. Storch, and to affirm that not a part, but the whole of the poverty which he and others have attributed to division of labour, is caused by "*vexatious regulations*". As far as I see my way in this complicated question, I should say that division of labour is an admirable means by which each person may *know* all things; while to enable him to subsist, he is required to perform only one small part of social production.

The application of steam-engines to working power-looms, enables one man to perform the operations of several; or to weave as much cloth as three or four persons can weave by the hand-loom. This is a complication of employments. But if things are allowed to take their natural course, this complication will be again separated, and it will become in a short time the business of several hands to perform what one now performs. The different parts of power-looms and of steam-engines, which are at present perhaps all made by one or a few persons, will each, as the demand for them increases, be made by a different person, and the making of these different parts will become separate and distinct trades. The application of the *power* to the weaving instrument will be another business, and the actual business of weaving will all be comprised in looking after the working of a machine, which is made and set in motion by almost numberless distinct tradesmen. In many arts, therefore, we find, in consequence of new inventions, a perpetual complication and subsequent simplification of the productive processes performed by individuals; or a perpetual renewal of occasions for the farther division of labour.

This beneficial effect, it should perhaps be noticed, is the necessary consequence of the invention and employment of machines. By their use, food and clothing are obtained with less labour; and the whole quantity of labour not being diminished, more food and clothing may be produced. If there be more food and clothing there will also be more people, increased demand, or extended markets, and farther division of labour.

14 The Well Paid Artizan and the Half Starved Labourer
Official Gazette of the Trades Union, 1834

This radical analysis of value and skilled and unskilled labour shows the real basis of Smithian and Ricardian value theory (the idea that value was determined by a "common" labour). The writer here argues that the value of labour is determined by unskilled and unemployed labour. He argues, further, that with economic and technical progress there is an increasing tendency to reduce levels of skill and to bring a common character and value to labour. The *Official Gazette of the Trades Union* was the official organ of the Grand National Consolidated Trades Union, an Owenite inspired general union of the early 1830s.

The time for deliberation draws nigh. The representatives of labour will meet on Monday for the purpose of discussing its true interests, and determining the line of progress, which an increased experience indicates as that which must be pursued at the present moment. We have already expressed our deep anxiety that the true principle of unity and the power of wisdom may influence the decisions of that Meeting.

The old proverb says, "Well fed ignorance is always fat and contented " and certainly nothing but a lamentable want of correct knowledge can give rise to the apathy of a number of the well-paid artizans of this country, to the possible future that awaits themselves, if the means of the passing time be not husbanded better for the protection of others as well as themselves. Relief is generally sought with an anxiety proportioned to the amount of suffering, and where little is felt, experience unhappily teaches that still less is thought of its possible occurrence. These remarks are deemed applicable to what is termed skill-labour, or that which requires the combined efforts of mind and hand. This kind of labour is that alone which now meets with an adequate and compensating return for its exertions; and though, in some instances, those artizans have had the prudence and forethought to unite amongst themselves in union with the artizans of the *supposed* lower grades and denominations, is looked upon as impolitic and unnecessary. Though it is true, indeed, that on many occasions during the contests of the men against further reductions in trades, the wages of which were already below par, a liberal support has been rendered by different bodies of the well paid workmen, it is not the less true that in almost all cases such support was occasional, not continued, and granted rather as a boon to others, than as a duty to themselves. However praiseworthy even this might be, it would be matter of regret, at the present juncture, should such still continue to be the case. It is an important truth, which should never be lost sight of by those whose opinions influence the movements of the great body of artizans and labourers, that the value of labour is determined by the unemployed labour that exists in the market, not by the employed, and this is not less true of skilled than of unskilled labour. Nor is it less important to bear in mind that skilled labour itself, independent of the influence which the competition of its own class of artizans has in determining its value has also to submit to the practical influence of those circumstances which determine the value of labour in what are considered its *unskilled* operations. The continued improvements in machinery, which, though giving increased employment to hand work, is proportionably decreasing the labour of the head, except in the fabrication of the machine itself, have a natural and necessary tendency to give an almost uniform value to labour; and in a state of active competition, the scale of comforts which that value shall represent will be calculated from what is found to be absolutely necessary to subsist human machinery and continue its existence, not what it ought to receive. Under such circumstances the wages of the most skilled artizan will naturally be compared, not indeed with the wages of the least skilled, but with the grades more immediately below him; and he will always be considered as getting too much, while others are contented to subsist upon less. The usual arguments of proportion will be applied, and it will be demonstrated that he is too well paid, when compared with other artizans of an approximating grade and ability. And this same disposition to equalize the value of labour, as far as possible, will be applied to every grade, from the extreme high to the extreme low, and powerfully aided by competition in its endeavours to make those extremes meet, will find success in perserverance, unless countervailed by the power of a great *National Consolidated Union*. It needs little of common sense, therefore, to discover that the interests of labour, skilled and unskilled, are one and universal, to which the interests of capital under existing arrangements will constantly be opposed; nor does it require any greater powers of reasoning than are supplied by common sense to discover that the isolated attempts of particular trades to secure to themselves a permanently high rate of wages, must ultimately fail from the operation of the circumstances above explained. The interests of the well-paid artizan are bound-up with those of the ill-paid artizan, they are both sailing in the same vessel, and though the former may have the advantage of being a cabin passenger, one cannot sink without the other, though there may be a little difference in the time. Let the well-paid artizan reflect on this, and let him hesitate no longer to join his brethren in union.

The interests of labour, present or absent, united or not united, are still the same, and the mind that takes a part only, and not the whole, into its considerations, is wanting in the most important element of success — *correct knowlege*. From the old principles of Strikes, it is idle to expect permanent relief; it is criminally mischievous to teach such an expectation. The power of securing permanent relief, depends upon our becoming capitalist; the primary element in the production of which is *labour*. To that end, therefore, must our attention be especially directed; the adoption of the most judicious means is the all-important matter for the consideration of the assembled Congress of Labour. The operations should not at first be too extensive. *Success* not *display* is the end to be achieved, and for this end security demands that capital be not confined to a centre, but be proportionately fixed and employed in the various districts, and above all things, credit should be a term not understood among the managers of the capital of united labour.

Next to this subject, in importance, is that of general education. The working man's child will never be well educated until his interests become the only limit to its extent. Want of knowledge at the present moment is the great barrier to progress, let us not forget to make some provision for the development of the intellectual capacity of those to whom we have given existence but not secured its pacific and happy continuation. True, physical comfort is of primary import, but next to this is the knoweldge to secure it.

15 On the Effect of a Machine introduced to Supersede Manual Labour The Journeymen Bookbinders, 1831

The journeymen bookbinders wrote this pamphlet to express their own feelings of resistance to mechanization in bookbinding. They regarded mechanization as a threat to their skilled craft. The pamphlet takes up various remarks, published by their employers on their original 'memorial' which they print here. The employers' remarks appear in quotes.

The Memorial humbly showeth that your Memorialists, since the introduction of machinery to supersede the beating of books, as performed by manual labour, have been suffering under many grievous privations, —and that the rapid progress such machinery is now generally making in the trade, must inevitably tend, not only to reduce a considerable number of our body to actual want, but, by a continuation of its use, prevent your Memorialists from using their exertions in endeavouring to earn a honest subsistence for themselves and families.

In confirmation of this, we respectfully solicit your attention to the following facts:—

That our Trade Society, founded especially for the support of its members out of employ, has been enabled, during a period of *forty years*, to possess ample funds to meet all demands which the depression of trade, at any time, might call upon it to provide for.

Your Memorialists, in laying before you an extract from the printed audit of last year (ending May, 1830), beg leave to state, that the sum of 488*l*. 18s. was paid to men out of employ; and if, in addition to that sum, be added, the voluntary contributions to their sick members, amounting to 150*l*., at the lowest calculation, making a total of 638*l*. 18*s*. paid to their suffering brethren, from May, 1829, to May, 1830.

That, during the months of May, June, and July, of the present year, we paid to men out of employ nearly 220*l*.; clearly demonstrating the rapid effects of machinery in destroying manual labour; reducing many of your Memorialists to subsist on casual bounty, and finally reducing them to the greatest distress.

Do not, we beseech you, let ill-will or discontent arise between us; let us still think our best exertions you have a right to claim: and that you, in return, feel that interest for our welfare, that the comparative small profits the use of machinery brings to each employer (using it separately), and which, acting collectively, your Memorialists so severely feel, rendering our distress permanent. We, therefore, sincerely hope you will not allow its destructive effects to operate any longer against us.

Is not the process by manual labour equal to the effects produced by the use of machinery, depriving your Memorialists of a certain part and portion of their employ, which they claim by their legal apprenticeship to be justly entitled to?

Gentlemen, your Memorialists join, with an unanimous voice, in soliciting your attention to the foregoing statement of facts; and very earnestly entreat you will take them into your most serious consideration; and your Memorialists, as in duty bound, will ever pray.

———

That this memorial was not altogether "folly", is proved, by the fact, that some of our employers have partially done away with the use of the machines; and, feeling a praiseworthy commiseration for our distress, have agreed to abandon it altogether if they can obtain the concurrence of the other employers, with the sanction of the British and Foreign Bible Society (by whose order, as we were informed, it was originally introduced).

Is it then right to stigmatise with folly what has occupied the serious attention of employers, who practically understand the subject, and who are equally as respectable, and doing as much business as any of those who have turned a deaf ear to our complaint: as one of them sometimes employs seventy journeymen bookbinders.

"The workman is relieved from the only portion of his employ which was sheer drudgery — from the only portion, of his employ which was so laborious, that it rendered him unfit for the more delicate operations of bookbinding, which is altogether an art."

The workman is *not* relieved from the only portion as there are many other "portions" (as our author pleases to term them) necessary to the binding of books equally as laborious, if not more so, than the use of the hammer, — to give but one instance, out of the many that might be adduced, the whole of the finishing of the books for the British and Foreign Bible Society, and the Society for Promoting Christian Knowledge. We refer to the sprinkling, the burnishing, the polishing, etc.; and yet these are a part of the more delicate operations to which our author alludes. Indeed, in all that relates to the mechanism of bookbinding, he has evinced an entire ignorance of his subject. But what has this to do with the question, excepting so far as it proves the want of knowledge of the writer. Mechanics are well aware it is by their daily toil alone they can support themselves, and families, with credit; and if any portion of their property (for their labour is their only property) is taken from them, without producing any benefit to the community at large, is it wrong to represent the evil to those who have the power to remove it?

"The greatest blessing ever conferred upon bookbinders, as a body, was the introduction of this machine. Why? It has set at liberty a quantity of mere labour, without skill, to furnish wages to labourers with skill."

It would be almost impossible to convey more misrepresentation in fewer words. Can there be a greater insult to suffering humanity than to tell a body of men that the greatest blessing ever conferred upon them is, the introduction of a machine, that has reduced them, from industry and competence, to idleness and want?

It has *not* set at liberty a quantity of mere labour without skill, for it required skill; for proof, refer to any master bookbinder, who understands his business (even supposing him to be an advocate for the rolling machine), and he will tell you there is no part of our trade that requires more skill than the use of the hammer. And, as to furnishing wages to labourers with skill, it is a well known fact, that while great numbers have been deprived of their bread by the introduction of the machine, not one journeyman bookbinder (as far as our information goes) has reaped the slightest benefit, either in increase of wages or extra employment.

"The master bookbinders of London and Westminster state, that they cannot find good workmen, in sufficient quantities, to do the work which the consumer requires."

We should like to know who these masters are; as it is an undeniable fact, that, for many months past, there has always been, at the house of call, men of the first-rate abilities wanting employment. He cannot have written this from his own knowledge; and whoever so scandalously imposed on his credulity is certainly not the friend of truth.

"The beating of books was a mere drudgery, which the better men paid others to perform."

Such language as this requires no refutation. The author has placed himself in the situation of an over-anxious witness in a bad cause; he proves too much. Among the reading public, there is scarce an individual but understands human nature too well to believe, that any body of men would humbly petition to get rid of such a benefit as this writer wishes to make the rolling-machine appear to be. It is not common for men to strive to do away with what is advantageous to their own pockets, which must be the case if they have no longer to pay these mere drudges. But the fact is the reverse of this author's assertions; beating is *not* a mere drudgery, as it requires skill, — and the better men never pay others to do it.

16 To the Working Builders of Great Britain and Northern Ireland
The Pioneer, 1833

James Morrison's *Pioneer*, was in turn an organ of the Builder's Union in Birmingham, a general Owenite socialist newspaper, and an organ of the Grand National Consolidated Trades Union. It continued to maintain a strong following among building workers, and this piece indicates that the building worker too feared the encroachment of machinery upon his craft, even as early as the 1830s. The address mentions the threats already being felt by sawyers, brickmakers, and cabinet makers.

Many of you are disposed to flatter yourselves that machinery, which has already wrought tremendous evils amongst the manufacturing classes, cannot seriously operate against you,—notwithstanding that you have seen it make its way in comparative quiet, invading the territory of the timber-sawyer and the marble-mason; there being now not less than a dozen establishments in this country for making chimney pieces, etc. by machinery; — notwithstanding this, I say, and seeing also, as you may, that the various improvements in pegging mortar, hoisting materials, grinding clay, etc. have superseded the employment of labourers in a great degree; yet with all these things before our eyes, there are thousands of you content to loll in fancied security, — to laugh away the day of your power *"until the night cometh,"* and then you will have learned the bitter truth, that *"no man can work." "Unless you see signs and wonders, you will not believe."*

Working carpenters and masons, let me tell you, in the voice of prophecy, that machinery is close upon you, and unless you divert its operation — turn it to your own account, instead of suffering it to go against you — you may have your ruin completed by thousands. Some of you, in the frenzy of your rage, may burn the machinery and the shops, as the foolish sawyers did; — you may struggle with the gigantic oppressor for a time; — but you will at last sit down vanquished by it. — I tell you distinctly, that all the preparation of your work previously to putting together, will speedily be done by machinery. Ah, but you will say, Who shall put it together? Who, let me ask you, superintended the machine saws? Working sawyers themselves! Who put together machine chimney pieces? The marble-masons themselves! And working masons and carpenters will put together machine masonry and carpentry, spite of the ruin of thousands.

A machine is also in progress for brickmaking, and it will succeed. Painters will suffer by the introduction of oak and mahogany instead of pine; indeed, it is hard to say which class will not be directly affected, and it is certain that all will be remotely injured.

The cabinet-makers are the present victims of the self-love of the capitalists. Already there are considerable establishments being formed for dealing in German furniture, because English labour is dearer than German labour. — The last consideration with the capitalist is the interest of the English Labourer. Next we shall hear of ready-made joiner's work from the ports of the Baltic. — Nay, there is nothing which sordid avarice can invent for its own enrichment which it will not stoop to. The labourer is to them the goose with golden eggs, and they will rip up its body to hasten the crisis. Enriching themselves — they will exhaust the store — and all must pull together. Working Builders of England, you may avert it. — Your example will be followed by all the industrious classes.

A Brother Chip.

17 Machinery
The Pioneer, 1833

This short passage, written in the form of a catechism, indicates the agreement among radical workers on the analysis of the impact of machinery under capitalism. It is not an anti-machinery piece. Its argument is rather that the gains of technical progress ought to go to the working man.

Machinery

Q. What is the effect of Machinery?

A. To do that labour which must otherwise be done by hand, and to do it more perfectly and expeditiously.

Q. To whom then ought the machinery to belong?

A. To the men whose work it does — the labourers.

Q. What would be the effect of machinery in such a case?

A. If, in a community of one thousand men, a machine were invented to do the work of five hundred, it would enable the thousand to add five hundred to their number, and the whole would subsist as well as the thousand formerly did; or the thousand might either work half the time, or do the work twice as well.

Q. But how is machinery applied under present arrangements?

A. The capitalist takes it in hand, so that those who are already rich make it an instrument to increase their riches; while those who are poor, and who can only live by their labour, have that labour supplanted, and are made poorer.

Q. Then in fact, the capitalist, in the instance you have supposed, not only opposes the maintenance of the additional five hundred hands, but takes from the five hundred formerly employed their legal means of subsistence?

A. Yes, and plunges the whole in misery and destitution.

Q. Who are the inventors of machinery?

A. Almost universally the working men.

Q. But why do not the working men use machinery for themselves?

No answer!!

18 Science and Labour
The Pioneer, 1834

The universal benefits expected to flow from the great advances in scientific knowledge during the eighteenth and nineteenth centuries did not materialize. In middle-class voluntary societies such as the Mechanics Institutes and the Society for the Diffusion of Useful Knowledge, working men were told that they must help not hinder scientific progress, and that they would soon feel the economic benefits it brought. But hopes soon turned sour, and radicals now critical of the claims made for science counselled concentrating on organization and political power for the working class.

To The Editor of The Pioneer

It is only by the extraordinary combinations of science with genius and capital, that the working man is furnished with employment, or enabled to support his family; and without a body of men whose labour consists simply of thinking, society would fall in pieces, and poverty visit the firesides of the artisan and peasant.

The above is taken from a work lately published, entitled the Rights of Industry. Now, I would inquire of you, Mr. Editor, being a plain working man, when we possess in this country, in an extraordinary degree, the aforementioned combinations, and a host of thinkers into the bargain, whose occupation should have prevented such a calamity, why is the fireside of the mechanic robbed of its comforts, and instead of its being a little Eden, as it was wont to be, is now more like the picture of another place, of a far different description, which I need not name, with a number of half-fed, half-grown, dingy children, cowering over a few sparks, driven by necessity to labour years before their time of life fits them to endure it? It must be, that the thinking class have been mostly employed in thinking for themselves, and further, have put their thoughts into action, and have been scheming for themselves; and of this particular we have abundant proof by looking around us.

It is high time the working man began to think for himself, seeing that the thoughts and actions of others turn so little to his advantage, and I am happy to see the spirit of inquiry that is stirred up in our little town by the introduction of your excellent work; though we have our enemies — those who say that, by uniting we shall so raise the prices of manufactured articles, we shall not be able to compete with foreigners, and shall drive away trade, etc. Then be it so: trade at present brings us nothing but misery, and the want of it can do no more. But I trust my fellow-workmen will not be misled by such remarks; (they are only used by those who profit by our degeneration;) but pursue the straightforward course they have adopted, and unite; for in union there is strength and security. Mark persons who possess property in building or land, how carefully they fence and wall it in, aye, and more, plant man-traps and spring-guns to punish intruders: follow their example. Labour is your property, your only property, and a paltry pittance it is; fence it around by union, secure the benefit of it to yourselves and children. Generations to come will bless you, and if you let slip this opportunity it may never occur again. If you consider these remarks will serve the cause in which you labour, making them public will oblige yours etc.,

A. Willenhall Locksmith,
Feb. 8.

19 Radicals Debate Machinery
The Magazine of Useful Knowledge, 1830

This reports on a meeting of radical groups to discuss the machinery issue. Passages printed here indicate some of the efforts of a group of political radicals, including Lovett, Hetherington and O'Brien to dissuade workers from resistance to machinery in favour of political resistance. The speakers express an important strand in radicalism which saw utopian possibilities in the progress of science and technology, as long as this progress took place for the benefit of the working class. This could only happen if working men had political power. Note the discussion of such issues topical to the day as the 'tax on machinery' and the Swing riots.

The report having been adopted, the chairman announced the following question for discussion : "Machinery under competitive and co-operative arrangements."

Mr. Warden expressed great pleasure at the opportunity of meeting his brother co-operators, and observed that the question before them was one of great importance, and that the public in general were beginning to feel it to be such, but more especially the working classes, who had been thought to know little or nothing about machinery. There was shortly to be a meeting on Kennington Common, of the working classes, to discuss the very subject of machinery. The *Times* newspaper one of those "best instructors" of the nation, had taken up the question, and had endeavoured by some very specious arguments to prove, that machinery was beneficial to the working classes. After pointing out the fallacy of these arguments, Mr. Warden continued — time uselessly spent was an injury to society; but if it were in our power to devise any means whereby labour could be abridged, and yet more effectually applied to our purpose so that time was saved, we could then afford in the leisure thus secured, to cultivate our moral habits and mental faculties. Following out this argument, it would be seen that machinery would, under proper regulations, prove a benefit to mankind. In his opinion, machinery was not the primary cause of the misery at present existing among the working classes. He begged they would not misunderstand him — he meant machinery abstractedly considered. The purchase of labour was in his opinion little better than slavery, and was the primary cause of all the misery to which the working classes were subject, and had laid the foundation for all the injurious effects which machinery had introduced. We saw that the working classes sold their labour to the capitalists, who had now become possessed of the power of machinery, and they alone; but if machinery, could be equally available to the working classes, it would matter little about their being thrown out of employ. Under Co-operative arrangements, then, machinery would enable every one to procure wealth, and prove equally beneficial to all. For instance, in regard to printing: the *Times* newspaper, by the introduction of machinery, had thrown three-fourths of the men out of employ; but suppose those men had belonged to the proprietary of that establishment, machinery would be a benefit instead of an evil to them. (Hear.) They would have to labour only three hours a day, instead of twelve, and they would equally participate in the profits. But now fifteen men had been thrown out of employ, and for what? To get greater gains for the capitalists. Not only were these men thrown out of employ, but the price of the article they manufactured was not reduced; it remained at the same price, now it was printed cheaper, and five men were employed where twenty were formerly paid; therefore society was not now benefitted by machinery. On the contrary, under Co-operative arrangments the introduction of machinery would have done injury to none, but would have benefitted all. Further, these men so thrown out of employ, must seek it elsewhere; they had nothing to sell but their labour; they were only human machines. (Hear hear.) They must get employment, and in so doing, they throw out others, and so on with the rest. But a leading article in the *Times* says, "Machinery is, in the long run, beneficial to the working classes." How did the writer attempt to show this? He says, "Destroy machinery, and what follows? Why, human labour being dearer than machinery, a contraction of the markets will be produced." The writer had forgotten, or pretended to forget, that the competitor against human labour — machinery consumes nothing but the first cost. When high prices cause a contraction of the markets, how did it orginate? Were they not caused by high wages? For example, leather was at the same price as it was thirty years ago, yet the manufactured article was cheaper, because inferior labour was put upon it: namely, that of women and children. This cheap labour caused a reduction in prices. Machinery was still cheaper, and if it was destroyed, human labour would be better paid, and the working classes would be placed in a situation to consume more than when the prices were lower. Machinery then, was not, in the long run, beneficial to the working classes. And since it was clear that under the present arrangements, where one individual was benefitted by machinery, twenty were injured , it was better even that it should be destroyed than remain under those arrangements

(Hear, hear). He did not wish to be misunderstood; he was no advocate for destroying any person's property. (Hear.) But what was the remedy proposed for the evil by the writers in the *Times* (for they admitted that it was an evil) of the excess of number of those who offered themselves for employment? They said, reduce wages still lower, give cheap bread, and remove the Corn Laws; so that a working man who receives ten shillings a week, when reduced to five will be able to buy a loaf a fourpence instead of eightpence. (Hear, and applause.) Their remedy, then, was no remedy at all. They also said, if machinery were destroyed the value of articles would be lessened. Now, would not human beings exist in as great numbers as before the extermination of machinery? And there would be a greater demand for human labour, consequently the working man would be better enabled to purchase those articles. (Hear.) Such arguments, then, were most futile. They said, also, that the more wealth capitalists possess, the more funds they had to pay wages. But who were the real participators in the increase of wealth thus produced by machinery? He might be as rich as Roths-child, but was it to be therefore said, that he would employ more of his capital than he thought necessary? It did not matter to the working man how much wealth was produced if he was not a participator in it. Of what conseqence was it if England were full of wealth, if the working population still wanted the necessaries of life? — He thought he had fully answered all the arguments of the supporters of the competitive system. He had been lately told by an aristocrat, that if a rail-way were established from London to Liverpool, a great benefit would ensue to all the working population, because a greater number of packers and porters would be necessary. (Laughter.) But, he forgot that when he arrived at the height of consumption, he could go no further. He forgot that if he threw forty thousand man out of employ, they must press upon others, until neither employment nor wages remained. (Hear.) Machinery and its supporters would go on until they were brought to a point, which must produce an alteration, and the sooner we obtained information on the subject the better. This might be a revolting idea to those who employed machinery; but it would never be used to their permanent advantage until such a change took place. The accumulation of individual wealth would not ward off the blow. There must be an equality of liberty; and of instruction for our children and servants; there must be no aristocrats to monopolize the road to knowledge and the best clothes that could be manufactured: all must have comfortable clothing, a good education, and participate in the productions of machinery, or any other contrivance for the good of mankind; and, un-til this was the case, machinery would work tenfold more ruin and misery than at present existed. (Hear and great applause.) Mr. Warden concluded by moving the first resolution:—

That, in the opinion of this meeting, the use of machinery under the com-petitive arrangements of society, accompanied as it now is with individual accu-mulation of capital, is highly injurious to the working classes, and directly inimi-cal to the happiness of the whole population. This meeting is, further of opinion, that the use of machinery under Co-operative arrangements, accompanied with united interests and common capital, would be the means of diffusing plenty and happiness throughout the world.

Mr. Lovett begged to make a remark or two respecting the taxation of machinery. It has been said, the government would be partial if they did not tax machinery. So they were partial now; that is to their own interests. (Hear and laughter.) He objected to the taxation of machinery, for who would be benefitted by it? Why, those gentlemen! (holding up a well known paper entitled "Nice Pickings," which excited considerable merriment.) Instead of proposing a tax, said Mr. Lovett, let us direct our powers against *this* machinery. (Hear and laughter.) Against those monsters who prey upon the vitals of society. (Cheers.) Instead of adding to their power, and another link to the chain which already bound us, let us try to break the chain asunder. (Cheers.) Instead of praying them to tax — in fact instead of praying at all — (applause and laughter) — instead of praying and bowing and cringing, let us stand erect, conscious of our own worth, power, and importance in society, and say "You who have constituted yourselves our rulers, we have created all the wealth by which you are surrounded, and if any are entitled to it, above the rest, it must surely be those who produce it. (Hear and applause.) What was tolerated through the blindness of our forefathers has been justified by antiquity; and power has usurped the place of liberty. We their sons have bowed to the yoke, and you have formed our minds, politically, and religiously as you thought proper; you endeavoured to keep us in a state of mental blindness, but in spite of your efforts to prevent it, our eyes are opened. (Hear and cheers.) In spite of gagging bills—in spite of attorneys-general, (hear and tremendous applause,) we see, we feel, and we are determined to endure the evils to which we have been subjected no longer. (Overwhelming applause.) As you have betrayed the trust reposed in you, and instead of protecting, have preyed upon, and devoured those who relied on you, henceforth we will manage for ourselves." (Loud applause.) Henceforth, we should tell them, "as you have caused us to become a by-word and a reproach among all nations, enjoy the honey we have gathered for you, but now we will gather for ourselves. (Hear and applause.) We will prevent you from obtaining any more." Thus we should act, instead of praying. He concluded by urging the necessity of unity and firm attachment to the principles of Co-operation.

Mr. Rosser said, he rose in the spirit of Co-operation, which, while it deplored the evils existing in society, was anxious to bring about a change which would entail no evils upon any. He was induced to address them in consequence of the speaker who held up the paper ("Nice Pickings"), and drew forth, he feared, their disapprobation and distrust towards the individuals whose names were there inserted. Those men were to be pitied rather than condemned, for they were equally with the other classes of society the victims of a bad system. With all their wealth and luxuries they were not really happy. (Hear.) They were more entitled to commiseration than hate. That machinery was an evil, at present, no man could doubt, because it competed with human labour, and conquered it, and simply for this reason, because it was not so expensive. If a remedy were attempted it should be done by setting forth a correct statement of facts, in order to set right the public mind; with this view, he did not approve of those appeals to the passions, rather than to the mind; nor the neglect of inculcating those principles without the influence of which man would still be the enemy of man. (Hear.) If such a state of things existed as in France, previous to the memorable three days, there might be cause for loud and unlimited appeals, but he trusted that the appeals here would be made to reason, and that the arm of reason, and the union of knowledge, not physical force, would achieve the conquest. (Hear.) A change violently effected might last for a few years, but the evils would return with double mischief. He would have a better watch-word than "Swing," and a better union than that of mere discontent. (Hear.) Those men (pointing to "Nice Pickings") acted under the influence of the circumstances in which they were placed; from the nature of the stations and their education, they were as they were. They and we must remain the victims of a bad system, until error gave way to truth, and tyranny to liberty. He would have them, then, not attack men but measures. (Hear and applause.)

Mr. Lovett explained.   He did not speak against the men, but against the *machinery* — the system. (Hear.) But he could not help thinking that the men supported the system. (Hear.) While they pitied the poor men under their present circumstances, (laughter) he thought it advisable to surround them with such circumstances as should compel them to become serviceable members of society. (Hear and applause.)

———

Mr. Hetherington thought, those persons had done very wrong, who had prayed for taxation on machinery. His friend (Mr. Lovett) seemed to have a great aversion to praying. (Laughter) He (Mr. H.) had not quite so much, for he had heard that praying was in some places done by machinery. (Renewed laughter.) They would soon hear, he supposed, of cast-iron parsons, preaching by steam. He had heard of a heathen tribe, who prayed by machinery. (Laughter.) They put their prayers into the machine, and then sat round it smoking and regaling themselves. (Laughter.) He should like such machinery, and such praying, too, as this. But to the point: if machinery were taxed, would it give mere employment to the working classes? Who would have to pay the tax? The consumers. (Hear.) We already complained of the taxes on knowledge, and why desire more? As to machinery, if it were in the hands of the people, it would be a benefit, but while used only for the purposes of monopolists it was a curse to them.

20 On Improving the Moral and Physical Condition of the Working Classes Henry McCormac, 1830

Henry McCormac, an Owenite from Cork, here makes a novel claim for the possible benefits that the introduction of machinery could bring He argues that the machines could become one of the conditions for the emancipation of women. Ideas about the education of women and the need for their equal participation with men in economic and political affairs were an important part of Owenite social perspectives. McCormac here argues that the introduction of machinery, by reducing demands for physical strength, would make it possible for women to be employed on an equal basis with men.

The next great obstacle to the increase and diffusion of knowledge among the working classes, is one which, although it has been at work amidst every class of society, has, I conceive, been most so among them; I mean the non-education of women. Among what are called the higher classes, the training of the female mind in some branches at least, is a good deal attended to: in the middle, save in the perusal of works of fiction, little is done; but in the working classes, in these countries at least, reading and writing, together with a little arithmetic, form in most instances the extreme boundary of mental instruction. So that women in general for whatever knowledge they may acquire, are principally dependent for it on society; to which they are on that account among others rather partial; and for what they do acquire in this way, and their ability, and almost peculiar tact in using it, I do for my part give them the fullest credit. Many of them do indeed possess wonderful talent in employing such acquirements, and hence are able to render themselves infinitely more agreeable than many of their clumsy rivals of more solid attainment in the other sex; for what is knowledge, if, like the miser's store, it prove neither useful nor agreeable to the holder or to those around him? Blue-stockingism or literary vanity on the smaller scale is contemptible enough; but if females in general, as so many of them have done, were to add solid information to their other recommendations, would they prove less agreeable as mistresses or friends; worse companions or advisers to their husbands in the ordinary scenes of life, or during the storms of adversity, or less affectionate mothers to their children, when able to foster more cheerly their budding intellects, or stifle in their early growth, those germs of vice and passion which uninstructed maternal tenderness is neither able to stifle or control? Surely no; and I much fear that the generality of those who would say nay to such acquirements, must either themselves be deprived of the precious light of knowledge, or have the purer sentiments of their hearts steeped and drowned in sensuality and vice. It is hardly possible however for women generally, to surpass or even equal the other sex in the depth of their acquirements or the cultivation of their intellect, so long as their present unjust and barbarous position in the moral and political scale of society continue. Are they not made subordinate in their powers of action to man in almost every public and private capacity? It is true, that by some extraordinary, and to me unaccountable anomaly, they are made capable in this and some other countries, of becoming the heads of empires; while, miserable absurdity, they have been considered unequal to fill any inferior public office. Thus they may be placed in the most, responsible, momentous,

and important situation which a human being can occupy; requiring if it could be obtained, an accommodation of every excellence in the person selected for it; and yet are deemed unequal to hold any lower grade of employment. Let me then add the unit of my scorn towards the abolishment of this relic of the barbarity of other days, and even evidence of its continuance during our own. Let not artificial restrictions exist to prevent women from enjoying that just equality with the other sex, to which by nature and by God's award they are in everything entitled: nor can their inferior physical strength, (which now that machinery has superseded hand-labour, can make no practical difference), the original source and only pretext for their degradation, any longer afford us any unmanly pretext for its continuance. Let them buy and sell; make contracts and annul them; deny or affirm; represent or be represented;

exhort or condemn, whithersoever their talents or their inclination may extend; in a word, let them have the same voice in society which men have, and the same liberty to go and come, with equal independence of each other, and of the other sex. That this will one day be the case in society who can doubt? And the sooner the better; but let not the voice of themselves or their advocates ever be silent; means must be taken to effect any thing, and the most vigilant and strenuous employment of those which are most fitting must not be neglected in a matter of such importance as this. Who would not now be ashamed to allege their physical inferiority or their sexual peculiarities as proper motives for

PIN MONEY.

this unjust extinction of female rights? Yet such I affirm to be the exclusive reasons. People generally, however, in the exercise of injustice, which, while it sears the heart obscures the intellect, make little scruple to adduce false reasonings or false facts in support of their inclinations; and some have dared to assert that the intellect of women was naturally inferior to that of man, but this I scruple not to pronounce one of the most infamous libels on the majesty of human nature that has ever found utterance. The long galaxy of starry names which adorn the page of history; and the bright constellation of female worth and talent which showers down the rays of its soul-illuminating light on us at the present time, would amply prove to the most incredulous, were they haply capable of appreciating intellect of any kind, the untruth of this most unjust assertion, which would thus condemn one half of the human race to everlasting sterility of mental produce. I affirm, then, for my own part, that the intellect of woman is capable of every kind of cultivation, and that, whether as regards the perception of truth, and the combination of ideas, whether of the most subtle and abstruse, or the most light and ordinary nature, and in whatever form or manner expressed, it is equally apt with that of man. Why then should the janitors of the portals of knowledge keep the gates for ever closed against our sisters; or will they wait till an arrayed force shall snatch them from their unjust guardianship? Why not open wide the portals to all of them who wish to enter and slake their thirst at the waters of the holy fountain of truth; or bask in the regions of the highest empyrean, where the blessed sum of knowledge sheds the rays of his everlasting light?

21 The Women's Page
The Pioneer, 1834

In this Owenite journal we find one of the earliest demands for wages and unionization for housework. The writer, however, has a limited view of women's involvement and emancipation outside the home.

The rights and privileges of women, says our correspondent, may be found in the *oldest* book in the world, "that they be *discreet*, chaste and keepers at Home, not gadding about or busy bodies; and how can this be exemplified if they go out to *legislate*." This is the opinion of a male unionist. It only belongs to men to *gad about and be busy bodies*. Women have nothing to do but to keep at home, and remain in ignorance of everything but cooking, washing, scrubbing pots etc. Men alone are busy bodies; men alone should go to meetings, etc; for men alone have rights and privileges: all the rights and privileges of women are absorbed in the male and he will protect women, provided she only be obedient and keep at home. Now, this oldest book in the world, which has been quoted against the women by a master, may be quoted with equal authority against the men. It says, "Servants, be subject to your masters with all fear, not only to the good and merciful, but also to the perverse; for this is thankworthy, if a man for conscience-sake endure grief, suffering wrongfully." Again: "Let as many *as are under the yoke* count their masters worthy of *all* honour. Then, if men are going to bring the oldest book in the world against the women, we hope the women will bring it against the men, and down with the

unions." But we want no partial quotations; if our opponents quote from the master's page let them quote from the servant's page also, or we shall do it for them.

But we are pretty sure that our correspondent misunderstands us. We do not want to set women a-gadding, but to prevent their gadding and their tattling. What is it that makes woman a tattler and a busy body, but the confined sphere in which she moves? She is individualised by the narrowness of her knowledge and experience. What is it that makes a villager less liberal than an inhabitant of the city? His confinement certainly; the little variety of character and circumstances which present themselves; and therefore we find that, in small villages, the tittle tattle of private families is much more prevalent than in large cities; the only way to cure women of tattling and gadding is the way by which men are cured, enlarging their views and widening their sphere of activity. It is a physical and metaphysical absurdity, to suppose that the mind can be liberalised by the confinement of the body.

But what do we recommend, for women that can annoy anyone but a Tory? We do not recommend politics or trade to matrons. If they are not traders, why should they interfere with trade? Neither do we advise them to go and spout at meetings, or make themselves public in any way.

We only advise them to associate with each other, and commune with each other upon subjects connected with woman alone; and if they find themselves aggrieved in any respect by the *mal*-administration of the male, to express in clear and determined language their opinion and resolutions upon the subject. It is to create peace, that we made the proposal; it is to prevent individual quarrels at home, by forming regulations, and for the proper management of families, that we recommend the social intercourse of women.

But our correspondent would have women scattered; each woman subject to her own husband so that if a working man should make thirty shillings a week he may drink tea if he pleases; go to a coffee-house every night, and read the papers, and bring in fifteen shillings a-week to keep home and pay the rent withal. *He has a right to do this*, for he makes the money. But what is the woman doing? She is working from morning till night at house-keeping; she is bearing children, and suffering all the pangs of labour, and all the exhausting of suckling; she is cooking, and washing, and cleaning; soothing one child, cleaning another, and feeding a third. And all this is nothing for she gets no wages.

Her wages come from her husband; they are optional; he can give her either twenty shillings to keep the house with, or he can give her only ten. If she complain, he can damn and swear, and say, like the Duke of Newcastle "Have I not a right to do as I please with my own?" And it is high treason in women to resist such authority and claim the privilege of a fair reward of their labour! Good God! if we thought that the sex *woman* could patiently endure such a yoke of bondage, we should hate her most heartily! But how is she to prevent it? Why, by the very same means by which the men will prevent the tyranny of the master. Women will save themselves abundance of labour by association. We shall have an idea of what might be done by union.

22 To the Straw Bonnet Makers
The Pioneer, 1834

The Owenite journal, *The Pioneer*, which carried a substantial amount of material on the experiences of women workers during industrialization, also included this interesting comment on a women's traditional craft, straw bonnet making. The craft was apparently being broken down by the division of labour, and being 'diluted' by the introduction of male labour. It provides a good counter-example to the more common case, that of underpaid, unskilled female labour diluting male crafts.

Fellow-Workwomen — I am happy to inform you we are on a straight road towards our emancipation; but it is necessary that we take a right position, and most resolutely keep it. Let no man laugh you out of your claims to liberty; nor let flattery deter you from the hope you have now of gaining your freedom. At the same time, let the woman of the Union be known by her modesty, virtue, sobriety and cleanliness — not usurping the man's power, but wisely defending her own.

I have seen in the *Pioneer* a notice from the Blackers and others calling a meeting of the trade. As we hope for support and protection from our brothers in union, and their wives (for we do not mean to let our money lie idle) it is but just they should know what right we have to demand the whole management of our own affairs. A titled lady in Essex, nearly a century since, wishing to employ her own sex, ingeniously invented the platting and sewing of straw bonnets. In the reign of George the Third, his queen, Charlotte, seeing the number of industrious women supported by that one article, and most likely being wise enough to know the capital it would raise for the British realm, patronized it. Seldom the queen or her daughters were seen in public without a straw bonnet. Under these circumstances, the business was brought to the highest perfection; and there are those, whose fathers were mere beggars, now in the city, who keep carriages from the produce of women's labour. When the war ceased, in the year 1815, many useful men were thrown out of employment, their wives having to support them. The men, not wishing to be idle, were taught by the women to block; and in a very short time these men went round to all the principal houses in London and offered to take home the work, and finish it for less money than the master gave indoors, the latter finding everything for the girls' use. It was soon discovered by the women that these men were more tyrannical than their former masters: and to get the business out of their hands, they offered to take it for less still. This mad competition has sunk the business from one of the best to one of the worst a woman can have. The men will, perhaps, attempt to deny the charge; but was it not against the principles I hold sacred to throw public odium on any individual, I would give the names of the first men, and those who have been actively engaged this spring in lowering the price of our labour. Yet these men we will forgive, if they are willing to take their proper place; and we will be proud to own them as brothers, and to promote their interest: we will go hand in hand together with them to attain the full reward for our labour, without contention or fear.

My next letter will inform you where to find our Grand Lodge, to give you publicly our intentions and laws, and to show you the advantage of being a member.

P.A.S.

Part II
Mid-Victorian Capitalism

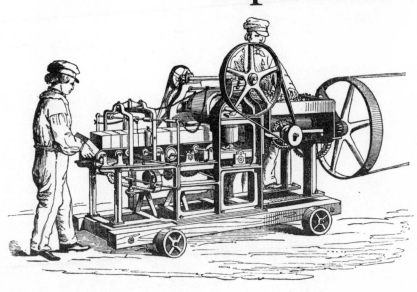

Chapter Three

Automation
and Skill Hierarchies

The period of British economic history which seems most eminently suited to fit Marx's concept of modern industry was the mid nineteenth century. By this time, steampower was widely used and there were conscious attempts to apply science to industry, and to develop the new possibilities for self-regulated mechanical systems including the mechanization of the machine-making process itself. Yet such features of modern industry developed alongside other, apparently antagonistic features such as the new social position of the skilled worker. Whether their trades remained important or were being undermined, skilled workmen emphasized the indispensable nature of their labour, and the 'customary' and even 'mysterious' methods of learning necessary skills. Some trade unions became highly exclusive as workmen tried to protect themselves against the further inroads of mechanization and dilution.

Such splits within the working class were also often encouraged by employers seeking to separate the respectable working class from other casual and unskilled workers. For the 'respectable' skilled workers had learned the middle-class values of thrift and ambition through such agencies as evening classes, mechanics institutes, sunday schools and chapels. Self-help organizations such as the friendly societies and co-operatives stores further encouraged such virtues. But organizations such as these could also function as radical alternatives to middle-class values. Friendly benefits and co-operation were also important to the large and powerful new model trade unions—the name given to the large amalgamated unions which emerged at the time—and voluntary societies could also foster a sense of working-class community.

Strong craft unions and the new model amalgamated unions were able to enforce machine manning and workshop rules. Apprenticeship, the long years of learning both the techniques and the social customs of the trades continued to hold sway and even to spread in some cases to the new industries and new skilled jobs which arose in the period. The capitalist dream of an unlimited, unskilled labour market was not to be, for if some craft skills were destroyed, many new skills were created in the mid nineteenth century, especially in the engineering and metallurgical industries.

23 The Workshop of M. Froment
Dionysius Lardner, 1852

Dionysius Lardner was a ubiquitous writer and lecturer on popular science and technology during the second third of the nineteenth century. This particular piece shows an aspect of the highest phase of machino-facture, i.e. the self-manufacture of precision tools for the machine-making sector. It shows the application of precision techniques and automation to the production of the most delicate instruments and tools, vital in their turn to the technical basis of the rest of the industrial sector.

The visitor to the great Exhibition, in turning over the leaves of the Official Catalogue, would probably pass without notice an item, No. 1609., in the French Department, consisting of three lines, as follows:—

"*GUSTAVE FROMENT — 5 rue Ménilmontant, Paris.*
Scientific Instruments. Theodolite; and various models of electro-motive power."

Assuredly brevity could no further go. Never was presented a more conspicuous example of modest reserve on the part of artistic genius the most exalted.

———

The inventions and improvements of M. Froment, in the construction of instruments of precision, and of scientific apparatus generally, can nowhere be so advantageously seen and appreciated as in his own workshop in Paris. There may be seen not only the finished instruments and machines, but their practical application *in the construction of each other!* There may be seen electro-magnetism applied on a large scale, as a permanent and regular moving power, in the fabrication of mathematical and optical instruments.

The electro-motive machines of M. Froment, which are very various in form, magnitude, and power, derive, nevertheless, their motive force from one common principle, which is the same that has been applied in certain forms of electro-magnetic telegraph.

An electro-magnet and its armature are placed so that when the electric current is suspended they will rest at a certain distance asunder, and when the current is established they will be drawn into contact by their mutual attraction. When the current is again suspended they will separate. In this manner, by alternately suspending and transmitting the current on the wire which is coiled round the electro-magnet, the magnet and its armature receive an alternate motion to and from each other, similar to that of the piston of a steam-engine, or the foot of a person who works the treddle of a lathe. This alternate motion is made to produce one of continued rotation by the same mechanical expedients as are used in the application of any other moving power.

The force with which the electro-magnet and its armature attract each other, determines the power of the electro-motive machine, just as the pressure of steam on the piston determines the power of a steam-engine. This force depends on the nature and magnitude of the galvanic pile which is employed.

The pile used by M. Froment for the lighter sort of work, such as that of driving his engines for dividing the limbs of astronomical and surveying instruments, and microscopic scales, is that of Daniel, consisting of about 24 pairs. Simple arrangements are made by means of commutators, reometers, and reotropes, for modifying the current indefinitely in quantity, intensity and direction.

In the apparatus for engraving straight scales and standard measures of the larger sort, the scale to be divided is fixed, and both motions above described are given to the cutter. In this case the cutter is fixed upon a frame which is moved by a fine screw, parallel to the scale to be divided. The revolution of this screw moves the cutter from division to division, and in the intervals during which the screw is at rest the cutter receives the other motion by which the division is engraved.

All these machines are self-acting. The limb or scale to be divided being placed on the table of the dividing engine, no further interference of the human hand is needed. The machine of itself begins its works at an appointed hour, minute, and second, and when the last division of the scale has been engraved, it not only suspends its own action, but stops that of the electro-magnetic machine by which it is impelled. These automatic arrangements must not be regarded as mere mechanical superfluities, upon which the boundless fertility of invention which characterises the genius of M. Froment has been lavished; they are of great practical value and importance. It happens, for example, that in these delicate operations, the tremor of the ground on which the workshop stands, produced by the movement of vehicles of transport in the adjoining streets, affects in a sensible degree the motion of the cutting point. It is therefore always preferable to execute the most delicate work in the dead of the night. Now, by the automatic contrivances above mentioned, this can be accomplished without imposing on the superintendent the necessity of watching. A clock, provided with an apparatus similar in principle to a common alarum, is put in mechanical connection with the dividing machine, and is set so as to start the machine at any desired hour. This being done, and the limb to be divided being fixed upon the table under the cutter, the apparatus may be left to itself; the superintendent may retire to rest, and, at the hour of the night which has been selected, the electro-motive machine will be started by the clock, and the dividing engine will commence, continue, and complete its work with the most admirable certainty and precision, and, when completed, the electro-motive machine will be stopped, and all reduced to rest.

George Dodd, continuing his popular series on British industry, fully evokes the sense of middle-class, mid-Victorian wonder at the intricate working of the machine. Here in his view of the *Times* Printing Machine he combines discussion of the central and irreplaceable skills of the compositor with the factory system in printing.

The Compositor and his Apparatus

It is scarcely necessary to inform an intelligent reader in the present day, that a *compositor* is one who puts the types together, for printing.

The labours of the compositor certainly require as much exercise of mind, eye, and fingers, as any of the ordinary handicraft employments. He is expected to decipher the writing, good or bad, of the author whose manuscript he is putting into type. He has to manage the punctuation, which authors too generally care very little about; and he often rectifies an occasional error arising from haste in writing or from transcription. His eye guides his fingers (or his fingers almost guide themselves) to the cells where the proper letter-types are to be found; and the formation of letters into words, words into lines, lines into columns, columns into pages, and pages into forms or sheet-surfaces, taxes all his powers — mental, visual, and digital. He has to "mind his *p*'s and *q*'s," not only in the literal sense of that phrase, as the *p* appears on the type like a *q* to the unpractised eye, but in many a figurative sense also.

The compositor has his types placed in small *cells*, which are combined into a *case*, and two pairs of cases occupy a *frame*. He has one pair of cases for Roman, another for Italic, or a smaller type for notes. The upper case of each pair contains large and small capitals, numerals, accented vowels, and a few other types; the lower case contains the small letters and the space-types. Some of the cells are larger than others, to contain the letters most in use. In the English language the letter *e* occurs more frequently than any other; then *t*; then *a*; then *i*, *n*, *o*, and *s*; *z* is the least in use, there being sixty times as many *e*'s as *z*'s. In a 'fount' or complete set of types, consisting of 106,000 there are 12,000 *e*'s, rather more than one-ninth of the whole. The letters are not arranged alphabetically in the case, but those which are most in use are placed nearest to the hand of the compositor: a conventional arrangement, wholly dependent on practical utility. So well does the compositor know this arrangement, that his fingers dip almost intuitively into the proper cell for any required type; no labelling or inscribing being at all necessary.

Step by step does the compositor build up his letters into words, and his words into sentences. Let his first word be "Industry:" he takes an

I from the upper case, or case of capitals, and then his fingers dip successively into the cells of the lower case which contain n, d, u, s &c. Each type, as he picks it up, he places against a ledge in a little implement called the *composing-stick*. When he has arranged side by side the eight types for the word "Industry," he takes a 'space' out of another cell, and uses it as a boundary between this and the next word—the 'space' being a blank type, too shallow to come under the action of the inking apparatus. Then he proceeds to the second word, and so on till he has words enough to fill one line of a page or column. He then begins a new line, and by the time he has thus collected about a dozen lines, his composing-stick is full; the contents are carefully lifted out in a mass, and placed in what is called a *galley*. He then gets another stick full, and transfers it in a similar way, until at length the galley becomes full. Thus he proceeds; at the rate of about fifteen thousand letters in a good day's work.

Can the aid of machinery be brought into requisition in compositor-work? This question has been many times asked; and many ingenious persons have endeavoured to give an affirmative answer to it. About ten years ago the attention of the printing fraternity was much attracted towards two rival machines, one by Messrs. Young and Delcambre, and one by Captain Rosenberg. Both machines could compose type by automatic agency, and both were highly ingenious; or, more correctly, both substituted mechanism for human fingers in certain parts of the apparatus.

In these two machines there is a key-board on which the compositor plays; he has not to deal with *flats* and *sharps* and *naturals*, but with the letters of the words transmitted to him by the author. To use our former illustration (the word 'Industry'), the compositor, instead of dipping his fingers into eight little cells, presses his fingers on eight different keys of his silent pianoforte. What, then, is the result? In Young and Delcambre's machine, the key moves a lever: the lever pushes a type out of a little receptacle; the types slide down an inclined plane into a funnel or spout, and thence into a box, where the compositor takes them up and arranges them in his composing-stick. In Rosenberg's machine, the key detaches a type from a vertical rack; the types, when detached, range themselves on an endless belt; they leave the belt and range close together in a receiver; and when one line-full is thus formed the machine rings a bell, and the compositor takes away the line of type, and leaves room for another. In the one, the types require to be distributed in the same piece-meal way as in ordinary composing; while Rosenberg's machine was accompanied by another for effecting the distribution also. Rosenberg's machines were therefore more complete than that which was invented shortly before them; and very high anticipations were formed of their value. But these anticipations have not been realised. Men are still required to attend on the machine, and to do part of the work; it is found that the machine cannot *think* sufficiently, and that nothing is saved by the time all the corrections and adjustments are made.

————

The Printing Machine and its Wonders

But the great, the crowning effort to advance printing has been by the application of the mighty power of steam.

Sixty years have now elapsed since the first attempt to produce a printing machine which should economise hand labour. Mr. Nicholson took out a patent in 1790, for a machine which—in theory, if not in effect — bore a strong resemblance to the last refinement in printing apparatus; for he proposed not only to distribute and apply the ink by cylinders, and to place the paper on a cylinder, but also to arrange the type on a cylinder, as in the most recent of Applegarth's machines. Whether this machine ever went beyond the patent, whether it was ever in actual work, we do not know; but it may be concluded that practical difficulties interfered with the general introduction of the machine. More than twenty years afterwards the composition inking-rollers were brought into use; and a plan was suggested by Messrs. Donkin and Bacon for arranging the types on oblong prisms. In 1814 the first notable advance was made, by the introduction of König's machine into the *Times* printing office; on the 28th of November in that year the readers of this celebrated journal were informed that the printing of that day's broad sheet had been effected by a steam-worked machine; and the (then) astonishing speed of eighteen hundred copies per hour was stated to be within the capabilities of the machine. It was quite right that the proprietors should speak in a gratified tone of their achievement; for it was one which greatly increased the power of the daily journals, and which laid the foundation for subsequent advancements.

The printing machines now employed at most of the large establishments in this country exhibit a harmony of movement most striking. Steam gives motion to the whole; but how numerous are the concurrent movements into which this motion is broken up! There are shafts and riggers, bands and spindles, wheels and axles, cogs and pinions, ratchets and levers, cylinders and rollers — all the paraphernalia of the machinist's labours; but it is not until we trace the numerous delicate and precise movements which these bring about, that we can appreciate the control which the master-power — steam — exerts on the whole assemblage. Several things are being done at once. While one form of types is being inked, another is impressing a sheet of paper; while one sheet is being thus impressed, another is travelling along to prepare for a similar process; while one set of inking rollers is doing its work, another is supplying itself with a coating of the unctuous compound.

Let us see whether a few words may suffice to convey a general idea of the action of such a machine. First for the inking. The thick ink is placed in a reservoir, in contact with which rotates a roller called (we know not why) the *doctor*; by which this doctor becomes thoroughly coated with the black oily compound. Another roller, having a peculiar vibrating motion, touches the doctor at intervals of a few seconds, and robs him of a little of his ink, which it transfers to a flat iron table; other rollers spread the ink evenly over the table; and another set again feed their surfaces from this table, and spread the ink over the form of types, by rolling along it. All this is very curious; for the ink becomes diffused in a remarkably even manner by these numerous transfers from surface to surface. Meanwhile the paper has not been idle. A boy, perched up on high, places sheets of paper on an endless web or apron; the sheet is caught in between a cylinder and a row of tapes, and thus passes on from one cylinder to another until it leaves the machine. But in its progress it is exposed to two printing processes. When one surface is downwards, it is pressed or made to roll upon one of the two forms of inked type, by which the sheet is printed on one side; and then after two or three serpentine twistings — over one cylinder and under another — the other side of the sheet is brought downwards, and is made to roll over the other inked form of types. How to adjust the cylinders and the tapes, so that the sheet shall not be crookedly printed; how to arrange the 'doctor' and the other rollers so as to apply just enough ink and no more; how to make the type-form go and fetch its own ink, and return to the exact spot at the exact time; how to make the sheet of paper, in its travels over and under about half a dozen cylinders, present each surface exactly at the proper instant to the proper inked form — how to realise all these conceptions, has been a tax to the inventive powers of our Applegaths and Cowpers; but the result shows how triumphantly they *have* been realised.

Great as these achievements unquestionably are, however, the *Times'* printing machine of 1848, and the *Illustrated News'* machine of a later date, are still greater marvels in the art. To what pitch the speed of printing will ultimately arrive, it would be vain even to guess; but these *vertical* cylinder machines seem to have a power of expansion (so to speak) which will lead, step by step, to further increase of efficiency. As it was the *Times* which introduced König's machine in 1844: as it was on the *Times* that Cowper and Applegath's improved machine first exhibited its powers in 1827; so was it the same journal that enabled Mr. Applegath to display the wonders of his new conception in 1848, by printing eight or nine thousand copies of that newspaper in an hour.

———

If we were about to attempt a minute description of this new machine, we should at once ask the reader to suppose the large cylinders of an ordinary printing machine to be turned up on their ends, and to be revolving on vertical instead of horizontal axes; and further to suppose that the types are arranged round a cylinder, instead of being packed together on a flat surface—for these are the two pervading principles of the new machine. And though we cannot go into technical details, a recognition of these two principles will do much to render the action of the machine intelligible. The monster machine at the *Times* office, then (for it is this of which we are speaking), has the type ranged round the surface of a cylinder more than five feet in diameter; or, more correctly, the surface is a polygon, each side of the polygon being equal to the width of a column. This type cylinder rotates, and presents its several polygon facets to the sheets of paper. The inking rollers are vertical and they feed themselves from a reservoir, which is also vertical. There are eight cylinders, about a foot in diameter, round each of which a sheet of paper coils itself; eight boys place the sheets upon stands or

platforms, and the eight sheets are drawn down and made to wrap round the eight cylinders. The inking rollers receive their dose of ink; they touch the types as the type cylinder rotates; the paper cylinders press the paper against the inked types; the printing is effected before the spectator can well tell what has become of each sheet; and the eight printed sheets fall from the eight cylinders; and are received by eight boys who are seated at the lower part of the apparatus.

In this most beautiful machine, Mr. Applegath undertook to provide a power adequate to print 8000 copies per hour; but he conceived it probable that, by a few slight improvements, such a machine might attain a speed of 10,000 or 11,000; and some such increase has been obtained.

Besides two of Applegath's great eight-cylinder vertical machines, there are three of the older four-cylinder horizontal machines in the *Times* office. There are nearly a hundred and fifty compositors and pressmen employed in the evening and night. The types in constant use weigh no less than seven tons. Each day's impression consumes about four or five tons of paper, presenting a printed surface of thirty acres, much exceeding the area of the Crystal Palace. One copy of the *Times*, including a four-page supplement, contains nearly a million types. There have been more than fifty thousand copies printed in one day, at a period of great political (and consequently news-reading) excitement.

Whether printing will ever be done by the furlong or the mile is a question destined (probably) to receive an answer ere long. When paper was rendered capable of production in endless lengths, it naturally became a speculation whether printing could not be conducted *before* instead of *after* the cutting of this paper into sheets. Some slight approaches in this method have been made; and patentees are looking out sharply in the same direction. Mr. Rose, of Glasgow, for example, patented such a machine in 1849. In his machine there are two horizontal cylinders, with the types arranged on their surfaces, one for each side of a newspaper or sheet; there are ink-supplying, ink-distributing, and printing rollers ranged around each of these cylinders; an endless web of paper is drawn through both machines, printed on both sides; and a cutting apparatus severs it into sheets after it leaves the machine: there are thus required no 'laying-on' boys, or 'taking-off' boys. Such at least is the specification of the patent; and, whether this particular machine has been found available or not; there can be little doubt that something of analogous character will astonish the world before long. Mr. Bodmer obtained, about the same time, a patent for an invention almost identical in object with Mr. Rose's, but intended to print two webs of paper at once instead of one. Again, in 1850, the ingenuity of Mr. De Witte was shown in a patented machine for printing endless webs of paper from cylinders having stereotyped surfaces.

Printing Establishments, in Modern Days

Few comparisons would present more curious results than that between a printing office in past days and one in 1851. Everything *was* done by hand, and on the domestic-manufacture system; much is now done by steam, and all on the factory system. Our Clowes, Hansards, and Spottiswoode's, at the present time exhibit the factory system in its best aspects; that is, combination in some departments, subdivision in others.

The French, and foreign countries generally, are more accustomed than the English to form large establishments, wherein the printing as well as the publishing of books is carried on. Perhaps the remarkable freedom of individual efforts in England may tend to explain this difference. The establishment of Alfred Mame and Co., in Tours, is one of those in which printing, binding, and publishing are all combined, and where they have been so combined for nearly half a century past. All the works relate to religious and moral subjects, and undergo a sort of general editorial supervision: such as educational books, sanctioned by the Roman Catholic Church; missals and other books of piety; and educational books for primary schools. The ware-rooms of the establishment are said to contain a million and a half of small books, pamphlets, and tracts; besides another store in unfolded sheets. There are about twenty machines, worked by steam-power, to carry on such of the printing and binding operations as can be brought within the scope of this power; and these machines are adequate to the production of fifteen thousand volumes per day, each containing ten duodecimo sheets. The sewing, boarding, and binding of the books, occupy many more hands than the printing, being less within the scope of steam-power. It is said that there are no less than one thousand persons of both sexes and various ages employed in this 'bindery' (the innovating but convenient name that our friends across the Atlantic give to a bookbinding establishment), by whom books are bound in styles varying from the most sumptuous magnificence down to the most economical plainness. All the copper and steel-plate engravings introduced into the illustrated works, are also printed in the establishment. It does not appear that type-founding is carried on, and in this respect the Tours establishment must yield precedence to a few great printing firms in England; but the combination of printing, binding and publishing, on so large a scale, is certainly note-worthy.

25 The Paper Trade and Printing
W. Glenny Crory, 1876

W.Glenny Crory in his collection on the industries of East London chooses an East London paper-making and printing works to express his wonder — twenty years after Dodd — at the amount of labour-saving machinery available to industry.

One of the most valuable branches of commerce in the United Kingdom is that known as the "Paper Trade". It has many branches, and several of these are represented in East London. There is paper-making, printing, lithographing, and paper-bag making done to a sufficient extent East of Aldgate Pump to deserve a prominent place each as an Industry of the locality. For my facts I have visited Mr.Edward Lloyd's paper mills, Bow, where paper is extensively manufactured; and also the Works of Mr. A. T. Roberts, Hackney-road, which is one of the places where a considerable quantity of printing is done. Had I attempted to go fully into the paper trade in East London, I should have noticed Messrs. Thomas Forrens and Co.'s mills at Ilford; also paper-bag making, as carried on by Mr. Pitt, Leman-street; Mr. Brandon Joses, Devonshire-square, and others in that line, as well as the publishing of newspapers. But I must pass most of these over without further mention, taking Mr. Lloyd as representative in his line, and Mr. Roberts as a fair specimen of those in the lithographic and letter-press printing business. If I mentioned printers of newspapers I should, in common justice,

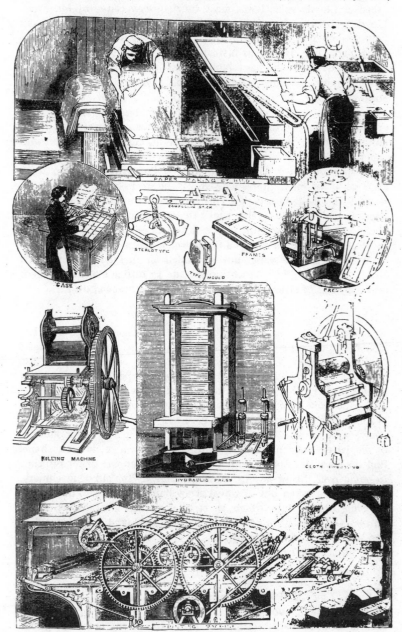

place the *East London Observer* as decidedly foremost of all in the locality in its special work. I should also be constrained to state, that in every respect it has steadily progressed for many years; but within a very short period, it has increased in circulation, as well as improved in typography, and in the quality of the paper on which it is printed. When I called at Lloyd's mill, I was most courteously received by Mr. Frank Lloyd, who showed me over the premises. Mr. Edward Lloyd is not only an employer of labour in East London, but is also a merchant in the Esparto line. He brings his supplies of this valuable fibre chiefly from Algeria, where he has establishments in connection with his East London business, namely, at Blockhaus d'Orleans, Oran, and Oned Magoun, Arzew. He has places for gathering Esparto at Calle de la Marina Espanola, Cartagena, Almeria and Aguilas in Spain. The gathering and utilising of this plant is a most important enterprise, on public grounds, and Mr. Edward Lloyd has made his mark in connection with Esparto even more clearly than as a paper manufacturer, printer, or newspaper proprietor. The mill premises at Bow cover some ten acres; and one of the most interesting sights is the stacks of Esparto piled up, ready to be made into paper. This fibre costs considerably more than wages in gathering it. It takes a long time to go out of the soil, and produces annually; and when it is in a sickly state, burning is good for it. It sells f.o.b. in the Thames at a figure which makes it a formidable rival to straw in paper-making. But it needed all that energy for which Mr. Lloyd is remarkable to bring a trade so difficult of management into that state of efficiency in which the Esparto branch now is.

Lloyd's paper mills, at Bow, have been established since 1860. They have been growing steadily and still show an elasticity which promises further expansion. There are about 200 hands employed. I am also happy to find these employés of a very good type; in fact, the whole place is orderly, the people at work are attentive, and the mill is most ably conducted by a manager, whose venerable appearance and general bearing offer an assurance that all goes well. In addition to Esparto and straw, there are piles of old ledger covers in one place, and mountains of old letters and envelopes in another, all of which, in some shape, find their way into paper, either suitable for wrapping or for printing. In going over the premises, I observed that, by the aid of machinery, the knots are taken out of wheat straw before it gets into one of the revolving boilers, into which all straw materials must go, as a first process. Oat straw is too valuable for fodder to be used in paper making. But seeing the demand for paper is so great, it is well that there are so many fibres to be had.

But as I passed along I could not but pay attention to the easy and efficient methods adopted for cleansing the pulp, washing it as it approaches towards paper, letting the dirty water escape, and keeping such as contains valuable chemicals. The blue used here for clearing the tone of white papers is made in East London. . .The process of converting straw into paper depends much on chemistry. But a wood pulp has already been produced by mechanical means instead of chemicals. Tints get into paper while it is in pulp and wet. The machinery at work at this mill is remarkably well kept, and the best of its kind. There are several engines and some four or five boilers. One of these is being fueled by one of Dillwyn Smith's mechanical stokers. This is a most ingenious contrivance, and though it saves coal and lessens labour, it also economises heat, as no cold air can get in while the boiler is being coaled. Appliances are visible all over the premises for the lessening of manual toil and elevation of industrial labour. The system of machinery at work is the best of its kind, and evidently capital has been invested with no miser's reserves in getting up every part of the Works. There is a reservoir which covers an area of probably between an eighth and fourth of an acre constantly full. The water as it comes from the River Lea is full of earthly matter, which rapidly finds its way to the bottom, from which one deposit or another has to be cleared out. This water is purified by passing over stones, and at last finds its way filtered into tanks, from which it is pumped into the several parts of the Works in which it is required. Even these storing and filtering appliances prove that no cost is spared, and no pains considered too much in doing everything attempted in the best possible way. The amount of money at stake here is very large. Therefore, altogether this mill is well worthy of a place amongst the chief of East London Industries. I must not, however, pass over what I take to be the most important feature of the Works, namely, the Hoe machine, which is here at work. I am happy to find that I am justified in holding this opinion by no less unquestionable authority than Mrs. Brown, who, having visited the Works in 1870, was struck by a sight of the "O printing macheenes," and says: "Why they makes the paper by the miles here for *Lloyd's News*, then they cuts it up into bits for the O machine to turn into fires, and murders, and baby farmers' triels." Now, I should take leave to add that there are miles of paper made here for other journals, both in London and the provinces, as well as Lloyd's. Also that Mr. Lloyd was the first to adopt the machine which admits of the reel instead of sheets of paper in printing. The advantages of this machine is obvious, even to one unacquainted with the trade. The same amount can be done by it as is done by Hoe's machine, which does not admit the reel; and the doing of it requires only three men instead of sixteen. Perhaps there is no fact more important than that progress owes a great deal to invention, but it owes more to the enterprise of capitalists. I regret, after all, I have not had space to describe the paper-making process as I find it here. But I feel that, interesting as such information would be to many readers, it must be much more so to learn that invention and capital have certainly combined all over East London, and in no place is there a more striking instance than the one before me. I must not close this portion without mentioning that when I visited this place a new strainer was on trial, in the last process of paper-making. Also that sometimes twenty-four miles of paper is reeled without a break. The woollen felts used have found a rival in cotton fabric, which I am told promises great things. The reeling process is a most interesting one, and the use of the indicator, marking lengths, is a striking feature. There is a machine and fitting-shop attached to the mill, and taking the paper-making, printing, and every other process, as a whole, the Works of Mr. Lloyd, are amongst the most important, in a commercial and industrial sense, in East London, and probably are as well managed as any other in that division, or elsewhere in or out of the metropolis. In giving a line or two to details as to Mr. Robert's Works, I include not only those before-named in his line but others, to mention the whole of which would be impracticable within my space. These have been established about thirty years; and it is a fact creditable to both master and men that some who entered twenty years ago as apprentices are still working on at the "old shop". The printing business has risen rapidly within the past quarter of a century, and in no part more than in East London, and probably a fairer specimen could not be given of all other places than the one I have chosen. It is certainly amongst the largest, if not the largest, in the locality, there being from sixty to seventy hands at work on the premises, besides engravers on copper and wood, machine-rulers, book-folders, plan-colourers, etc., employed elsewhere. Wages have risen very much, and yet those who need to employ a printer, can get their work done at prices which twenty years ago whould have been considered impossible. These remarks apply to printing generally, but the department most altered as to cheapening of cost is the lithographing, or that of letterpress and lithography combined. All this is owing to a more liberal outlay of capital in plant, to better machinery, and a more general adoption of mechanical instead of manual labour. As one passes through these Works such things naturally arise before the mind. Here is to be seen stacks of white paper, being reduced rapidly, while after passing through one or other process, there comes out of what is 'used up' handbills showing tailors' fashions, finished in a style which makes them look like pictures intended for framing; also show cards on which appear a perfect likeness of the interior of a room, or some other object most difficult of representation.

———

And if an example be demanded worthy of the whole, or of which the whole, with a few exceptions, is worthy, Mr. Roberts may, without offence to any other East London lithographer and printer, be fairly taken. I was told that at this place, if required for some emergency, such as an election, or to meet the sailing of a ship, one million or more of any reasonable sized lithographed circulars could be produced on a day's notice. On circulars printed here I saw Glasgow, Newcastle-on-Tyne, Truro, Bristol, Sheffield, and other addresses figured quite freely. These printing and lithography Works are most efficiently conducted. Both the driving machinery and printing machines include the latest improvements. For example, I find Tangye's patent engine at work, driving Conisbee's, Payne's and Hopkinson's machines, with others recently invented, by which manual labour is saved and efficiency secured. The "dead register" improvement in printing is one of the most important of recent inventions. I saw it tried on a large sheet of Brown and Polson's bills, and so accurately did it act that I venture to say that if every one of the many millions produced for this House at these Works were examined, few, if any, would show a double working. The value of this in working in colours is beyond the possibility of exaggeration. But not only in respect to these, but in regard to cutting, numbering, perforating, and every other class of machine, the best of its kind is the one selected, and so the turning out of work well done and with despatch is only a natural result.

26 The Unskilled Labourer
A Working Man, 1879

This essay expresses the feelings of the skilled worker on the great social distinctions to be found between those with a skill and those without. As this writer makes clear, the man without a technical skill, was also a man without a trade community, and without a union.

Relatively speaking, the workman of this class may be regarded as the great unknown of the workshop world. That he is a man, or at any rate like the murdered in Macbeth, "in the catalogue goes for such," the artisan class would of course be fain to acknowledge; but they would scarcely count him a brother, and certainly not an equal. As his title of "unskilled" implies, he has no handicraft and he has no union; while if he has grievances, either real or imaginary, he has not, like the artisan, special means and appliances for so "working" such grievances as to bring the fact of his existence prominently before the public in connection with them. A servant unto servants is he, the Gibeonite of the world of manual labour, the hewer of wood and drawer of water to society in general, and to the mechanic, his immediate lord and master, in particular.

Unskilled labourers are divided into two leading types — labourers attached, and labourers unattached, each type having its own especial characteristics, and especial advantages and disadvantages. The first is attached to the *Trades*, to the skilled "hands" whereof he is the unskilled assistant. Connected with most of the handicrafts there is a good deal of sheer "slogging" to be done, sheer digging and delving, pulling and hauling, fetching and carrying, and the like. At what they hold to be the slogging point the craftsmen take their stand on the thus-far-and-no-farther principle.

T.T.— I

Thus the need for the unskilled labourer and a field for his operations in connection with the skilled labourer are created.

———

On the whole, and by the general body of the skilled hands, the unskilled labourer is treated with kindness and consideration, if he only prove himself a willing worker, and shows that he "knows his place." This latter is a cardinal point. Notwithstanding all the talk anent equality, brotherhood, the federation of the world, and the like, that flow so trippingly from the tongue of many who profess to speak in the name of the working classes, there is no place in which class distinctions are more sharply defined, or strongly, or, if need be, violently maintained than in the workshop.

———

The unskilled labourer unattached is engaged in work that is all labouring — dock labouring, coal-portering, and the like. He has not, like the other labourer, that definiteness of position and reflected glory that a trade is supposed to give to all within its circle, nor is his work as a rule so steady, or so much under shelter. On the other hand, he is more free than the attached labourer, is subject only to his employer and his ganger, and may himself rise to be a ganger. He might be free from the evils of strikes, too, but as though there were some law of universality in the strike madness, the unattached labourer will sometimes get up a strike on his own account. His strikes, however, are seldom important, or of long duration. Living from hand to mouth when in work, he has nothing to fall back upon, and is soon starved into capitulation. Or, failing that, it is comparatively easy to replace him by others.

27 On the Inner Life of Workshops
Thomas Wright, 1867

This selection depicts the workshop culture of Victorian England. It indicates the great significance to learning a trade of the social dimensions of skill and work.

———

In all phases of life, there is, I fancy, a sort of inner life — a life behind the scenes — that is known only to the initiated.

———

There are traditions, customs, and usages interwoven with, and indeed in a great measure constituting, the inner and social life of workshops, a knowledge of which is as essential to the comfort of those whose lot is cast amongst them, as technical proficiency is necessary to obtaining or retaining employment. To these unwritten, but perfectly understood and all-powerful laws of workshop life, all working men — whatever may be their private opinion — must in some degree bow. The social phase of life in a workshop — the phase embodied in the customs and traditions of "the trade" — is generally the first into which the beginner is initiated. When an apprentice enters a shop, he will in all probability be taught to "keep nix" before he is told the names of the tools; and though the apprentice, everything around him being novel, would prefer being enlightened regarding the elementary mysteries of his trade to being put to keep nix, this merely shows his want of wisdom. Keeping nix is a really important job, and one the efficient discharge of which is supposed to imply the possession of considerable ability on the part of the apprentice, and which elevates him in the estimation of those who are to bring him up in the way he should go. Keeping nix, consists in keeping a bright look-out for the approach of managers or foremen, so as to be able to give prompt and timely notice to men who may be skulking, or having a sly read or smoke, or who are engaged on "corporation work" — that is, work of their own.

For, though it is nominally the master to whom he is bound, who has to teach him his trade, it is on the goodwill of the skilled workman of the establishment that he has really to depend for being initiated into those little "wrinkles" and specialities the knowledge of which makes the difference between the good and the bad or only ordinary workman. Having by a more or less painful experience obtained a knowledge of those phases of the inner life of a workshop that apply more especially to boys, and having by a fight or two settled which of the *other apprentices* may or may not venture to fag him, and having selected a mate with whom to go for walks in the evenings and on Sundays, and exchange confidences concerning their respective sweethearts (for by this time he will have learned that in order to be in any degree worthy of his age and generation he *must* have a girl—even if he has to invent one)— the young apprentice may begin to think of settling quietly down to the study of his trade. He will now be left unmolested to practise with the simpler tools at this time entrusted to him, and to wonder within himself whether he will ever be able to acquire that extraordinary degree of deftness in handling them which he sees possessed by the workmen around him; he will be left to learn by observation and inquiry "the ins and outs" of the strange things that he sees going on around him, and otherwise to generally qualify himself to witch the world with noble workmanship, and realize his idea of becoming in time one of the great men of the profession. For the next two or three years he will go on pretty smoothly, gradually improving in proficiency as a workman, and, as a rule, getting "disenchanted" as he becomes familiar with the intricacies of the trade. During this period he will get upon terms of equality with most of the apprentices, and be in a position to lord it over some of the younger of them, though himself not as yet allowed to mix as an equal with the journeymen. From some of these he will in the meanwhile recieve kind and considerate treatment, while from others he will get ill-treatment.

———

But while the payment of a footing with a boy is never thrown away, the treatment which an apprentice receives from the men in a workshop will depend in a great measure upon himself. If he is lazy, ill-tempered, or impudent, and stands to the letter of the law in obliging or yielding obedience to the men, he will be treated accordingly — that is to say, the men will stand to the letter of the law in teaching him his trade, and complain of him whenever his conduct gives occasion for doing so. Boys who are at once willing and dull are the ones with whom men, from a twofold motive of kindess and a regard for their own credit, take the most pains; but they naturally have the greatest degree of pleasure in teaching those who are sharp as well as obliging. Nor does their concern for the welfare of their apprentices cease on the boys becoming journeymen, as the "old hands" will continue for years to take the warmest interest in the progress of those whom they have taught their trade. On completing his term of apprenticeship, and springing at once from a wage of eight or ten to one of thirty shillings or upwards per week, the new-fledged journeyman is generally as eager to pay his footing to those who are now his brother journeymen as they are to receive it; and a newly-married man is generally found to be liberally disposed towards his shopmates.

———

From the talk of the old hands about strikes, locks-out, nobsticks, and other kindred subjects, the apprentice obtains an insight into those technical trade points which are so frequently the grounds of disputes between masters and workmen. He will learn at what times and under what circumstances he will be justified in demanding and holding out for "walking money" — money claimed in consideration of men being sent to work at such a distance from the shop as necessitates their rising earlier in the morning and getting home later in the evening than usual; or "dirty money" — money demanded by men who are put upon repairs, or other work that involves extra wear and tear of clothes; and on what kind of jobs it will be advisable to "kick" the master for "allowance" — allowance being drink or money to get drink, asked for by men who are employed upon work requiring an unusual degree of physical exertion, or that has to be carried on in very hot or very cold places, or upon the successful completion of any unusually large or difficult piece of work. He will learn exactly how far he may go in doing any work that does not strictly fall within his own branch of trade; what rate of payment to demand for overtime under various circumstances; with whom he may or may not work; in what jobs he may demand or object to the assistance of a labourer, and a variety of other useful matters pertaining to trade and workshop etiquette.

And while at this time and in these things he may see much of the weaknesses and prejudices of his class, he will during the same period learn things that will show him that his class, as a class, have their noble as well as ignoble qualities. He will be taught to consider the intimation "he's in the trade," an all-sufficient reason for extending the hand of friendship to all fellow-craftsmen, irrespective of position and appearance, and he will find that the greatest kindness is extended to a brother of the craft at the time that he stands most in need of it — namely, when he is out of work; and he will see that whenever special misfortune overtakes a man, his shopmates are always prepared to enter into a subscription to relieve his wants, so far as a little money will do so. He will see men "pitching into" their work in the hardest style, in order that they may be able to give a hand to a mate who through illness is unable to do his full share, but who, from having a family dependent upon him, must stick to his work as long as he possibly can; and he will not unfrequently see a young man — even when trade is at the dullest — voluntarily offering himself for "the sack", in order to save a married man from it; and when, as sometimes happens in times of dull trade, the men of an establishment are called together, and it is put to them whether they will all agree to go upon short time until trade gets brisker, to save some of their number from being discharged, he will invariably find the old hands, those who are sure of being kept, the first to advocate short time. Apart from such general matters as these, no one can be long in a workshop without witnessing special acts of generosity between mate and mate. And upon the whole, while the apprentice who has entered a workshop entertaining great ideas concerning "the dignity of labour," and the superiority of the "intelligent artisan," will as he nears the termination of his apprenticeship, find that workmen are not all that his boyish fancy had painted them, he will probably conclude that, all things considered, their virtues outweigh their faults.

———

The life and education of the workshop, as I have attempted to show by briefly epitomizing the career of an apprentice during his "seven long years," is twofold — technical and social. What a knowledge of the world is to the man of the world, a knowledge of the social life of workshops is to the working man; it will enable him to push through where others would stick; to make friends readily; to avoid those whose acquaintance would be unprofitable; to get mates to put in a good word for him when he is out of work; and to go on smoothly with those with whom he is connected when in work. On the other hand, a man who is ignorant of the social part of workshop life, or who lacks tact in practising it, will, although he may be a good man and clever workman, find the workshop world a harsh, unsympathetic, and unjust world to him.

Chapter Four

Mechanization and the Trades

The effect of mechanization and the responses to it were immensely varied in mid-Victorian Britain. In the building trades subcontracting and division of labour had the most far reaching impact on the organization of work, but mechanization was also a significant factor, and was met by violent protests from sawyers and brickmakers. Resistance to the moulding machine in brickmaking, as well as attempts to enforce apprenticeship rules, the employment of only union men and the payment of union dues all contributed to the Manchester Outrages in the building trades in the latter part of the 1860s. There were similar reactions in the old cutlery trades of Sheffield, where wage reductions and unemployment also provoked trade union sanctions to prevent further mechanization, and to enforce trade union rules on employment and apprenticeship. Until well into the nineteenth century the Sheffield trades formed a bastion of domestic and workshop production based on hand techniques. A piecemeal process of mechanization affecting in the first instance the saw grinders evoked fierce resistance from workers. They imposed demands with work-centred sanctions, including the theft of tools and the destruction of materials, the so-called 'rattenings'.

Even in the newer engineering industries mechanization and division of labour affected the stronghold of a newer group of skilled craftsmen spawned by the industrial revolution. The great engineering industrialists, themselves trained by earlier craft toolmakers, concentrated their efforts on creating large-scale engineering works, in using their ingenuity to mechanize as many processes as possible, and in raising productivity through the use of piece rates, systematic overtime and manning new machinery with unskilled labour. This provoked the manning of machines issue which underlay the 1852 Lockout in the industry, and which in turn brought about the emergence of the Amalgamated Society of Engineers.

Yet the rapid spread of the industrialization and the great boom of the mid-Victorian economy cannot be accounted for only in the expansion and mechanization of old crafts, and in the emergence of new sophisticated mechanical industries. For perhaps the most important basis for this rapid economic expansion was one of the oldest established and most primitive of all industries—coal mining. Perhaps no other input was so important to most mid-Victorian industries, and the output of coal nearly doubled between 1854 and 1874 from 64.7 million tons to 126.6 million tons for the United Kingdom as a whole. Such an enormous expansion of output was not, however, based on technical improvement, but on the opening of new mines, and the use of deeper pits and more men. Total UK employment in the mining industry rose from 307.5 thousand men to 538.8 thousand men in the decade 1864 to 1874 alone. The hewers at the coal face were backed up by a whole series of gradations of labour including men, women and boys. Most of this was sub-contracted labour hired through the butty system. The butty, who hired his own labour and used his own equipment, contracted with a proprietor to deliver coal at so much per ton. The great demand for coal combined with militancy among the men prompted coal owners to seek mechanical devices for mining, but they were still unsuccessful even by the end of the century. The major technical improvements that did successfully affect the industry were those which allowed for deeper mining, that is, systems for draining shafts, and for improving haulage and ventilation.

Marx drew on the mid-Victorian economy for many of the characteristics of his phase of modern industry, but what is most impressive about the period is the variety in the forms of technical change embraced. In the midst of hitherto unheard of possibilities for mechanization, tradesmen maintained their domains of skill, and such basic industries as mining expanded enormously the hard physical labour which had characterized the lives of workers in this and other industries for centuries before.

LOCOMOTIVE FACTORY

28 Saw Mills and Wood Working
George Dodd, 1862

The sawyers' trade was threatened in the 1860s by the introduction of the steam saw mill. George Dodd describes its effect in displacing the old sawpit. The saw mill was, however, very slow to take over the country areas of the trade.

Saw-mills and wood-working — The cutting down of timber trees, and the shaping of the wood into pieces of convenient size, are necessary preliminaries to the work of the carpenter. The cutting down is simple enough, though laborious; it is effected almost wholly by means of the axe. When once a tree is lowered, and the shoots and branches lopped off, it is converted into baulks or square beams by the combined action of the axe, the adze, and the saw.

The saw is one of the oldest of tools. However easily timber may be rent in the direction of the grain by cutting tools and wedges, it is difficult and wasteful to divide it across the grain except by a saw. There are pictures extant, showing that the ancient Egyptians used hand-saws at a very remote period. At the present day, saws are made of well-tempered steel, with teeth made chiefly by filing; they display a multitude of sizes and forms, according to the purposes which they are to subserve. Thus there are *cross-cut, pit, frame, hand, panel, tenon, sash, dovetail, compass, keyhole saws*, etc., all used by hand, irrespective of the larger kinds worked by machinery.

Everyone has seen a saw-pit, and the manner in which two men manage a long saw to cut a large beam of timber into planks. It is not to be wondered at that, when the steam-engine came to be a prime mover in so many departments of industry, some one should have hit upon the idea of working large saws by its means. Saw-mills driven by horse, by wind, and by water, preceded those driven by steam; but now the latter have nearly superseded them. In some of these mills, any number of saws, from two to a dozen, are arranged vertical and parallel, at distances equal to the thickness of the planks or boards which are to be produced. The saws are fixed in a frame to which a reciprocating or up-and-down motion is given. The log of wood is placed horizontally in a frame so adjusted that it can travel from end to end; that is, the log can advance up to the saws as fast as the latter can effect the cutting. A still more complete kind is the *circular* saw, sometimes nearly twenty feet in diameter. This saw is made of a number of thin pieces of steel ingeniously adjusted; it rotates on its axis with great rapidity, and the wood is driven up against its edge to be cut.

Besides saws of various kinds, numerous machines of most ingenious construction are now used for the cutting and shaping of wood. *Planing,* dowelling, dovetailing, grooving, tenoning, moulding, rebating, and other carpentering processes, are in the present day effected very rapidly by machines specially invented for those purposes, and with greater accuracy than by hand.

In such undertakings as the Great Exhibition building at Brompton, it would be impossible to execute the work in the stipulated time or at the stipulated price were not the aid of machinery obtained in shaping and preparing the wood. Where flooring is estimated by the *acre*, and sash bars by the *mile*, the necessity for mechanical aid becomes apparent.

Not only is the timber-work of buildings now prepared by machinery; but even such trifling articles as *firewood* and *lucifer-matches* are cut by steam-worked mechanism of a highly finished and elaborate kind, such as can only be rendered profitable by an enormous demand. There are machines now at work which will cut and shape *millions* of lucifer splints in a day.

29 Brickmaking
George Dodd 1869

Brickmaking, one of the building trades, was organised according to a strict job hierarchy based on skill. In the 1860s the introduction of machinery for replacing the pinnacle skill of the moulder provoked violent protest from the brickmakers. George Dodd here describes the process of making hand- and machine-made bricks.

Brick making. In this, as in many other branches of manufacture, the articles are not only made more rapidly by machine than by hand, but they are more equable in quality and regular in appearance, owing to each one being an exact type of all the others.—*Hand-made Bricks.* All the ancient bricks were made by hand. It is supposed that the Babylonian bricks were burned in a kiln; that those which the Israelites made in Egypt were baked in the open air; while in many countries they were merely sun-dried. The Romans were skilful brick-makers, as many ancient buildings in England still testify. In making bricks by hand in the present day, the clay is first tempered by long exposure to the air; and, if too stiff, sand or ashes are mixed with it. When kneaded to the proper consistency, it is separated into lumps, each large enough for one brick; the moulder dashes it into a wooden mould sprinkled with sand, and then removes the sides of the mould, leaving the brick on the bottom. The bricks, as made, are removed to a field, where they are dried in air and sunshine. Finally, they are burnt in clumps or in kilns.—*Machine-made Bricks.* The machines employed have been many in kind, due to differences of opinion among the inventors as to the best mode of achieving a particular result. The chief machines employed are those of Oates, Clayton, Norton, and Tweeddale. The clay is spread out on the ground, and tempered with water until brought to a soft moist state, being turned over and over several times to expose new surfaces. It is thrown into a hopper, from which it falls between two crushing rollers, where any hard particles in it are thoroughly crushed. The crushed clay passes at once into a *pug-mill*, the revolving arms or screw blades of which mix it up thoroughly into a homogeneous and smooth mass. — *Wet Making*. The clay thus prepared for the *wet* process is forced through an aperture from the pug-mill into a horizontal clay-box; from this it is forced in a continuous horizontal stream or band to a delivery table. At regular intervals a wire descends and cuts this band into separate bricks. The shape of the orifice in the clay-box determines the height and width of the brick, while the intervals in the descent of the wire determine the length. — *Dry Making*. Although more labour is required in grinding the materials, less drying and burning of the bricks are needed in the *dry* process than in the *wet* : the former is gradually coming more and more into use. The moulds for forming the bricks on the dry process are ranged round a circular revolving table. The machine is so placed that it discharges the prepared clay into two moulds at one time; they travel on, and receive pressure by the action of a square piston or plunger, while two others are receiving their quota of clay; and so on. The bricks gradually rise out of their moulds as the table revolves and then pass over to a revolving endless band, which conveys them away. — *Burning*. Some bricks require to be dried before burning, but not all. In the ordinary brick-kilns there is a great loss of heat occa-

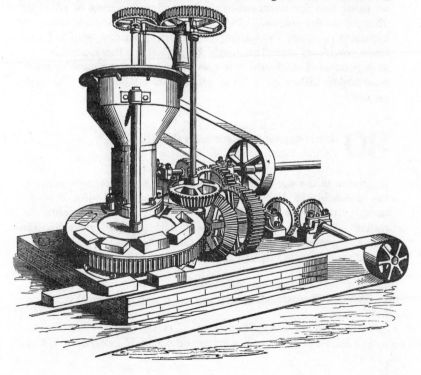

sioned by the escape of hot air and smoke into the open air, no arrangements being made to economise it. To obviate this loss, Hoffmann, of Berlin, has invented a very improved kiln, capable of burning 25,000 bricks per day. The kiln, 160 feet in diameter, is a kind of tunnel or arched passage running in a cricle. Round the outside are twenty-four doors, opened or closed as may be needed; these belong to twenty-four compartments into which the ring-formed passage is divided; and twenty-four flues lead from these compartments to a central chimney, with valves to cut off communication. There are dampers, easily opened and closed, between the several compartments. The compartments are filled with newly-made bricks at different times, and are empted at different times, in such a way that the heat, when it has done its work, travels on to other compartments, and is never wasted by escaping into the open air. The bricks do not travel round the ring, but the hot air does. — *Ventilating* bricks and *hollow* bricks, having cavities of various sizes in or through them, are now much used. They are easily produced by modifications of the machinery.—Messrs. Peto and Betts, during the progress of their works on the Chatham and Dover Railway, on one occasion made 200,000 bricks in a fortnight with one of Oates's machines; but the average is usually 80,000 per week. Mr. Cola affords an idea of the cost of brick and tile machinery adequate to the production of a certain quantity of these articles. He sets down £750 for the hoisting, grinding, pagging, moulding, cutting and other apparatus necessary for making 12,000 bricks per day by the wet process; and about an equal sum for steam-engine, boiler, and mill gearing of all kinds. Then, by the dry process, £1,050 for the hoisting, grinding, and moulding apparatus necessary for making 14,000 bricks per day, with £750 for steam machinery, etc. This would be £3,300 for the apparatus for a large permanent work. There is a second estimate for a *portable* series, according as the machines are to produce from 9,000 to 14,000 bricks per day.

30 Testimony on the Manchester Outrages
George Taunton, 1867-8

Resistance to the use of moulding machines in brickmaking was one of the causes of the Manchester Outrages during the 1860s. This and many more passages of the Inquiry into the Outrages describe the feelings of the trade about the use of machine-made bricks, and the sanctions imposed by brickmakers on those who transgressed.

Mr. George Taunton sworn and examined.
    14,586. (*Chairman.*) I believe you are a master brickmaker, are you not? — Yes.
    14,587. Do you live at Cheetham? — Yes.
    14,588. I believe there is a master brickmakers' association, is there

not? — Yes.

14,589. And I think you are chairman of it?—Yes.

14,590. How long has this association existed? — I think nearly 20 years.

14,591. Have you been a member all that time? — No.

14,592. How long have you been a member? — About 10 or 11 years I think.

14,593. Can you give me any notion of how many members it has?— There are about 70 members I think.

———

14,613. Do you come to any agreement between yourselves or with the operative brickmakers' union as to the price of labour? No, they do all the dictation in that matter.

14,614. Who do?—The operatives.

14,615. But do they dictate to you? — Yes, they tell what we are to pay them.

14,616. That is what I wanted to understand? — Yes, they charge us so much per 1,000.

14,617. Then you have, if I may so call it, your directions from the operative union as to the price which you are to pay for labour? — Just so.

14,618. And if you do not pay them what happens? — We should have a strike.

14,619. And sometimes a little more?—Yes, very likely, perhaps.

15,620. Of course that comes into part of the question of labour, and the time of working comes into the same consideration, I suppose? — Yes, the hours are fixed, that has been latterly done.

14,621. Had you ever any bricks spoiled yourself? — Yes.

14,622. When? — On the evening of the 24th of June 1864, I believe it was.

14,623. Where were your works then? — In Bank Street, Cheetham.

14,624. That is in the Manchester district, is it not? — It is in the Manchester district.

14,625. Have you any notion why your bricks were spoiled? — I have no notion at all.

14,626. After three years' reflection upon it you cannot give any reason why your bricks were spoiled?—I cannot, unless it was that I strongly advocated machinery; I had spoken pretty freely, perhaps, upon machinery amongst our association at different times.

14,627. That we understand is a deadly offence?—That is obnoxious to the brickmakers; it is the means of lowering wages, and it will naturally be obnoxious, no doubt.

14,628. But you exercised your freedom of opinion, and you can give no other reason why your bricks were spoiled but that? — I cannot, and I only surmise that.

14,629. It has been said that the invention or employment of machinery tends in the end to increase the labour and the number of hands employed, although it may not at the moment have that effect; has that been your experience? — I believe it would increase hands, perhaps, but then they would not get so much wages as they do.

14,630. They may or they may not; but you know that it is said among political economists that the result of employment of machinery has been of a considerable benefit to the operative classes, and that they have gained by it, not only in wages, but in the number of hands employed. You have heard that, I daresay? — That point is very right.

14,631. But it may be attended with immediate loss at the moment to the person who may be employed in making whatever may be the article in question without machinery?—Yes; you see there is a great difference between clay being worked in machinery and cotton and silk and all those matters, because it is a heavy rough material, and there is a great deal of wear and tear on the machinery for little value.

14,632. What is your experience with regard to machine-made bricks and bricks made by hand? In your judgement, as far as that particular trade is concerned, would fewer hands be employed throughout the country if bricks were made by machinery? — In my experience in machinery I have not seen any machines that could compete with hand labour. I say that from the experience that I have had amongst it. Those machines which have been commenced here have all of them failed; the owners have all of them I think been insolvent.

14,633-4. But have there not been certain causes at work which might account for the insolvency besides the business? — Well, the frustration no doubt would have a tendency; but I can speak for other counties. I have a cousin that makes bricks by machinery in Nottinghamshire, where there were no unionists existing, and he was only telling me as he was looking at this machine up here, about a month ago, "I lost 500*l.* or 600*l.* by machine; it is in its infancy yet."

14,635. Then in your judgment are hand-made bricks better than machine-made bricks, or is it the other way? — Hand-made bricks are the best, with the exception of those made by Ibbotson and Platt's machines. I believe that would pay and make as good a brick and as cheap a brick if they could be mixed. It makes a class of bricks which we call stock and second bricks which are used for frontages; but that machine, and no other machine that I have seen, I think could compete with what we call the common bricks, which are mostly used, and of which there is the greatest consumption.

14,636. Have you changed your opinion then since your bricks were spoiled? — Well, I have rather changed my opinion since then, because all the companies are gone down, and I have thought they had not got the machine yet up to the mark.

14,637. Then I suppose there would be great difficulty in this district in making bricks by machinery for fear of damage? — There would be great difficulty. There is a very strong combination between brickmakers and bricklayers.

14,638. Against machine-made bricks? — Yes, it would take a great deal of capital to break through that combination.

14,639. And perhaps some physical force?—I cannot speak to that.

14,640. Have you an insurance company among yourselves to pay for damage? — We have.

14,641. Is that in case of any wilful damage being done by anybody? — That is the nature of the insurance.

———

14,668. There was no other occasion on which you remember that Kay or anybody else was employed to draw the men off, but it was done in the case of this man?—Yes, to inform us where these parties were.

14,669. Are there any machine-made bricks now in Manchester? — Yes, there is one going on with Johnson, the wire worker in Bradford, I believe. He has put one down lately, but with the exception of that I think there are not.

14,670. I suppose from what we have heard of the sort of things that have been done, and the outrages that have been committed, the machine-made bricks have never had what you call fair play in this district? —Not since the combination came with the brickmakers, but previous to that of course they had a better opportunity.

14,671. When was that combination formed? — I should think it is two or three years ago perhaps. It would be the time that Kettle's affair was on here, the gaol job. It would be the time that Mr. Brammall's affair was on.

14,672. They have never had fair play or fair competition since that time at all events? — No, but previous to that of course they had pretty fair play.

14,673. I think you explained to me that you considered that machine-made bricks for certain purposes are better than hand-made bricks, but that the hand-made bricks for certain other purposes are better than the machine-made bricks?—Yes, they are of different classes.

14, 674. Can a machine-made brick be made cheaper than a hand-made brick? — I question it very much; I never had a machine, and I only speak from what men I have seen employed about it. I have taken an estimate about it sometimes. I have had notions about it. When there is anything fresh you must go on with the times. When you are in a business you must keep with the times, and of course I have looked into it, and I have taken a calculation both of Mr. Atken's machine and this of Marsland's in Ardwick, and I thought really they were costing more than hand-made bricks, rating men at 3s. 6d. a day, or something like that.

14,675. You include of course the labour as well as the expense of the machine? — The labour as well as the expense of machinery.

14,676. Do they cost less in labour? — They would cost less I think by hand.

14,677. Then actually according to you the machine-made bricks would cost more in labour? — Taking labour and wear and tear both together, I believe they would, with the exception of Platt's; I do not know whether that would.

———

14,717. (*Mr. Barstow.*) As a matter of fact, do you admit a man who makes bricks by machinery to be a member of your masters' union? — No, we do not; with the contention that we should have we have thought it better not. We should have a great deal of contention, no doubt.

14,718. (*Chairman.*) You would get into a quarrel with the operative brickmakers immediately? — Yes.

14,719. (*Mr. Chance.*) In fact, brickmaking by machinery has never had a fair chance? — Well, it has not since the combination came on. Previous to that of course it had a better chance.

John Lomas sworn and examined.

14,720. (*Mr. Barstow.*) You are a clog maker, are you not? — Yes.

14,721. And you carry on business at No. 78 Oldham Road? — Yes.

14,722. In April 1863 were you building two houses near the Queen's Park, Cheetham?—Yes, right opposite the entrance.

14,723. Were you building them with machine-made bricks? — I began them with hand-made bricks up to the 1st of April, and then the party with whom I had made a contract for hand-made bricks could not supply me in consequence of not having them ready for me. I had five bricklayers at the time standing, and they declared they would have their wages whether I got them bricks or not. I applied to a brickmaker not far from the place, and he wanted 6s. a thousand more. I offered him 4s., but he would not take it. I offered him 4s., but he would not take it. I offered him 4s., and to cart them off the premises, and he would not take it, and so I declared that I would not give any more, and that the men should not stand, and I went to the machine brick-yard in Cheetham and made a contract with them for a quantity of bricks. On the 2nd of April, about half-past 8, Mr. Wogden delivered the first load of machine-made bricks, and at about 25 minutes to 9 I went to see how the men were going on, and when I got there one of the foremen said, "There has been a bother about those bricks going on." I said, "Never mind them; they will not sell me hand-made bricks, and I shall have machine-made bricks." A man of the name of Kay came. I did not know him; he was a stiff man. I had seen him on a picket job in the Oldham Road, not far from me. He asked me what I was going to do? I said, "I am going to build two houses." He said, "That is not what I mean." I said, "That is an answer to your question." He said, "That is not what I mean." So I said, "What do you mean?" He said, "You know me; you saw me on that job picketing in the Oldham Road. I may as well tell you straight out. You are going to use machine-made bricks, are you?" I said, "I am; I cannot get hand-made bricks unless I pay an extravagant price for them, and I am not willing to do so." He said, "Well, then, cart them back." I said, "Yes, if you will furnish me with hand-made bricks and pay me for what I have paid for the machine-made bricks." He said, "We shall not do anything of that sort, if you will cart them back we will forgive you." I said, "Forgive me for what?" He said, "Why, for having those bricks on the premises, and I will furnish you with as many as you want." I said, "I shall not do anything of the sort unless you pay me the money which I have paid at the machine yard." I have the receipts here.

14,724. (*Chairman.*) How much was that altogether? — The first is 23*l*. 1*s*.

14,725. But how much was it altogether that you paid for the machine bricks? — What I paid for the machine bricks at that time was 27*l*. So he refused to refund the money, and I said, "Then I will use them." We were standing in the middle of the field opposite the buildings, and he said, "If you do not send them back you may mark the consequences; I will shift your head."

14,726. (*Mr. Barstow.*) What did he meant by saying that he would "shift your head?" — I suppose he meant that he would blow my head off. I said, "You can blow away if you have a mind; that will make no difference to me." I said, "I shall not take them back for my right hand unless you refund the money;" and I said, "I will tell you what I will do with you; I will make a report at the police station as I go down," and I did so; and the superindendent came almost every day to see how things were going on, and on the 9th of May he called on the Saturday morning and said, "How are you going on, Mr. Lomas?" I said, "All right, we have not been interrupted yet." He said, "Have you seen any of those brickmen about?" I said, "I have seen several," and then about half-past 11 on the same Saturday evening a girl came running down and said the buildings were on fire.

31 The Cutlery Trade of Sheffield
Frederick Callis, 1903

The Sheffield metal trades experienced violent resistance on the introduction of mechanization after centuries of hand techniques. Frederick Callis gives a survey of the history of the trade. He is concerned to emphasise the enhancement in the position of cutlery workers by the end of the nineteenth century, and regards earlier anti-machinery attitudes as backward looking.

A Century's Progress
It is, however, during the last century, and more especially the latter portion of it, that the most remarkable developments have taken place, alike in the manner in which the business is conducted, in modes of manufacture, and in the conditions of life of those engaged in the trade. A variety of causes have contributed to bring this about. They are, the greater energy and enterprise of manufacturers and the increasing

steadiness and intelligence of workmen; the reliable use of steam in place of the uncertainty of the old water power; the free adoption of machinery whereby much heavy manual labour has been saved and the output vastly increased; the operation of the Factory Acts, securing better sanitary surroundings and, as a consequence, improved health and longer lives.

A Manufacturer's Views

An admirable illustration of what has been said is furnished by the history of the firm of Messrs. Harrison Brothers and Howson. Their business was established over a century ago by Thomas Sansom and Sons, and in 1847 it was purchased by Messrs. J.W. Harrison, H. Harrison, and W. Howson. In that year the cutlery trade was so depressed that the workmen were glad to sweep the streets for a living. A change came, and the new firm began to prosper. Their premises in Norfolk Street were extended again and again; additional works were acquired in another part of the City; and still more accommodation was needed. Some six years ago the firm purchased property in Carver Street covering about an acre of ground, and thereon they have erected a thoroughly up to-date manufactory replete with all modern appliances and conveniences. The internal arrangements are as complete as skill and long experience could suggest. A prominent feature of the new works is the power-house with its engine of 250 h.p.; its powerful dynamos, and its motors scattered through the place, furnishing alike force and light. The firm employ about seven hundred people. The progress made by this firm is typical of that of others mentioned.

There had been progress in the output of high-class goods in the last fifty years, but not by any means to the same extent as in medium and common qualities. This was probably to be attributed to the introduction and free use of machinery which lent itself with more satisfactory results to the production of the lower than to the higher grade wares. Best table cutlery is made now after very much the same methods as it was a century ago, and there is little probability of change, as it is not an article that lends itself to alteration. High-class steel is so hard that attempts to manipulate it by machinery break the tools, and heating it to make it work easily would destroy its temper and reduce it to common steel. For the production of medium and common goods machinery is most valuable—indeed, a necessity of the times. While a forger is making a handful of blades, a machine will turn out a barrow full.

Coming to the position of the workers, Mr. Howson compared it with what it was in 1847, when his father commenced business, and stated that not only in money wages, but also in the conditions under which the workman does his work, and indeed in all directions, there has been distinct improvement. The introduction of the emery wheel has relieved the cutler of much exhausting labour. "Half a century ago you did not see," remarked Mr. Howson, "a cutler wearing a collar, and it was most unlikely that he had a Sunday suit. I have heard my father speak of one workman of his earlier days, an ivory cutler, who was known as 'Ivory Bob.' He was dubbed 'the gentleman of the firm' because he wore a collar and a top-hat! You may take it generally that the workman now is twice as well off as were his forefathers." Mr. Howson spoke most approvingly of the working of the Factory Acts and of the judicious manner in which they have been administered in Sheffield.

A Chat with a Working Cutler

These opinions of a prominent employer can be amply confirmed by the reflections of the older workmen. Take, for example, Walter Barnes, an admirable type of the self-respecting working cutler. His memory travels back to the days when the position of workers in the cutlery trade was totally different from what it is now. He remembers very distinctly how his father was "chaffed" for going to live in a house which was £10 a year. That was in the days of the £10 franchise, and his father wanted a vote, and had to pay for it by an increase in his rent bill. Now we have household suffrage.

"In those days," said Mr. Barnes, "the cutler was very poor, and in his poverty was often addicted to drink. Not one in twenty had a second suit of clothes, and the only change in his dress on a Sunday was that he put on a clean apron! All that has been altered. Now in the homes of many you will find the floor covered with oilcloth, a good table and sofa, and even a piano — although perhaps purchased on the hire system. Yes; the position of the cutler in my time has altogether changed. He is a steadier man, earns higher wages, and he has comforts and sources of enjoyment unknown in former years.

"There was no School Board with its free education in my young days," continued Mr. Barnes; "and before I was ten years of age I started to work. I had to leave home at a quarter-past five in the morning and was kept at work until nine o'clock at night. If I got off at four o'clock on Saturday I felt as though I had secured a day's holiday. Now we begin at half-past eight and stop at six, and at twelve o'clock on Saturdays. The cutler and all his surroundings have undergone a complete change for the better."

A Master of the Old School

Another master whose opinions it is interesting to quote is Mr. Charles Ibbotson, one of the old school of cutlery manufacturers, who was once a workman himself. He can recall the days when most of the common goods, and especially the well-known Barlow Knife, of which enormous quantities used to be sent to America, were made in the surrounding villages — Stannington, Wadsley, Worrall, Dungworth, and Hillsbro. Forgers, grinders, cutlers in the employ of "Little Mesters" were scattered all over the district. In many instances the men had a bit of land attached to their house or their shop and were able to eke out a living by growing vegetables. There were no Factory Acts in operation then, and when there was a big rush of orders men and apprentices would

139

STEEL CASTING FURNACE — FILE CUTTING

FORGING AND STRIKING

work from four or five o'clock in the morning till nine or ten at night. The masters might have been seen rushing round and offering bounties to men to work for them.

"I used," said Mr. Ibbotson, "to work every day in the week, never taking a holiday or going on the drink, and my wages averaged a guinea a week! I used to make seven dozen Barlow Knives a day, and was paid sixpence a dozen. By the way the material is put into his hands a cutler can now make eight dozen where I made six dozen. I remember once when trade was bad and my master had stocked all his money I went on working for him on credit until he owed me £33. The 'Little Mesters' at the end of the week used to bring the goods down to Sheffield on donkeys to sell, and when trade was good the merchants would meet them on the road and bid against each other to get the knives. Barlows were sometimes sold at 11s. per gross and at all prices up to 21s. per gross. If you had met some of the 'Mesters' going home you could have told by their appearance how Barlows had gone. I need not say anything about the masters, but with regard to the workmen their position in my time has wonderfully improved, and the improvement is going on."

Views of a Prominent Labour Leader

There are few men in a better position to form an opinion of the cutlery trade of the present as compared with the past than Mr. W.F. Wardley. He is a member of the City Council, and a very prominent worker in all movements for the advancement of the people. For nearly thirty years he toiled as a table blade forger, and only left the hammer and the anvil to take up the duties of Secretary to the Table Blade Forgers and Strikers Union. In this position he is brought into personal contact with employers and employed alike throughout the City.

"I can remember well," he said, "hearing conversations between my father and the older members of the trade of what they had passed through in the 'good old days of protection.' There were then, as there have been since, periods of good and bad trade, but it was evident from what they said that when bad trade did come the sufferings of the people were very much worse and more widespread than they would be now.

"And why? Because all the necessaries of life were so much dearer and the little money obtainable from parish relief or any other source would go practically no way in what it would purchase. A man, his wife and family would want three stones of flour a week, and this at 4s. 6d. per stone, as it was in my father's younger days, would mean 13s. 6d. per week. The price of flour to-day is 1s. 6d. per stone, so you see the difference in the bread bill alone. The fact is the poor could not obtain sufficient money to buy all the bread they needed, leave alone meat and other necessaries. The acute sufferings of the poor cutler when trade was bad in those days can hardly be realised by us.

"Of course, in some branches of the trade, such as table blade forging, fewer men are employed now; but that is not because of any falling off in the demand, but because of the wide introduction of machinery.

Many classes of goods are now made by machinery that used to give employment to a large army of hand forgers. They have found other and better paying work. There can be no doubt that the general condition of the working cutler during the last half-century has decidedly improved. He works under healthier, easier, and less exhausting conditions altogether. To-day he would not submit to some of the inconveniences and annoyances which his forefathers thought belonged to their stand in life. For instance, an apprentice in the old days recognised it as part of his duty on a Saturday to break so much sand to scatter over the floor of his master's house after it had been washed, or fetch water from the wells for use during the following week. I had to break sand in my apprentice days. As far as his means will allow, the cutler has moved upwards. He is better educated; his wife and family are better dressed, and he has a more comfortable home. Many things he then regarded as a luxury, only obtainable at intervals at the best, he now claims to be a necessity, and gets them."

The "Little Mester"

Under the reign of Free Trade that very ancient institution the "Little Mester" is rapidly disappearing, partly from the different way in which production is carried on, and partly from the operation of the Factory Acts. He made very cheap goods; his people worked often amid most insanitary surroundings; he was dependent upon the sale of his output at the end of the week for the wherewithal to pay even the poor wages he could afford; and the income of both employer and employed was of a very precarious character. The trade is being concentrated more and more in the hands of men of capital, who own large, light, airy shops, who have the most efficient up-to-date machinery, and who have plenty of capital at command. While alluding to the "Little Mester," with all respect for the part he played and the work he did in the past, it has to be admitted that he was a great obstacle to progress. He would not be convinced that the markets of the world were changing, and that what suited the grandfather and father would not please the son and grandson. The head of one large firm remarked, "We spend considerable sums of money in sending our travellers to the four quarters of the globe for orders, and when we have received their reports and samples of what was wanted, the 'Little Mester' has stood in the way of the suggestions being carried out." There are many instances in which the "Little Mester" is now being employed by the big firm as ganger over a team of cutlers. They work in a large shop, and by co-operation and subdivision of labour, goods are produced in enormous quantities at a minimum of cost.

Pen and Pocket Cutlery

Although it has not been found possible to introduce any very great variety of patterns in table cutlery, there have been endless developments in pen and pocket knives, and the introduction of new designs is still going on. Up to the end of the seventeenth century the spring cutlery, though good in quality, was extremely plain and sadly wanting in finish. The trade entered upon a new era in 1820, when what is known as the 'Wharncliffe Knife" was invented. Since then leading firms have devoted unremitting attention to the production of novelties and specialities, and such knives are made to-day of the most costly material by the most skilled of workmen. In addition to steel goods, the cutlery trade of the present day embraces the manufacture of silver or plated knives and forks for fish, dessert, butter, etc., with handles of pearl, ivory, and other costly material. By stamping, chasing, etching, and similar processes, the ornamentation of these goods has been brought to great perfection, and the increased wealth of the nation admits of a very large business being carried on in all these productions. The trade no longer has to depend on the wants or whims of a few rich people, for these articles of comfort and luxury are now to be seen on the tables of the many.

Scissors and Razors

The branches of the cutlery trade devoted to the manufacture of scissors and razors have passed through a period of serious troubles, that were largely of a preventable character. Instead of recognising the necessity for change in methods of production in face of growing competition of foreign rivals, the men generally fought against it, and trade was literally driven away. A prolonged strike some thirty years ago in the scissor trade let the Germans into our home and foreign markets, and it was found impossible to drive them out. By the tardy adoption of machinery which the foreigner had long been using much of our trade is being gradually won back. Another trouble was caused by a change in fashions. The days are not long past when there was a brisk demand for the most expensive and elaborately worked scissors Sheffield could produce; but they are not much wanted now, either for the home or foreign markets. Russia, for example, was once a good customer for fine scissors, and bought largely at sixty shillings per dozen; now they want them at about six shillings per dozen. The demand is for a useful, rather than an ornamental, article at a moderate price, and Sheffield manufacturers are endeavouring to meet it.

Again, the development of the razor trade was checked by the introduction of the German hollow-ground razor. For a long time the Sheffield grinder refused to take it up, and makers had to send their blades to Germany to be ground. He has come to a better frame of mind, and now hollow grinding is done in Sheffield in as great perfection as can be turned out on the Continent. The Sheffield-made razor is regaining its position of supremacy not only in our home market and Colonies, but in India, South America, and elsewhere. Some houses still do a good business in fine razors with America. Here again it has been of immense advantage to have the world as a market rather than two or three countries only, for the output by many firms is far in excess of anything possible in olden times.

Reference has been made to the introduction of machinery to the cutlery trade. This was not done without much misgiving on the part of manufacturers and the keenest opposition from the workers, who believed they saw in it the ruin of the industry. It is scarcely half a century since Mr. Michael Hunter put down a trip hammer for forging blades, the work having hitherto been done by hand. The men were so incensed at his action that there was danger of his place being blown up, and the manipulators of the new tool had to be under police protection. Those were the days when men's tools were "rattened," when houses and works were blown up with gunpowder, and murders were committed. The machine, however, had come to stay, and developed into the steam hammer, the automatic air hammer, and the spring hammer, each introducing an improved system of forging and cheapening production. Then came the machine for "flying" blades, i.e. cutting them out of the bar of steel; and so extensive has this mode of manufacture become that the supplying of blades to the trade is a separate industry. As an example, reference may be made to the manufactory of Mr. Samuel Staniforth, of the Central Cutlery Forge. His machinery includes forty hammers and five pairs of eccentric rolls. His output is a thousand gross of blades per week — more, probably, than all the hand labour in Sheffield could produce. This free use of machinery in turning out blades, springs, scales, and other parts, has saved the labour of large numbers of workmen who are now employed at other work, and at the same time it has enabled our manufacturers to compete successfully with foreign rivals in almost all the markets of the world.

Satisfactory as the cutlery trade is, it might have been even more prosperous if masters and men had co-operated more heartily together. There is, however, much to be said for the men in the attitude they often assumed. They were poorly paid; much of their time was often wasted in waiting for work or in collecting the material to do it; and when employers suggested change of patterns or the utilisation of machinery the men were exacting in their demands, and consequently valuable improvements had to be abandoned or postponed. It is the opinion of many that if the Sheffield cutlery manufacturers had had to face the foreign competition that has prevailed without the advantages of Free Trade neither they nor their workpeople would be enjoying the measure of prosperity that now prevails.

32 Testimony on the Sheffield Outrages
G. Colley and J. Thompson, 1867

The highly organised trade societies among the Sheffield cutlers fought all challenges to the craft. This included the machine, and the use of non-union or non-apprenticed labour. They imposed their demands with work-centred sanctions, the so-called 'rattenings'. The 1867 Commission of Inquiry into the Sheffield Outrages discovered that twelve of Sheffield's sixty trade unions were implicated in the employment of henchmen to perform their rattenings. There was widespread support for those involved, and for the maintenance of the customs and sanctions of the trade among Sheffield's trade unions and workers.

George Colley sworn and examined.

1220. *(Mr. Barstow.)* You are a scissor grinder?—Yes.

1221. Where do you live? — I live in Allen Street.

1222. Have you been an apprentice to the trade? — Yes.

1223. And you are now a journeyman? — Yes.

1224. How long have you been a journeyman? — Since 1855; 11 or 12 years.

1225. Are you a member of any Union? — Yes.

1226. What Union is that? — The Scissor Grinders' Union.

1227. How long have you been a member of the Union? — About five years.

1254. *(Chairman.)* I suppose that rattening is a thing which is understood very well in Sheffield, is it not? — Grinders understand it well enough.

1255. And they understand that rattening is when their bands are taken away, because they have done something against the Union; that is what they mean, is it not? — I believe so.

1256. That is how it is understood in the town, is it? — Grinders understand it so.

1257. And it often happens amongst grinders when they do anything against the Union that they find their bands are gone?—I have known it to be the case.

1258. How often have you known it to be the case? — I have known it once.

1259. Yourself? — Yes, some five or six years since for owing 12s.

1260. *(Mr. Barstow.)* What did you do when you lost your bands? — I did not do anything at all about them.

1261. You did nothing? — No; I did not see anybody about them. I did not bother about them.

Joseph Thompson sworn and examined.

1315. *(Mr. Chance.)* Where do you live? — No. 80 Allen Street.

1316. And what are you?—I am the secretary to the Scissor Forgers' Society.

1317. What are you by trade? — I am a scissor forger by trade.

1318. How long have you been a scissor forger? — I served my apprenticeship to it.

1319. Is it a Union? — It is really a Union but that is the name we give it, the Scissor Forgers' Provident Society.

1320. You say you served your apprenticeship? — Yes.

1321. And then you became a journeyman? — Yes.

1322. And then did you progress from a journeyman to become a master, or are you still a journeyman? — I was a journeyman until the trade took me from the shop to devote the whole of my time as secretary to the trade.

———

1459. Will you describe to me what your notion of rattening is? — I think it is a very arbitrary mode of enforcing law, but at the same time it is the best way that we have got.

1460. How do you mean that it is the best way you have got? — Because we could not summon the man for his contribution.

1461. As you find you cannot summon a man for his contribution, you say rattening is the only way of enforcing the payment of contributions? — I am speaking of trades generally.

1462. I am speaking of rattening; is it done by the trade? — Rattening in our trade is not recognised under any circumstances.

1463. Do you mean to say that rattening has never taken place in any case of scissor forgers? — I do not mean to say that, but I expect afterwards to be examined upon that point.

1464. I daresay you will, presently, but I want to come to the gist of the thing. Have you seen the "Independent" of this morning? — Yes.

1465. I saw in it a statement this morning; it seems a very clever and well-written article, and I daresay the gentleman who has written it knows a great deal about trade. I want to known your opinion upon this. They say that "rattening is the coercive power which unions use to enforce compliance with their rules by neglectful or refractory members." — Yes.

1466. Then the rattening is used by the trades generally? — Certainly.

1467. You know that as a matter of knowledge? we may take it as a matter of course we all know Mr. Leader, and I suppose he is the person who has written this. He knows trade, I suppose, as well as you do, and he tells us that it is known in the town that rattening is resorted to by the trade? — Yes; I believe it is an old established law in Sheffield and the neighbourhood.

1468. How do you mean an old established law? — I have read that before Unions were in force to anything like the extent they are at the present day, supposing that a man refused to comply with the rules of a factory, they would take away his tools.

1469. Where have you read that? — I think it was in one of our local papers.

1470. That is some years ago? — Yes; many years ago. I did not read it many years ago, I read it in a paper a short time since. It was speaking of rattening generally, and it laid it down as being an old established. and, in fact, an ancient custom.

1471. This is very useful, because if your mode of enforcing the penalties is not right, we hope to have law to enable you to enforce your penalties in some other and more desirable way, and if this is wrong it can be put an end to? — That is what we desire.

1472. Quite so. I knew I was speaking to an intelligent man. You say that this rattening is the ancient system. It is a bad mode of enforcing your rules, but it is the only mode you have got? — Quite so.

1473. Supposing that a man is a defaulter, what course do you pursue? — Are you speaking of my own trade?

1474. I am speaking of any trade you know of? — We take away his tools and hide them.

1475. You say that in your Union you do not know that it is being done?—Just so; will you ask me the question again, if you please, and then I shall understand?

1476. Has it never been done in your own Forgers' Union? — It has been done, but it has never been recognised by the committee.

1477. What was the instance in which it was done in your Union? — In the case of Mr. Darwin.

1478. Who is Mr. Darwin?—I think that he has a case to bring here.

1479. Who is Mr. Darwin?—He is a scissors manufacturer.

1480. Can you tell me how he had offended the Union? — I am rather afraid that we are drifting out of the argument, although you should know better than myself.

1481. I only want to know how this rattening is used; what had Mr. Darwin done? — I have a statement to make which will implicate my own conduct, if you think well that you should have it now.

1482. If you please. It may save us a great deal of trouble. If there is misconduct, we will give you, if you make a clear statement, a certificate directly which will protect you.—Mr. Darwin, scissors manufacturer, in Snow Lane, had in his employment as a forger, a person named Hague. He worked in the factory on Mr. Darwin's tools, I believe. He left, not Mr. Darwin's employment, but the firm.

1483. How is that; I do not quite understand that? — We have in our trade in-workers and out-workers. If a man works in he is supposed to work on the manufacturer's own tools, if he works out he works on his own tools, a journeyman's tools. By working out he would receive a little extra for his work.

1484. Then you mean that he left the factory and became an out-worker? — Just so; in order that a brother of his (Hague's) might come from the workboard branch, and commence forging, having served no apprenticeship. I waited upon him several times and asked him to commence contributing to our society, and to become a member of it. He rather objected, and said that he would see me again on the matter. As he became more efficient in his workmanship the consequence was, that instead of there being, I may say, three men working for the firm, there were four, on account of his coming in, and it had a tendency to cause one of the men to become short of employment. Mr. Darwin then took the advantage, and said, "Now I am very short of work, but I will find you work if you will do it at something less." I believe the man lowered the price of his labour 10 per cent., through Mr. Darwin's influence. Mr. Darwin said, "I will give you so much less," and he paid them 10 per cent. less.

1485. (*Mr. Barstow.*) All the men? — The one that I will mention named Clarke.

1486. (*Chairman.*) That was less than your list prices? — Yes; I believe then that the other men settled the price of labour at 10 per cent.

1487. You are not quite clear about that?—I am not quite clear about it. Mr. Darwin then appealed to Clarke to settle another 10 per cent., and Clarke refused to allow the 20 per cent., and the consequence was he turned him without work. He must then come on the box. Clarke was exasperated at the trade allowing the young man to come in without contributing. He appealed to me and said that we ought to do something. I said, "What can we do?" He said, "Here you have so many men on the box, why "not set them to work?" I understood what he meant— to commit some outrage. In order to draw him into conversation, I said, "What can thou do?" He replied that if I would give him permission he would rip open Hague's bellows, which really belonged to Mr. Darwin, and take away all the tools that he could carry. The smaller tools are supposed to belong to the journeymen.

1488. Then he could damage Mr. Darwin by cutting up the bellows?— Yes.

1489. And he could damage the journeymen by taking away their tools? — Yes. I replied, "If there is one thing above another that I detest it is this "knife business," meaning cutting and destroying bellows. The conversation that followed I could not repeat exactly, but we came to the agreement that he should carry away the smaller tools.

1490. Did you tell him that he was to cut the things or not? — I distinctly told him not to do any such work.

1491. But you told him that he was to take away the tools? — Yes; at the same time I made this observation, that by destroying the tools we should cause enemies in the employers. By destroying the bellows Mr. Darwin would naturally be an enemy to our society, but by carrying away the smaller tools and hiding them we might return them when the men had commenced paying. For this piece of business I was to give him a sovereign. The result was that he went in the night and took away the smaller tools and destroyed the bellows likewise. He was taken into custody and brought before the magistrates, and after being remanded once he was sent to Leeds assizes.

33 Special Diseases of Artisans
Dr. Wynter, 1870

Another light is thrown on the implications of mechanization in the cutlery trades by Dr. Wynter's study of the work-related diseases of cutlers and miners. Dr. Andrew Wynter (1819-1876), the well known physician and author, is usually remembered for his special attention

148

and enlightened views on the treatment of the insane. But he also published many social and medical essays in the *Edinburgh Review*, the *Quarterly Review*, and *Once a Week*.

The fact that one of the last Reports issued by the Commissioners for the Employment of Children treats mainly of the evil conditions under which a large class of the adult artisans of Sheffield labour is significant. It must indeed have been a very serious case that could have induced them to transfer their own proper sphere of inquiry to another quarter; but, in truth, the case of the Sheffield knife-grinders has been so long notorious that we are by no means surprised they have at length brought the matter officially before the Government. Indeed, there seems to be no reason why Government should delay turning their attention far more than they have done to the conditions under which adult artisans labour. They are supposed, it is true, to be free agents, but, practically, they are little more so than the children Government has so properly taken under its protection. Artisans working in factories, mines, etc., are, to a certain extent, subordinate to conditions over which in many cases they have but little control. They are but part of a great machine, the human cogs in a system of labour employed for the production of certain articles. When, indeed, they possess the means of obviating the adverse conditions under which they labour, they are often so ignorant or so indifferent to the evils which affect them that, to all intents and purposes, they are no better than children with no wills at all. Let us instance the knife and fork grinders of Sheffield, whom we have heard so much about in the late Social Science meeting in that town. Dr. J.C. Hall, who, by his persistent efforts on behalf of those poor people for the last ten years, has at length forced the public to listen to him, in his late address, which we have before us, presents a startling picture of their sufferings. For instance, he tells us that the loss of metal in grinding a dozen razors is five ounces on the dry stone, and that the stone of seven inches in diameter will be reduced nearly one inch. This mingled mass of jagged steel and stone is thrown off by the very nature of his work directly in a line with his mouth. "When at work the grinder mounts what he calls his 'horsing.' This is a long, narrow, wooden seat. His elbows rest upon his knees, and his head, particularly when employed on very small articles, is bent over the stone." Not only is he forced to maintain this position in the ordinary course of his work, but by some extraordinary misarrangement he is forced to prepare his principal tool, the grindstone, himself. Dr. Hall tells us that the grindstones are received from the quarries in a rough state, and the artisan, before using, is obliged to "hang and race" it. This operation is performed by causing it to revolve slowly against a bar of steel in order to make its surface smooth and level. This operation fills the room with dust. Here, then, we have a contrivance directly calculated to produce consumption, and the result exactly tallies with the care taken to bring it about. In fact, the average age of a dry grinder is twenty-eight years. When they get much beyond this age it is considered a notable fact. A young man, aged twenty-six, once remarked to Dr. Hall that he reckoned in about two more years at his trade he might begin to think "of dropping off the perch; you know a fork-grinder is an old cock at thirty."

We all know that there is a stringent Act of Parliament compelling masters to box off dangerous machinery. Now, the danger to life from this source is trifling compared with an arrangement by which volleys of siliceous gritstone and steel dust are being driven into the worker's lungs during the whole period of his working life. It is, we know, urged by the masters that fans have been contrived which act very effectively in conveying this dust out of the hall or work-room; but it is useless to leave such preventive means to the men themselves; neither, indeed, do we see that the masters have any right to expect it. The labourer certainly has a right to demand that every precaution should be taken to secure him from dangers resulting from the tools he is using; and the Legislature, indeed, admits as much by the careful inspection it makes of miners in their workings. The Sheffield knife-grinder, from long habit, appears to be reduced to such a hopeless state that it is useless to look to him to take the least care of himself. "Generation after generation are ground off on the wheel," to use Dr. Hall's expressive term, and yet the wheel goes on doing its deadly work as of old. When a young man of twenty-two came ill to the dispensary, to the inquiry, What is the matter? the reply was, "I grind razors, and have got what I shall never get *shut* on." To ask such men to take any precautions to save their lives is a farce; indeed, some of them rejoice in the deadly nature of their occupation. "Trade is bad enough," they say, "and if men lived longer it would be so over-full that there would be no such a thing as getting a living." Can there be any question that Dr. Hall is right in suggesting that it should be made a finable offence to allow any man to grind without a fan, and that the fan should be provided and kept in order by the master? Surely, when a metal wheel is not allowed to revolve in an exposed condition for fear of causing an accident, a stone wheel should not be permitted to send a race of workmen to their last home in the days of their youth for the want of a simple fan, which would not cost the master £5 at the utmost. We are informed that the Messrs. Rodgers, whose cutlery is known the world through, and the proprietors of the Union Wheel, will not permit their men to work without a fan, and that, as a result, the average ages of their workmen, working at the wet and dry wheel, were respectively forty-nine and forty-six. The neglect of all precautions is mainly attributable to the poverty of the small masters, who abound in Sheffield, and in order to secure the enforcement of the use of the fan in the halls of those manufacturers a system of inspection would, without doubt, be necessary. That almost perfect immunity from the effects of steel dust, even when grinding with the dry stone, can be effected, we ourselves know. The needle-makers of Redditch, in Wordestershire, equally with the razor-grinders of Sheffield, use this stone, but the artisans are a healthy, robust class, in consequence of the use of the fan in all the large manufactories of the town.

It may, perhaps, be possible to include all the dust-making employments injurious to health under one enactment. Wherever small particles are plentifully given off, without the means of thoroughly flushing them away from the worker by strong currents of air, there the artisan is sure to suffer some of the more serious symptoms of lung disease. The making of cocoa-rind hafts or handles for knives in Sheffield is an instance in point. The workmen, says Dr. Hall, suffer from a species of hay asthma, or from a skin disease, the result of the sealing up of the pores of the skin. Stonemasons, again, are a comparatively shortlived class, especially those in Edinburgh, who work upon granite, and thereby fill their lungs with the ragged pieces of grit detached by the chisel. Millers, working in places filled with flour-dust, pearl-button makers, the shoddy-grinders, and foreign hair preparers or dressers, are all sooner or later damaged in their lungs by reason of the irritating dust they inhale while at work. The shoddy fever is as well-known a trade disease among the shoddy-grinders as the grinders' rot is in Sheffield, the process of tearing up old rags by means of the devil filling the air with fine particles of dust, frequently of a very filthy nature. The fluff of flax-mills, again, is very destructive to health; and, lastly, we would refer to the scourers in the Potteries, who work in an atmosphere loaded with the dust of pulverised flints, one of the most irritating foreign bodies that can be received into the lungs. The extension of the Factory Act has given the power to inspectors of earthenware manufactories to enforce certain rules of ventilation and cleanliness in the workshops, and we see no reason why the Legislature should not extend its provisions to all workshops in which dirt is given off to the detriment of the workers. In all open-air trades the wearing of the moustache and beard — those natural respirators — would be an admirable preservative against disease; but because it is a natural one, easily adopted, and entirely dependent upon the will of the workman, we fear it will be little put in practice. The manufacture of arsenical paper is so highly injurious to the workmen, the hangers, or the purchasers of these papers, that we really see no reason why it should not be prohibited by law. After sitting in a room hung with this emerald-green paper, a feeling of languor creeps over persons which they little understand. The eyes and nose run, and the individual suffers apparently under the effect of a bad cold; the throat becomes sore, and the general health is seriously affected. The hangers of these papers always complain of feeling ill after putting up pieces of the paper, and the artisans employed in its manufacture are affected in a like manner. The reason is obvious. The large amount of the aceto-arsenite of copper, which produces the brilliant tint, is easily detached from the paper by the clothes brushing against the wall, and this settling upon the furniture, books, etc., is set floating in the air with every movement. Why should such a deadly poison be allowed upon our walls, while the individual would be denied the smallest dose at the chemist's without a medical man's order? The use of this pigment, again, in the manufacture of artifical flowers is, we know by the coroners' inquests, but too often fatal; but we suspect that the fashionable fair will be the last to care what becomes of the poor girls who minister to their vanity. There is, however an emanation given off on another manufacture, which we are all interested in, from the highest to the lowest in the land. The common lucifer match is responsible for one of the most terrible diseases which can afflict humanity. In the act of manufacture the phosphorus becomes volatilised, and the fumes attack the bones of the jaws of the workers, and in some cases entirely destroy them. The process in which the workmen are liable to this emanation is that of dipping the match into the melted phosphorus. Without doubt the law would enforce precautions which would protect the artisan from this shocking disfigurement, and in some cases the painful death, resulting from working in the present factories. At all events, the public may take the matter into their own hands, as there is now coming into use a well-known match produced without the use of phosphorus at all, and in which, consequently, the workmen escape all danger. But what shall we say of the workers in lead? Dr. Hall has given us in his address a picture of the file-makers' disease in Sheffield, which arises from the dust given off every time the file, which rests upon a bed of lead, is struck with the chisel, and from the habit the men have of handling the lead with the rest-finger and thumb; but this incidental contact with lead is by no means so injurious to health as the process of manufacturing white-lead. In fact, in one form or other, the use of lead is so interwoven with our manufactures that its effect upon the nervous system is especially injurious, because so insidious in its action. The file-maker suffers from it, as we have said, the part usually affected first being the finger that rests upon the lead, which becomes numbed or paralysed in the nerves of sensation; the house-painter's finger which touches the brush suffers in a like manner; the potter, again, who dips ware in the glaze—a preparation of lead and flint—suffers in the same manner; even the compositor finds that his fingers which pick up the type become cold and feelingless. In all of these cases the artisan should take timely notice of this fact, as it is the sure precursor of that distressing complaint to the working man—the "dropped hand," or paralysis of the extensor muscles of the wrist, where the hand falls helplessly forward, like the forepaw of a kangaroo. But there is still another danger from working in lead: the effects we have spoken of are the results of touch, but there are constitutional symptoms, such as colic and obstinate constipation, arising from reception of the lead directly into the mouth. The painter, for instance, will eat his dinner with his unwashed fingers; the file-cutter, as we have seen, wets his finger and thumb, while handling the lead for the dipper, through the contact of the metal with his skin, brings on saturnine poisoning, which in extreme cases ends in fatal mania. These constitutional symptoms are wholly preventible by changing the dress or washing the hands before taking meals; but this, again, is so simple a preservative, that it cannot be depended upon unless the master is induced to enforce these precautions.

152

These diseases, however serious to the individual, cannot well be prevented by any systematic Governmental inspection. It is only where men work in large numbers together, such as in factories and mines, that the conditions under which they work can be controlled and directed by law. Possibly the metalliferous mines of Cornwall, Devon, and the North of England present examples of evil conditions for the workers in them second only to those existing in the Sheffield halls of the dry grinders. The amount of mortality among these miners has long been a scandal, and we rejoice to find that the Commission appointed by her Majesty to inquire into their condtions has issued a Report which cannot fail to produce an amelioration of their condition. The life of a collier is not to be envied, working as he does in the dark, and in many cases in foul air, breathing a dust that fills his lungs with carbonaceous deposits, and giving him what is known as the "black spit;" but his occupation is a healthy one compared with that of the Cornwall or Devonshire miner, employed in procuring copper and lead from extreme depths. The Report which lies before us discloses a most dismal state of things, — a very large segment of the population devoted to occupations in which a man is considered old who reaches the extreme limit of fifty years! The metalliferous mines, as a rule, are very badly ventilated. The air in various portions of different mines having been analysed by Drs. Taylor, Angus Smith, and Bernays, we find from the Reports that only in 10.65 per cent. of these the air may be considered normal, that is, possessing 20.9 per cent. of oxygen, while 24.69 per cent. are impure, and 65.63 are noted as exceedingly bad. Perhaps some of us have ventured for curiosity into the gallery of a London theatre, and speedily escaped, half poisoned with the vitiated air. Now, according to Dr. Angus Smith, the air in the gallery of a theatre at half-past ten P.M. contains 20.67 per cent. of oxygen; in nineteen of the specimens of air extracted from these houses there was only 19 per cent.; and in one instance it was as low as 18.27 per cent. Gentlemen who yawn and retire with a sick headache after the languid enjoyment of the opera may therefore guess at the conditions under which our metalliferous workers labour for eight hours of the day for the term of their natural, or more properly speaking, unnatural lifetime. But bad air is not the only difficulty they have to contend with. The heat of some of the deep mines is so great that they are obliged to work naked, and to have cold water thrown over them at times to revive them: 80° or 90° is not an extraordinary temperature for a deep mine, and in one case it reaches to 110°! The perspiration of the poor miner is so great that he sometimes loses as much as ten pounds' weight during his day's work. The only test the miner has of the condition of the air in his working is the burning of his candle: as long as it lives he thinks the air is good, but it often happens that at the end of workings it goes out from want of oxygen; but even this warning is not heeded by the men, for they will often place the candle eight feet or ten feet distance, where the air is pure enough to allow of labour, and then they will go on working by its light in the foul air. It would really seem as though the perversity or the ignorance and neglect of men had heaped together the greatest number of adverse conditions to health: poisoned by the lack of oxygen, weakened by the intense heat, rendered asthmatic and bronchitic by the carbonaceous matter received into his lungs, after his exhausting work, day by day, his only means of reaching the upper air is by a system of ladders, up which he has to climb, in some cases a height of from 1,200 to 1,680 feet; or perhaps the reader will be better able to realise this labour if we say that he has daily to climb, in many instances, higher than Snowdon before he sets his feet upon the grass or begins his journey home. This perpendicular climbing, in the miner's exhausted condition, is the cause of an enormous amount of heart disease, and this, together with the pulmonary affection which he contracts in the course of his daily labour, produces a mortality, the frightful nature of which will be best estimated by the comparison the following table affords with other males at the same ages of life, calculating the deaths per 1,000:—

Ages	Metal Miners	Males, Exclusive of Miners
Between 15 and 25 years	9.53	7.57
Between 25 and 35 years	12.38	9.19
Between 35 and 45 years	17.64	10.13
Between 45 and 55 years	33.11	16.18
Between 55 and 65 years	78.34	29.38
Between 65 and 75 years	127.52	66.10

It will be observed that the mortality becomes enormous, as compared with other labourers in the same district, between the ages of 55 and 65, and 65 and 75. And the loss of life among middle-aged miners is not the only loss to the community; the loss of the labour of the best and most experienced men, in some mines, is almost total. After a certain time of life the miner can no longer climb the interminable ladders. Thus, just at the time their experience would be valuable to the proprietors, they can no longer work in the depths of the mine. In some cases, where there are man-machines to lift the men without exertion to the surface, these middle-aged men can labour as when younger—a proof that the present deficient mode of access and egress is not only a source of disease, but causes the loss of the most valuable mining labour.

Among the more important recommendations of the Commissioners, in conclusion, may be noticed the following: — That every mine should be provided with proper houses, conveniently situated, in which the men can change and dry their clothes; that in order to avoid the evils consequent on climbing ladders, mechanical means should be provided to convey the men to and from the surface when the mines are of great depth; and that, as a general rule, no boys under the age of fourteen years should work below the surface.

That these recommendations have been most imperatively called for there can be not the least doubt. Let us hope that the time is not far distant when human labour may be superseded in both coal and metalliferous mines by machinery, which can take no harm by either bad air or hard labour, and that the miner will be emancipated to a great extent from work which reduces him to the condition of a mole for the greater part of his dismal life.

34 On Machine Tools and Engineering
James Nasmyth, 1867-8

James Nasmyth was one of the largest engineering industrialists in the country. Trained in London by Henry Maudslay the celebrated tool-maker, he later set up his own large-scale engineering works, the Bridge-water Foundry at Patricroft between Liverpool and Manchester. Nasmyth was well known for his antipathy towards trades unions, and often wrote of the ways his technological improvements, such as the steam hammer, would help to dispense with the use of skilled, unionized labour. In this testimony he gives the employers' views on labour and mechanization a decade after the manning of machines issue of the 1852 Lockout.

19,133. *(Chairman.)* You have favoured us in this paper with a summary of your views on the subject of apprenticeship; will you state them?—I have a very strong opinion about apprenticeship, and I back these opinions by my own practice. After the great turnout, or lock-out of 1851, when the Amalgamated Engineers' Society tried to get the upper-hand of all the employers, there was a formidable resistance made to it by the employers, and I saw clearly that one of the most probable ways of resisting their encroachments upon the liberty of employment was to do away with apprenticeship *in toto*, and practically ignore the apprenticeship system, because in my previous experience of seven years, bound apprentices, I generally found that the lads, after they knew that they were bound by indenture, both you to them and they to you, took advantage of that fact. Whatever was their idleness or misconduct, you could not punish them for it, unless there was something so serious as to bring it before a magistrate by which you can break up an indenture. All the while a lad may be doing no good to himself, and he may be annoying every one around him, so that when that turn-out occurred I was determined to put an end altogether, so far as I was concerned, to the apprenticeship system; and I took all the boys I could get, and filled the works with as many clever lads as I could pick up here, there, and everywhere. The system on which I employed them was simply from day to day; that whatever was the worth of their labour, they got wages according to their worth. We generally commenced with them at 3s. a week when lads of 14 or 15. If in the course of a week or so they showed themselves worth 6s. they got 6s.; their remuneration was measured by their value to me, not by the length of time they took to learn the trade. It is remarkable, when they have emulation before them, how very rapidly those younger boys will get to great excellence in the management of machinery. I may make the remark in passing that one great feature of our modern mechanical employment has been the introduction of self-acting tools, by which brute force is completely set aside, and the eye and the intellect of the workman are called into play. All that the mechanic has to do now, and which any boy or lad of 14 or 15 is quite able to do, is to sharpen his tool, place it in the machine in connexion with the work, and set on the self-acting motion, and then nine-tenths of his time is spent in mere superintendence, not in labouring, but in watching the delicate and beautiful functions of the machine; and a boy with quick intellect can do it; he does not need to labour with chisel and file, and so weary himself out.

19,134. *(Mr. Roebuck.)* So that a boy of 16 is really as useful as a man?—I was fortunately the contriver of several machines for giving geometrical forms to metal work with such precision and rapidity, by certain modifications of the planing machine, that all that class of men who depended upon mere dexterity were set aside altogether, and I was able to move on with these lads. Instead of having the old proportion of one boy to four mechanics, I had four boys to one mechanic nearly. There were an immense number of labourers in the neighbourhood, bargemen and others, the Bridgewater Canal Company's servants, and I got them into my employment, and in a short time they were as good workmen as could be desired.

19,135. Was there any action taken by the unionists against that?—Yes, but we defeated all their combinations; their funds were so low that our three months' lock-out used up their funds.

19,136. *(Mr. Harrison.)* When did that occur?—From December 1851 to March 1852.

19,137. *(Mr. Roebuck.)* How many men did you employ?—My highest number was 1,500. When I began to introduce those mechanical contrivances that facilitated the production of work, independently of dexterity, enabling me to do the work with boys and labourers, I reduced the numbers fully one-half.

19,138. You have stated that the number of your own employés was reduced, do you believe that the number of those people employed in the same business as yours was decreased generally?—Not in the same proportion. I rather took the lead in this non-apprentice system.

19,139. I want to know whether your economy of labour really did not lead to a greater employment of profitable labour in other ways?—I should fancy that according to the usual principles of political economy it would be so, but I am not able to trace it out in that respect. Only my profits were so increased, that if I had wished to expand the establishment and build additional workshops, from the profits resulting from this new system, if instead of putting it into three per cent. consols I had put it into additional workshops, I might have taken on 400 or 500, or 1000 workmen, and expanded the business.

19,140. And would you have had work to do?—Plenty of work. The chief cause of the attempt on the part of the Amalgamated Engineers at that time to get the upper hand of us simply arose from there being two masters looking after one man; there was a dearth of labour in the market, and the consequence was that the men took advantage of that, finding that there was a great deal of trade going on and a great demand for their labour, to urge their unreasonable demands. The first open movement in the dispute of 1851 was a demand made upon Messrs. Platt of Oldham to discharge all labourers whatever from machines. They were going upon the same principle as myself, in respect of employing what was called unskilled labour to superintend those automaton machines, and this was a matter which gave great umbrage to the regular trade union workmen. They did not like it. They said, "If you "have a machine that a labourer could work, you must not employ a "labourer but a regular seven years mechanic to superintend or to stand "and look at that machine."

19,141. Was not that in reality the same sort of dispute as took place about the hand-loom weavers?—I fancy it was, but I do not know the merits of that question. This demand was made on Messrs. Platt of Oldham. They were determined to resist it, but as they saw that the whole power of the union would be levelled against them, they called a meeting of the employers and said, "Will you make common cause in "resisting this most unwarrantable infringement on our liberties, that "we are not to have the advantage of our machinery; that the economy "resulting from those improvements is not to go into our pockets but "into the pockets of the union men."

19,142. You broke down the power of the society, as I understand it, by increasing the area from which you drew workmen?—Yes.

19,143. And whereas before there were two masters bidding against one another for one workman, you turned the tables against them, and found so many workmen that the workmen were more numerous than the masters?—Yes, and the moment you have a natural balance of employers and employed you will have no strikes.

19,144. (Mr. Harrison.) Do you consider that a prosperous state of things?—Up to that point it is beneficial to the workmen.

———

19,169. (Mr. Roebuck.) I suppose, then, you would believe that what is called division of labour does not conduce to the strength of the intellect or the improvement of the artizan?—No, I think not.

19,170. Though you may get more work by it, you do not get so good a man?—Not so resourceful a man. I remember a favourite maxim of Henry Maudslay's. He said that to be able to cut a plank with a gimlet and to bore a hole with a saw (he had a very striking way of putting those things) was the great criterion of a thorough mechanic, a fellow that could not be beaten; and if that principle was inculcated from the earliest days of education, God only knows what a great nation we should be.

19,171. (Chairman.) Then I am afraid that any improvement in machinery must have the effect of diminishing the power of individual men?—Not altogether. I have often noticed the great effects of these improvements in intellectualizing a man. If you call for the brute force of a man you will degrade the man. He goes to his home so physically exhausted that it is an utter absurdity to say to that man, "Read and improve yourself." He would fall asleep immediately; he must go and take some excitement. But if you take the man who has been superintending some piece of mechanism all day, in which there is a very little or only a minimum of call for his brute force, you will find that that man's intellectual power if he has any at all, will come forth, and he will be a reader and a self-cultivating man. I have found that again and again. I think this is the result of machinery, that it takes away the necessity for brute labour, very much elevates the intellectual and moral position of the working classes.

19,172. *(Mr. Mathews.)* With respect to the division of labour, the labourer becomes part of the machine instead of an entire machine, but in the case of a man who has self-reliance enough to study his work, he becomes the machine in himself?—I do not say that exactly. The functions of all machines are most interesting, and after a time the men begin to feel it. Some of our modern machines are as exquisite in their structure and results as the finest astronomical instruments, requiring extreme accuracy and delicacy, and affording exercise for all the intellectual functions to meet the conditions constantly arising in dealing with the work, and that in itself is a most valuable kind of education. Then, again, there are the most beautiful geometrical forms always presented before the men, and the mere looking at anything absolutely correct or true in geometrical form, I think, has in itself a tendency to improve the mind.

19,173. *(Mr. Roebuck.)* In your experience of late years of the working man, have you seen any change in his manner and mind for better or worse?—Yes, I think a good deal for the better in regard to his habits of life.

———

19,191. When you reformed your works you said that you had something like the proportion of four boys to one man, did you not?—As many as we could get.

19,192. Do you think that your neighbours, if they had introduced the same system into their establishments, could have done the work on it?—Yes, and many have.

19,193. Do you think that, supposing improvements go on, and the wonderful machines which you yourself and others have introduced become more common, practically speaking, the whole of the trade might be carried on in that way by boys and labourers, with a very small proportion of skilled men?—Not to the entire exclusion of men. I think that you would have to cheapen the work done by machinery, because a manufacturer after taking considerable profits from these economical arrangements takes the proper course of lowering his price to meet competition from various quarters, and then both the public and the working man partake of the benefit.

19,194. Still you think that in a system which you can conceive of as practicable, the bulk of the engineering trade could be carried on by boys and not men?—Yes.

19,195. You think that we are coming to that?—In certain departments of the work.

———

19,301. *(Mr. Roebuck.)* In your time have you had any experience of any attempt at a regulation to prevent men doing as much as they could under the notion that they were hurting their health?—Not that they were hurting their health, but that they were doing what is called "chasing." If a very active fellow got forward in that way, you generally saw the intimidation begin by the men jeering him.

19,302. That was in your time, was it?—Yes. I saw instances of it; but when it was very annoying we generally met it by displacing that kind of dexterity altogether and taking a machine. Dexterity has an unhappy knack of getting drunk (at least it had in my earlier days) and not coming to work till Wednesday, because a man knows that he can make a living by his three days' work instead of six days'. But when he finds that there is a machine rising in the background which will displace him altogether if he goes on with those tricks, in the first place there is a great tendency to check that man in his bad career, and in the next place if he perseveres it will displace him altogether. That is the history of nine-tenths of the improvements that we have got. This is just one illustration of the way in which good often comes out of evil. I believe that if there were a debtor and creditor account made up of strikes and lock-outs with the interests of society, up to a certain point they would be found to have been a benefit. Such has been the stimulus applied to ingenuity by the intolerable annoyance resulting from strikes and lock-outs, that it has developed more than anything those wonderful improvements in automaton machinery that produce you a window frame or the piston rod of a steam engine of such an accuracy as would make Euclid's mouth water to look at. These things are pouring in in quantities as the result of the stimulus given to ingenuity through the annoyance of strikes. It is not being coaxed on by some grand reward in the distance, but I think a kick from behind is sometimes as useful as a gentle leading forward in front.

35 Putters and Hewers
A Traveller Underground, 1853

The extractive industries so fundamental to British industrialization expanded on the basis of traditional techniques. The process of coal-cutting required the organization of a whole series of different types of underground workers, each with its special place in the job hierarchy and special social characteristics. *Our Coal and Our Coal Pits* describes the jobs of Putters and Hewers, those closest to the excavation and movement of the coal. The selection also mentions some of the few mechanical aids that had come to the pits by mid-century, such as iron plates for the easier movement of coal trains.

But now, having passed the craneman or flatman, we are amidst a rough and roystering race of lads and boys, who seem but half civilized—they are the putters. Next to the hewers, they are the hardest labourers in the pit; and in some few places their labour is even harder. It was a long time before I became skilled in all the subdivisions of their labour, which are these:—The term "putter" includes the specific distinction of the "headsman," "half-marrow," and the "foal." Where full tubs or baskets are to be pushed along the rails from the hewers to the crane

and the drivers, the headsmen take the chief part; a half-marrow goes at each end of the train alternately with another half-marrow, while a foal always precedes the train. Where the inclination is steep, there are "helpers up" to assist at the worst. The foals and half-marrows often employ a pair of cords, called "soams," from two feet nine inches to three feet in length, for pulling up the loads. Before you can converse satisfactorily with the pit lads, you must have all these technicalities at your fingers' ends. The average weight of the loaded corf or tub put by putters, is from six to eight hundred weight. The greatest is ten hundred weight. The putters are paid by the number of tubs put, and can often earn (the eldest of them) from 3s. to 3s. 6d. per day. The half-marrows will make from 1s. 6d. to 2s., and sometimes 3s. 6d. per day, and the foal about 1s. 6d. or 2s. per day. The gains depending upon the scores of tubs put, they will differ according to the strength of the boys, and I have found some boys making only 1s. 3d. per day. All these lads come into the pit an hour or so after the hewers, and then find baskets of coal ready filled for them. In this pit the putters put full tubs down a descent of one and a quarter inches to the yard as maximum fall, and down half an inch as the average fall. Notwithstanding the severity of this toil, it does not commonly injure the boys' health very materially, if they be naturally strong boys. Such boys feed well, and drink water in large draughts down the mine, where no beer or spirits are ever permitted. You see casks of water placed here for their benefit; and they probably thus repair the rapid waste of the bodily fluids by perspiration. They stop "to bait" at fixed times, and then devour huge hunches of bread and cheese, with a bone or so of meat, drinking at that time cold coffee or milk out of tin canteens. When at home after work, they eat as much as they can get; and they generally get fat meat, or bits of "singing hinnies," which are rich kneaded cakes, that sing with their exuding fat when baking on a girdle or gridiron. Some prefer cheese and bacon to other food; and it is a common remark, that pit people have always white bread of the best flour.

I suppose that in no pit is putting so exhausting as in this: for here the heat of the unbroken mine averages about 78° Fahrenheit. Mr. Elliott has known the extreme heat to be 89°, where animal heat has been added to the natural. He tells me that, at the bottom of the pit, the mercury ordinarily stands in the barometer at thirty-two inches, and that water boils here at 220 degrees Fahrenheit. A curious medical fact is, that by some means boils are frequently produced in this pit. The putters are very subject to them at first. From the medical attendant at this colliery, I learn that, when a fresh man enters the mine to work, he is generally plagued with these boils, which may arise from the heat in the first instance, and become subsequently aggravated by the salt water found here. This salt water used to pour out from the dykes and troubles in large quantities in the early workings; and the water is exceedingly irritating, though not caustic. The great heat, too, affects the vessels and glands of the skin in new-comers; and therefore boils are found on parts of their persons which the salt water would not fall upon or reach to.

———

I have on different occasions, and in different pits, questioned a large number of lads engaged in the putting labours, but could not elicit from them very much more than a description of their present labours, their peculiar hardships (not always quite truly stated), and their past accidents. Taking in the class of drivers as well, it is at first quite strange to hear of the numerous accidents many of the boys have met with. This is alluded to by the driver in his stanzas, given above. These accidents are commonly called "lamings" by the boys; and I found that several of them had no other chronology than that formed by the occurrence of these disasters. Thus, while a Greek reckoned by Olympiads, a pit-boy reckons by limpings. "O," said one, in reply to my question about the date of a particular event—"O, I don't know when, but it was just after last laming." "No," said another, "I never learned to read till last laming but one." "I," would another say, "was lamed twice in Howden pit, and once in Walbottle;" and a little lad of some fourteen years of age, would speak of having been "lamed three times while he was a driver, and once since he has been a half-marrow."

Another had lost a finger in Felling Colliery, and broken his leg in Walker pit, and cut his face in Percy Main. These things they had suffered before they were perhaps eighteen years old, in any case, but the little hardy fellows soon recover, and go down to work again; and, if they are unacquainted with learning, they are well versed in laming.

———

A great improvement has, however, taken place both in their upper-ground behaviour and their under-ground labours. I met with a merchant at Newcastle who had himself known the severity of boyish labour in pits some forty or fifty years before. His description of that period was indeed sad, and it was very detailed. Then, according to his account, the boy would go into the pit to work at two o'clock on a Monday morning, and arrive at his home between eight and ten o'clock at night, entirely worn out. He would again repair to work the next morning at the same hour, half asleep, and sometimes half naked. This continued through the week, and he would not see much daylight from the Sunday until the next Saturday afternoon. Although this state of things might not be permanent as regarded the long hours, yet the labour was always extreme, and two boys were often bound to "put" together, without the adequate strength. Continued quarrels arose between unequally-matched boys, and though these were sometimes brothers, fights and foul language were frequent amongst them. One great cause of improvement was the employment of metal or iron plates for the trains to run upon, and another was the blasting of the coal with powder. Before this, the boys often had to drag their load over a fir plank, or even on the bare floor. Now the whole way is laid with metal plates, even up to the face of the workings, and by this improvement one lad can perform the previous work of two. To quote a verse from a poem in the pit *patois* —

"But heavy puttin's now forgotten,
Sic as we had i' former days,
Ower holly thill and dylls a-splittin' —
Trains now a' run on metal ways.

"Then bless the man wi' peace and plenty,
That first invented metal plates!
Draw out his years to five times twenty —
And fill his dishes and his plates."

I squat in the dark to give them their light,
And I hew while they are in slumber;
Tho' I don't think it rhyme, or reason, or right,
I shouldn't be one of their number.

Was there ever so slaving and slashing a trade,
Such a trade as this terrible hewing?
I wish I'd been born to the plough or the spade,
To building, or baking, or brewing!

> Well, marrows,* —come, marrows—come, put in the pick,
> And curve out the jud and the jenkin;†
> The seam is so thin, and the air is so thick
> That —*Maister your health should be drinking!*

You now observe the characteristics of these hewers, and their work of hewing the coal. This is the innermost workshop of the pit; into this place the hewers make their way at two or three in the morning, and here they work for eight hours, some one or two possibly a longer, and some few a shorter time, for they are paid by the amount of clear coals sent up. The pick and the spade are the hewers' only tools. You see one kneeling, another sitting, another stooping or bending double, and you may sometimes (especially in very thin seams) see them lying on one side, or on their backs—hammering at the coal before them or above them with their short and heavy picks. To hew coal well is a peculiar and difficult work. The men have been brought up to it, or brought into it, through the successive grades of trapping, teaming, and putting. Hewing is the topmost promotion—the colonelcy of the regiment. Gunpowder may be used to help the hewing, by tearing down or loosening the coal, where naked lights can be used with safety; and the hollow boom of the blasting sounds very singularly in the confined recesses of the pit, at first alarming one with the idea of an explosion of fire damp; but where Davy lamps must needs be employed, gunpowder must not.

The intensity of the hewer's toil is great—his confined position makes it worse. Where there are several props and stays to uphold the roof, he cannot well get his strength to bear on the coal-seam; and, if the seam be hard as well as thin, then you must witness his labour to know it at all. He is generally bathed in perspiration (though some practised ones are cool) and enveloped in coal-dust, and complaining of this "drouthy wark." If you wish to converse with him, and have learned the dialect, he will tell you all his hardships, and his master's hardness, with a glib tongue. The best hewers have learnt to do their work in quick time, and it is curious to watch them shifting their postures, and strangely adapting themselves to the exact form or figure required to bring down the coal with advantage and speed. I have never seen any labour like it, but its duration and voluntary extent must be measured against its intensity.

Marrows — that is, companions, mates.
† *Jud and Jenkin* — technical terms in hewing coal.

163

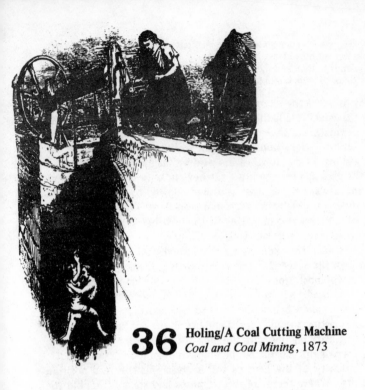

36 Holing/A Coal Cutting Machine
Coal and Coal Mining, 1873

By the 1870s the job of the coal hewer still existed just as it was in the 1850s. This document shows some of the inducements—thus far totally unsuccessful—to mechanizing the means of cutting coal.

Holing

The other operation is conducted by the use of the pick or wedge. This the miner has to do under the two-fold disadvantage of confined space and dim light. He is "holing" the coal—that is, digging away the lower part, so that the upper part may come down in large pieces. To do this, he has to be upon his side, and wield the pick. Even those who are not accustomed to underground life and who never saw a coal mine will readily understand the peculiar difficulty of using a pick while in the position indicated. It might not be amiss, perhaps, if some of my hearers would try the experiment and thus realise the difficulty. It can, of course, be readily done without going down the shaft, in the garden or even in the parlour. The miner, however, trained to this kind of labour from childhood, acquires great skill in the work, and does it with comparative ease. In fact, he realises the truth of the old proverb that use is second nature, and probably there are men in the mines of South Staffordshire who could more effectively labour in the odd and awkward position of a navvy in using the pick. This work is attended with special danger not only from the fire-damp, but also from the tendency of the coal, when partially holed, to suddenly break away and bury the miner.

Coal Cutting Machine

The purely mechanical operation of cutting, by means of a light pick, a groove of from 2½ ft. to 4 ft. deep along the face of coal which is to be removed is not only slow and laborious, but also wasteful, inasmuch as a considerable amount of the seam is necessarily cut into slack; and forming, as this process does, the chief item of expense in the excavation of coal, the idea of doing the work by machinery has of late been more seriously forced upon the attention of coalowners by the irregularities and strikes of the workmen, which have so often brought the operations of coal mines to a ruinous stand-still.

More than a century has elapsed since the first apparatus designed for the effecting of this object was patented, and since that time "iron men" and coal-getters in great numbers, and almost equally great variety, have been presented to the public. Additional impetus was given to the inventive genius by the appointment of a committee of the North of England Institute, commissioned to investigate the subject, and to report upon the value of existing patents; by the prizes offered by the South Lancashire and Cheshire Coal Association for the best coal-cutting machine; and by the encouragement afforded by mining engineers, both in their individual capacity and when incorporated into associations. It was felt that, looking at the success which in other departments of industry has attended the substitution of machinery for hand labour, there was good ground for the belief that machinery might also be advantageously applied to the cutting of so uniform a substance as coal, and the driving of air-ways through it.

The introduction of efficient machinery is also calculated to have an important bearing on the safety of mines, enabling them to be more rapidly opened out, and the seam to be intersected or the winning to be surrounded by air-ways so as to drain off the dangerous gases. It is not to be wondered at, therefore, either that an efficient machine for getting coal should have become an acknowledged want, or that so many ingenious inventors should have applied themselves to the production of apparatus to meet that want.

Part III
Climacteric
or Resolution?

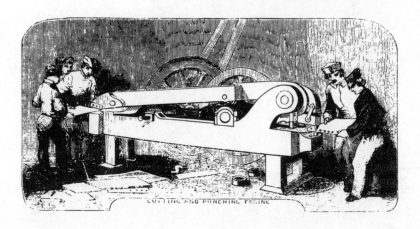

CUTTING AND PUNCHING ENGINE

Chapter Five

Tradesmen, Heavy Industry and the New Technology

The varieties of technical change and worker exploitation which so marked the mid-Victorian economy also characterize the late nineteenth century, but by this time the mechanization and automation of the trades and of the great new industries of the industrial revolution were becoming much more substantial threats to traditional crafts and skills. Older trades such as shoemaking remained largely unmechanized in Britain long after mechanical techniques had been successfully introduced into the American industry. The shoemakers' craft had instead been divided, and many processes were performed as outwork. The widespread use of the sewing machine and of women's labour concentrated in factories did at length come to the industry. But the sharp resistance of shoemakers to mechanization and a reasonably successful outworking system meant that the process took over fifty years. The factories were not general until the 1890s.

Newer industries also experienced an expansion of hand craft labour. Iron shipbuilding is perhaps the most celebrated example. The transformation from wood to iron shipbuilding started to become important from the 1860s. The contract system based on the shipwright passed away as the industry became heavily capitalized, but neither the new scale nor the new materials of the industry changed the basic organization of work, which was still carried on along craft lines. The major effect of the change to iron ships was to bring more crafts into the production process, for the myriad crafts of the engineering and metalworking trades were added. The involvement of more crafts meant more unions, and demarcation disputes arose as each group of workers sought to stake its claim to any new jobs arising through changing techniques and materials. The grip of the crafts on shipbuilding was not effectively challenged until the mechanization of many of its processes in the twentieth century.

The longstanding hand techniques of such old and new industries were complemented by the mechanization of important heavy industrial skills basic to the industrial revolution. This was to happen at the end of the nineteenth century and early in the twentieth century with the slow displacement of the iron puddler and moulder, and with the introduction of self-acting machine tools. The introduction of the Bessmer and related processes made steel a viable substitute for iron, but not until the late 1880s did the output of steel succeed that of puddled iron. Mechanized moulding was also at length introduced, but effective machinery did not even exist until the 1890s.

A much greater threat was posed by the introduction of self-acting machine tools. Engineering industrialists had long dreamed of such possibilities, but it was not until late in the nineteenth century that the introduction of new machine tools and the perfection of older devices in the engineering industry led to changes in skill requirements. The industry increasingly called on relatively unskilled workers. The old centre lathe was displaced by more automatic types of turret and capstan lathes. Machine tool operators were deprived of responsibility for determining correct feeds, speeds and angles and machine tools were displacing skilled fitters. There was great employment of boy labour and a certain amount of female labour in the industry in this period. The 'Machine Question', that is, the manning of machines by skilled or unskilled workers, dominated demands made by the Amalgamated Society of Engineers between the end of the nineteenth century and the first part of the twentieth century. However, British craft-orientated engineers were able to slow down, at least until the war, the transformation taking place under the system of Taylorism in the United States and on the continent.

The struggle within all these industries over the rationalization of production was soon reflected in Britain's comparative industrial performance. Other nations now took the technological lead. In Britain militant and well-organized workers' resistance met the automation, division of labour, novel flow techniques, speed-up and productivity incentives which Marx had predicted would form the characteristics of the higher phases of modern industry. The combination of these features soon to be defined as Taylor's system of scientific management was not to become a reality in the nineteenth-century British economy. Workers' resistance, heavy capitalization in older plant and equipment, and a perception of alternative technical and organizational possibilities prevented this eventuality at least until the First World War.

37 The Boot and Shoe Trade
John T. Day, 1903

Day, Editor of the Shoe and Leather Record, discusses the history of mechanization in the boot and shoe industry, comparing Britain's long entrenched hand techniques with the rapid mechanization of the industry in America.

In reviewing the progress of the boot and shoe industry under Free Trade it is only necessary to sketch very briefly the history of the trade prior to the complete introduction of the factory system. In 1846 the industry was in much the same position as the better class tailoring trade is in to-day. People were measured for their boots, which were made by hand, by or under the direction of the bootmaker who took the measure. There were a few so-called factories in Stafford and Northampton, and a few more scattered about the country. But these were not factories in the modern sense of the term. They were shops where leather was cut up by hand and given out to bootmakers working in their own homes, to make up by hand. The whole family was usually employed, the women and girls closing the uppers, and the men performing the harder and more skilful work of joining the uppers to the soles and heels.

The introduction of the sewing-machine modified this system. The manufacturers bought sewing-machines, and the women were taken into the factories to make the uppers, but the main work was still a home industry so far as the men were concerned.

In the early sixties riveted boots were introduced. These were made on heavy cast-iron lasts, which could not be conveniently carried to and from the workmen's homes, so factory accommodation was enlarged, and with some difficulty sufficient men were induced to leave their home workshops and enter the factories. Almost at the same time a sewing-machine was invented which would sew on the soles of boots, and this was the beginning of the revolution of the industry. More men had to go into the factories, but a great deal of the labour was still performed at home. The work known as the "finishing" of both machine-sewn and riveted work remained a home industry, and the old hand-sewn system of bootmaking was also continued—and is also continued so far as it has survived—as a home employment.

The Introduction of Machinery

The introduction of the sole-sewing machine not only helped largely to transform a home industry into a subdivided factory industry, but it had other important consequences. (It was an American machine known in the United States as the McKay Sole-Sewer, and in this country as the Blake.) While the patents existed no machines were ever sold, but thousands of them were leased on both sides of the Atlantic under a system whereby the boot manufacturers put down a premium of about £100 (the machine cost not more than £30 to build) and agreed to pay in addition a royalty equal to about a penny a pair for every pair of boots sewn upon it.

The profits to those exploiting the patent were enormous, amounting literally to many millions of dollars, most of which went to America. The result was that every Yankee inventor began to turn his attention to shoe machinery as the easiest way to fame and fortune. And to this day, in America universally, and in the United Kingdom partially, the royalty system has been maintained in connection with shoe machinery.

The supply of machinery is a practical monopoly in America, where the United Shoe Machinery Company of Boston levy royalties estimated to average five cents a pair on every pair of boots and shoes made in the United States, their royalty income amounting, it is said, to a million dollars a month.

Now this development of shoe machinery in America had nothing to do with either Protection or Free Trade, but it has had a considerable influence upon the industry in this country. The McKay or Blake machine, which made the money which has attracted so many inventors' brains to the shoe trade, was an invention which sprang out of the necessities of the American Civil War. As the men of the North were drafted into the army skilled labour became dear, and boots and shoes, articles of prime necessity in war time, could not be made in the old way in sufficient quantities. The McKay machine solved the difficulty by making a boot in an entirely new and very simple way, which might never have been discovered but for the pressure of the war, but which, once discovered, became of enormous permanent value. The thousands of inventions which have since been given to the trade are the outcome of the inventive talent kindled by the fire of the first great success, and fed in large measure by the money which it brought in. For the owners of the McKay patent were as active as their imitators in casting about for new machinery to replace the old as their patents expired. And the American manufacturer never seemed to object to the royalty demanded for the use of a new machine so long as it saved enough labour to pay the royalty and show him a profit.

High Wages and Low Cost

But on the other side of the Atlantic different conditions prevailed. In America weekly wages were quite double those ruling in the English shoe trade. Many machines which were profitable to use when they displaced labour at a shilling an hour were hardly worth investing in when hand labour cost but sixpence. And this was about the relative position in the two countries at the time the revolution of manufacturing methods was in its most active phase.

Further, the British boot manufacturer has a rooted prejudice against paying royalties. He prefers to buy his machinery outright.

Sometimes the American owners refused to sell. At other times they asked so big a price that few could afford to scrap their old plant and lay down new. In a brief sketch it is impossible to enter very far into detail, though much of it would be both interesting and instructive. It is enough to say that the play of circumstances brought it to pass that by 1890, or perhaps a little earlier, the factories of the Eastern States were so much better equipped than ours that the American boot manufacturer had the British market at his mercy.

But he did not know it.

Until about 1894 (so far as the shoe trade is concerned) the American manufacturer held very strongly to the view that he was only able to keep his domestic market to himself by maintaining a high tariff. When it was imposed he was told that it was for the purpose of keeping out the products of "the pauper labour of Europe." He was quite curiously unaware that in the course of about thirty years he had so improved his methods of manufacture that his productive labour was costing him (in some cases) less per dozen by 50 per cent. than it was costing the British shoe manufacturer for the same work. And yet the American boot operative was earning three pounds a week against thirty shillings for a similar man in Leicester or Northampton. And in the case of female labour the disparity was even more marked.

I give these figures broadly as the result of a most careful personal investigation which I made in 1891, when I visited the United States for the express purpose of investigating labour costings in American shoe factories. The whole of the details were published at the time, and, I hope, helped forward the much-needed work of shoe-factory reorganisation in this country. I may say that the result of the investigation came to me as a great surprise. It seemed impossible that such high weekly wages should accord with such low piece-work costings. I had heard the stories of the agents sent over here to sell or lease American machinery, but I thought them exaggerated. Finally I decided to examine the facts on the spot, with the result stated, and I now repeat with all seriousness that thirteen years ago the American shoe manufacturer had the British manufacturer at his mercy and did not know it.

The Trade Union Attitude

Today the opportunity has passed, for there are many factories in England as well equipped as any in America, and though trade union tyranny prevents the machinery being run to its full capacity, the chief losers are the men themselves. Their weekly earnings are less than they need be, but most smart manufacturers have been, by the aid of machinery, able to reduce the labour cost per dozen to somewhere about the American level. The men seem to think that if they did more they would get no more pay—which is a poor tribute to the power of their union. They also appear to adopt an altruistic attitude towards each other, one man fearing to do too much lest he should either rob his fellow-workman of employment or set him an inconvenient pace.

No one objects to working men doing all they can to improve their wages, but a man who deliberately does less than a fair day's work is injuring himself and injuring the whole community as well. If the policy of shirking work were really beneficial to the working classes, then no workman ought to do any work at all.

Here it may be convenient to explain that at the time of which I am writing (1891) productive wages in an English shoe factory would average about $33^1/3$ per cent. on the wholesale selling price of such goods as were then in demand.

A popular gentleman's boot was sold at about 8s., and a ladies' at 6s. (factory prices). This would mean that about 2s. 8d. and 2s. respectively would be distributed in the productive wages of manufacture. I have spoken of extreme cases in America where I found a saving of 50 per cent. in wages. This was in lower grade goods than are the subject of the present illustration. The productive wages paid in the best American factories on such boots as I have instanced were at the time of my investigations about 1s. 9d. and 1s.3d. respectively. This meant that the American shoe manufacturer had an advantage over his possible English competitor of 11d. per pair in one case and 9d. in the other. This would have been more than enough to enable him to swamp the market had he addressed himself energetically to the task.

A recent estimate issued on the authority of the Federation of Boot Manufacturers Associations places the annual consumption of boots and shoes at 100,000,000 pairs. This is probably within the mark. I estimate that the new machinery and improved organisation adopted by British boot manufacturers within the past ten years have enabled them to effect a saving averaging quite sixpence per pair. The whole of this saving has had to be given to the public, because the re-organisation of the factories has expanded their productive capacity and induced a very active state of competition. Indeed, at the present moment the trade is paying the penalty of its previous lethargy, and is suffering from a sharp attack of over-production. The changes came about so rapidly that the market has been glutted and is likely to remain so until the normal growth of demand has overtaken the increased capacity for supply. In such circumstances it has been impossible for manufacturers to keep for themselves any of the advantages derived from their new machinery. It follows, therefore, that the public has reaped a benefit now equal to about £2,500,000 a year for improvements in manufacture which would not have been adopted for many years under a protective system.

Competition and Efficiency

But let me hasten to add that little, if any, of this benefit has been conferred in the shape of reduced prices. It has mainly taken the form of improvements in the article produced. For example, ten years ago the great middle-class trade was furnished with a boot sewn on the Blake machine to which allusion has already been made. To-day the same class of trade is supplied with what is known as Goodyear or machine-welted boots at approximately the same price. This welted boot is made precisely on the same principle as the old-fashioned hand-sewn boot of thirty years ago, and which may still be obtained of a few fashionable West-end boot-makers by people who can afford to pay the price it commands. Its exact equivalent made by machinery is now within the reach of all, and it has largely supplanted what is known as the ordinary machine-sewn boot. In many other ways too, improvements have been effected in the finish and embellishment of the modern factory-made boot, which is also of better design and fit than its counterpart of only ten years ago. All these advantages have been given to the public without any extra charge, and it has been possible to give them because of the adoption of the American system of manufacture, which in turn was the outcome of direct American competition in the boot market. This competition would have been shut out by even a moderate tariff.

———

There has been some hardship experienced among the older men unable to learn how to operate the new machines. Younger men have had to be drafted into the factories and considerable displacement of labour has been inevitable. But this was the price that had to be paid. Regarded broadly, the position of the workman has been improved by the reorganisation of the factories. The most serious drawback has been that in filling their factories with new machinery manufacturers have been compelled to increase their trade in order to get the best results from the new appliances. This had led to an expansion of productive capacity which will presently find its proper level by the natural operation of the laws of supply and demand.

38 Iron Shipbuilding
W. Glenny Crory, 1876

The transformation from wooden to iron shipbuilding was one of the major changes of mid-nineteenth-century industrialism. The contract system based on the shipwright passed away as the industry became heavily capitalized. This did not, however, change the basic organization of work in the industry, which was still carried on along craft lines. The major effect of the change to iron was to bring more crafts into the production process. The myriad crafts of the engineering and metal working trades were added. W. Glenny Crory's essay on shipbuilding indicates something of the new scale, techniques and crafts attached to the industry. It also reveals standard middle-class prejudices in favour of disciplining the labour force.

One of the oldest firms, and one also of the most extensive in this line, is that of Messrs. Samuda Brothers. The works of this firm cover many acres of ground; about 1,000 hands are usually employed, though double that number are at times at work; and the wages paid on an average are probably £100,000 annually. This is not the only firm, however, in the same line, and when I mention, in addition, the names of Messrs. Green, Messrs. Wigram, Messrs. Dudgeon, Messrs. Yarrow and Hedley as well as the Thames Iron Works, as amongst the more extensive in this trade, some idea will be formed of its magnitude and importance. The capital at stake in iron shipbuilding is enormous. The amount of employment given is most valuable to a large industrial population, on whose purchasing powers, in turn, traders of every grade depend for support. This one trade is of itself sufficient to show that the Industries of East London are very important. But it is but one of many which, taken as a whole, enable this portion of the metropolis to cut a very formidable figure by the side of the other and often more favourably spoken of division of London. Not many "wooden walls" are now made anywhere in comparison with what used to be, and of these very few are built in the East of London. Messrs. Samuda build all sorts of iron ships, but their line is more especially yachts and war ships, in which they take the highest branches. They also build some for the mercantile marine and passenger and mail traffic. In several respects Messrs. Green are in a different line. This firm builds ships for their own trade. Messrs. Wigram also differ from Messrs. Samuda, and so does the firm of Messrs. Dudgeon. Messrs. Yarrow and Hedley confine themselves mostly to steam launch yachts. But while I must, for want of space, pass over these and other firms, without more specific mention, I am not in the least degree unaware of their importance in the trade, nor of the most efficient manner in which their work is turned out of hand. Besides, in selecting Messrs. Samuda's premises for special notice, I have taken it as a specimen, and not as a pattern in any invidious sense. It is true it is in many respects ahead of some others, or it may be, even above the average. It is an old firm, and more is to be expected of it than of some, though not of all, others. On visiting this place, I was politely shown over the works by Mr. Kelson, a new member of the firm. Some of the first things which caught my notice were the plates of iron in progress of preparation for the sides of ships. These are from 8 to 10 inches in thickness, of the best of Staffordshire or Yorkshire iron, and seem to the eye, as they should prove, impenetrable. But next to these I observed machines in size so big, and in aspect so formidable, as to strike an unpractised eye with astonishment. Nevertheless, these monsters are used with as much facility by the skilled workmen of the place as that with which a baby handles its toys. These are planing, plotting, and drilling machines, steam hammers, or such like. There is one machine, however, which deserves special mention, namely, a rivet-making machine. This very fine piece of mechanism was invented by Mr. Ould, a foreman in the works. It produces rivets in a most simple way, and of a better style than has ever been made by any other machine. It is fitted so as to make large, small, and middle-sized rivets, and produces them with either heads or cones, according to the purpose for which they are required. Mr. Ould has not patented this machine, though he informs me it has been copied. Perhaps this is not the only highly valuable piece of machinery which is unprotected by Royal Letters Patent. Be this as it may, one thing is certain, that many of the things patented are protected more because of their small value than on account of their very great importance to any one except the patentee. There are twelve trades carried on here. Amongst those engaged are engineers, mast-makers, shipwrights, blacksmiths, boiler-makers, riggers, boat-builders, cabinet-makers, joiners, painters, and plumbers; in fact, almost everything is done to their ships by the firm's hands, except upholstering. Over each department there is a responsible foreman. There are also in every branch several leading hands, to whom, as well as the foreman, much of the efficiency of the business is due. The workpeople consist of both men and boys. But whether skilled workers or labourers it is obvious there is nothing more important to any man, nor anything which renders him so valuable to the firm as a good character. In these days of educational movements we hear much of the importance of being taught not only the three R's but science and even classics. All this is very well, and so long as it is kept in its proper relation to the development—education in its strict sense—of the man, it must be good. But very little knowledge and not much observation are all that seems necessary to show that if the end of instruction be the making of its recipient merely a more marketable commodity, and not the raising of the *man* to a higher condition, be his calling what it may, the time will come when it will be discovered that educated people are not more trustworthy, not less eye-servants, and not in the least degree more truly *men* than were their uneducated progenitors. In the various departments of these works many branches of education, such as a knowledge of drawing, and it may be also of metallurgy and mechanics, must be highly valuable. But, after all, it is the man of original mind, industrious habits, unwavering rectitude, and who is never above his work, who is the best workman. I find that the wire ropes made by Messrs. Binks, whose works are in the Isle of Dogs, are used by Messrs. Samuda, and doubtless by many others. These deserve to be well spoken of, though I cannot visit the works where they are made. In the progress of my observations, I found, in addition to the machinery already named, saw mills, lathes, hydraulic presses, and many other appliances for getting materials for the ships into form. The most remarkable of these is a machine for bending armour plates. These are first heated, and then bent to any shape by a machine possessing a power of pressing equal to 4,000 tons. This part of the work is probably the most interesting to a looker-on, while, like all other parts, it seems quite simple and easy to the stalwart and intelligent men who are engaged at it. The power at work is steam-power, but the number of boilers and engines is too great for me to remember. The fuel used is large-sized steam coal. The engines are, on the whole, well kept, but the machinery immediately in use in preparing the iron for the ships is more attractive than the engines. In one part of the premises there are a number of men at work preparing bars of iron for the keels and kelsons of the ships. This is a most interesting process, and, like all branches of skilled labour, requires care, attention, and very considerable intellectual as well as corporeal power. But the ribs being shaped, then comes the shipbuilding in the strictest sense. Here we find everything done according to a plan, and that plan obviously modified to suit the class of craft calculated to do the work for which it is intended. There is nothing of a random character visible in all one sees. The draughtsmen must be accurate, those who work the machines must be equally so, and everything fits in, each part in its own place, and all portions alike well.

It seems a question of importance what should we have done without iron, and what use would it have been had we not had coal, and were the one to be had in lesser abundance than the other, what would have been the use of either? But there is a question behind this one, namely, what could we have done with coal or iron had we not had inventors, skilled work people, as also labourers, to engage in such undertakings as that under notice. Behind this question, also, there is still another, namely, what use would any or all these have been in the absence of capital? Or what would have been the good of them had the money of this great country been in the hands of usurers, or those who loved it for its own sake rather than regarded it, as all enterprising men do, at once as a trust to be employed for the common good, and a treasure which is only valuable when it is sown about like corn seed, with a view to fruitfulness, being also the more valuable the less it is coveted or desired, except for its utility and as a means of enabling a man to love his neighbour as himself.

It is a coincidence not unworthy of notice, that the Tower Hamlets are represented in Parliament by members each of whom leads in his line, and both of whom have a large stake in the East of London in that which is the *au comble* in this truly commercial country, namely, industry. The M.P., however, in his place, can do no more than it is also possible for any other man in his place to do also, in kind, however less in degree. But before a man can take his position aright he has first to feel and understand it; and then be his line of industry—the idler is ruled out of all positions—what it may, he is sure to do its duties in a way worthy of a man. How the occurrences of ten or a dozen years back affect the shipbuilding in the East of London at present it is hard to say. One thing is certain, that the workmen are far more likely than the masters to suffer by the custom of raising wages when a big job comes in. A capitalist can more easily change his line than can a blacksmith, a rigger, a boiler-maker, a shipwright, or any other skilled labourer. Consequently, if any mistake be made by those who protect the interests of labour—and I question not their good intentions—those whom they seek to benefit suffer first, unskilled labourers come next, and capitalists last of all, the community at large bearing a share with each. If those who lead East London working men, the evidence of whose skill and industry are to be seen not only in the place which I am attempting to describe but in every seaport of the globe, were to study Political Economy more and crude notions of sciolists as to the relations of capital and labour less, they would probably be more prosperous, and certainly more happy. I do not, however, mean to recommend those crotchety crudities by which simple minds are led into labyrinths of absurdity, and landed in mazes of mystification, out of which very few who have been entangled ever escape, but rather those rules of rectitude and laws of *meum* and *tuum*, amongst the formulæ of which "as ye would that men should do to you, do ye also to them likewise" stands foremost. Rightly or wrongly, it seems to me that East London Industries are only beginning to show their powers of expansion. If I am right the shipbuilding trade has yet before it a great increase. In any case, as it is, it is one of the most important trades of the United Kingdom, and in no place is it better carried on than in this locality, and in no premises more efficiently than in those of Messrs. Samuda Brothers.

39 Testimony on the Shipbuilding Trades
John Price, 1893-4

The addition of more and more crafts into the shipbuilding industry after the emergence of iron shipbuilding also brought more unions. The inevitable result was a myriad of demarcation disputes, as workers and their unions sought to protect what jobs they had and tried to extend their jurisdiction over any new jobs which arose, from the incursion of other craftsmen and other unions. John Price here explains from the employer's viewpoint just how demarcation disputes arose.

Mr. John Price called and examined.

26,280. Mr. *Dale.* You are the general manager, I think, of Palmer and Co., Limited?—Yes, I am.

26,281. They are Shipbuilders and Engineers, Jarrow?—Yes.

26,282. Is that firm a member of the National Federation of Shipbuilders and Engineers?—It is.

26,283. You propose, I think, to lay before us certain evidence on the subject of demarcation of work, of overtime, and of freedom of labour?—Yes.

26,284. I think it would be most convenient if you would kindly give it as you have prepared it?—Very well. The demarcation of work occurs wherever two trades work in the same materials, as, for example, shipwrights and joiners; engine-fitters and plumbers; engine-fitters and drillers; engine-fitters and caulkers and holecutters; engine-fitters and blacksmiths who are not in the same societies; plumbers and tin and iron plate workers; tin and iron plate workers and platers belonging to the Shipbuilders and Boiler-makers' Society; angle-iron smiths and blacksmiths; iron-shipwrights and caulkers; platers and caulkers (these two latter classes are members of the same Society; of course I am enumerating all those with whom we have actually had differences); caulkers and drillers; painters and red-leaders. The line is generally, but not invariably, drawn between the rougher and the finer jobs, or those in which the heavier as against the lighter masses of material are used and for which different tools are required, as in the cases of shipwrights and joiners, and of iron plate and tin plate workers, &c. The fitters and plumbers' differences are of a more complex kind. The fitters work upon products of other branches of the same Trade Society, the fitters' work being largely—as their name implies—the putting into place of these products, and in adjusting or adapting them by their treatment as to details to that end. In the shops where this work is performed, there is no collision with the plumber, but only on board ship, and chiefly on board war-ships of all kinds built in private yards, where the work on such fittings as water-pipes made of malleable iron, copper, or brass, and jointing up, is finally carried out. Here differences arise because, for certain purposes, iron, copper, or brass are used instead of lead, at the wish of the owner of the vessel, or by the specification or practice of the Government. The plumbers' trade is more what may be called an original trade than the fitters', for its work is chiefly in lead, which, except in pipes and sheets, is not manufactured into forms for them; and it is principally as to piping where differences with the fitters occur, and then only when iron, copper, and brass of certain sizes displace lead. In the bulk of their work the plumbers do not approach the fitters' domain at all. The use of iron piping has been much increased of late years. It has taken the place of lead for many purposes, as it possesses the great recommendation of being cheaper as well as stronger. It was first largely used for gas piping, and was fitted by the plumber because first used in dwellings. The jointing of the gas pipes together was by ferrules, or short pieces of piping screwed over the ends of the two adjoining pipes. On the introduction of iron piping on board ship the difference between fitters and plumbers arose on the jointing. The jointing of cast-iron and copper pipes by the fitters is effected by forming flanges upon them and pressing them together by bolts passing through the flanges. Whenever the plumber was called on to put a wrought-iron pipe in instead of cast-iron, copper or brass, so long as it was practically an adoption of the iron gas piping with the ferrule or screwed joint, no objection was raised by the fitter, but as soon as those pipe joints were of the flanged kind, the fitter objected that that was giving the plumber his work. The fitter did generally the jointing of all pipes fitted with flanges on shipboard, and when iron piping became so large, or was used for such purposes as to require flanges for jointing, the fitter claimed that as his work. That was the original point at which the dispute between fitters and plumbers first began. The dispute afterwards extended as the use of the iron piping increased, and it eventually was proposed to limit the fitting of iron piping by plumbers to that with the screwed joints, with certain exceptions, and to a maximum

CAULKING

BORING

STEAMING HOUSE

SPINNING

TREENAILS

SERVING

SAIL MAKING

diameter. As to what that diameter is to be is the great difficulty, as yet unsolved. The exceptions above referred to are in water-closet, urinal, lavatory, and bath piping, and the ventilation of all those spaces, which are admitted to be exclusively plumbers' work, no matter of what materials they are made, nor with what joints fitted. Although iron piping was the original and chief source of the dispute, other fittings have been drawn into it as the dispute became acute, and as the fittings of ships became more complex and required more men to carry them out. In war-vessels, for example, the tubes for the ventilation of the vessel, and the fitting of pipes for flooding the compartments, for accommodating the thermometers, and for the very large and extensive system of drainage in battle-ships, all of which are of iron piping; these have been fought for over and over on the ground of custom or prece- dent, or the size of the pipes, or the kind of the joints. There is also the strapping of all these pipes and tubes, apart from their fitting into po- sition and jointing, which has been claimed not by plumbers and fitters only, but by smiths also, and which has been finally divided amongst them. The details I am giving of the fitters and plumbers' trades, where they touch each other, are for the purpose of showing the complexity of the subject under consideration. The principal difficulty in com- posing the disputes has arisen from the variety of the practice in different works and districts, and from the trade societies wishing to bring them into a uniform practice. This difficulty has been enhanced by the practice in individual works and districts being different, and having been different at different periods, when the work now disputed used to be given to either trade, according to whichever was better able to undertake it, taking into account the amount of other work it had in hand at the time, and there being no regard paid to such matters at those times by the societies.

40 The Displacement of Hand Labour in Wood and Iron Manufactures , James Samuelson, 1893

James Samuelson (1829-1918), a well known liberal and working-class sympathizer from Liverpool, is best known for his support for the spread of trade unionism, and for his interest in popular science. He actively promoted the organization of dock labourers in Liverpool in the 1870s, and afterwards wrote on a wide range of labour and trade union issues. In this selection he indicates the continued progress of mechanization in the wood and iron industries, emphasizing in par- ticular the enormous numbers of men displaced by the introduction of mechanical riveting.

Both of these industries are so diversified and widespread that it will be very difficult to treat of the nature, and impossible to estimate the amount of hand-labour which has been superseded by mechanical appliances.

Incidental to the application of improved machinery to wood-working, mention has been made of machines for sharpening the tools so employed, and in relation to this feature, the following extract from a letter which I have received from a well-known firm—Messrs. Luke and Spencer, Limited, Manchester—may be of some interest:—

Our business consists entirely in the manufacture of machines for reducing hand-labour, chiefly in the finishing of metals and tools. . .We are unable to give you any information in figures as to the saving effected, but may say that some years ago we then made certain inquiries from our customers, whose replies are embodied in a number of testimonials we had printed at the time. These may be of interest to you, so we enclose one of the old catalogues with them in. We have not made similar inquiries since.

The machines referred to in the above extract are for grinding drills, saws, shear-blades, pattern-makers' tools, lathe centres and attachments, &c.; for "surfacing," cleaning the teeth of wheels, grinding bushes, bearings, chilled axle-boxes, &c. The chief agent employed is the emery wheel. The testimonials are very numerous and some from highly respectable firms of users personally known to me. They speak of a saving varying from 50 per cent. upwards in labour and files, and point to a considerable displacement of manual labour by such mechanical appliances.

Some of the front plates for large boilers (which I understood were made by Browns, of Sheffield) are bent by machinery, but smaller ones I saw still being bent by hand. The most important labour-saving machines, however, are the hydraulic riveting machines for large boilers, and the following may be considered an approximate estimate of the displacement of hand-labour and economy of working expenses obtained from the use of these machines.

Under the old system of hand-riveting a certain amount of work occupied 3 men 6 days at 36s. per week, and one boy 6 days at 8s. per week: making a total cost in labour of £5 16 0. The same work can now be accomplished by machinery by 1 man working 2 days at 38s. per week; helped by 3 labourers at 24s. per week, and 2 boys at 8s. (also for 2 days): making a total of £2 2 0. Saving on the work done: £3 14 0.

Thus one *skilled* labourer practically does the work of 9 men under the old system (doing in 2 days what 3 men were only able to accomplish in 6), and unskilled labourers and boys have to some extent taken their place. Of course the labour is not the whole cost. In the case of hand-labour the cost and wear and tear of tools; and in the other coal, interest, and depreciation of machinery, must be added. So much for the effect of fixed riveting machines such as are used by the firm above named; but so far as displacement of manual labour is concerned, the employment of *portable* riveting machines elsewhere appears to be still more striking, and I am told by disinterested experts that some of our greatest engineering works could never have been executed without these machines. I believe the most perfect of them is "Allen's Patent Portable Pneumatic Riveter" manufactured by Messrs. De Bergue & Co., Limited, Manchester. It is shaped like a horseshoe magnet with the arms placed vertically, and the dies fixed in the upper and lower "jaw"; and is driven by a cylinder and piston attached to the machine. It is worked by compressed air with a pressure of about 70lbs. per square inch; the air being supplied by an air compressor through a flexible tube. The manufacturers claim that the cost of "work done by their machines as compared with hand-labour is equal to 4½ to 1; that is, the cost in wages for the same quantity of work by hand would be 4½ times more than by the portable riveters, the work being reckoned as piece work in both cases." Amongst the testimonials sent to me by the firm was one from Mr. Gerald Barker, the contractor for the Overhead Railway at Liverpool, in which he said, "It is quite a regular thing for us to put in 3240 rivets in a day of 10 hours with this machine."

As I considered this an astounding result from the operation of one machine, I wrote to Mr. Barker asking him for certain further particulars, and this is his reply:—

Overhead Railway Works,
Hornby Dock, Bootle,
Liverpool, 10 March, 1893.

Dear Sir,—In reply to your letter of 9th inst., I have pleasure in giving you the following particulars respecting work done by the "Allen Patent Portable Riveter" on the Liverpool Overhead Railway. The rivets were 5/8 inch diameter. A full description of our method of applying the machine appeared in the *Engineer* of the 27th January, 1893.

"One boy attended the Lisle's patent rivet-heating furnace, and also carried the hot rivets to the man who put them in the holes, and 2 men manipulated the machine. In all 3 men and 1 boy.* In my opinion 24 men and 8 boys would have been required to put in the same number of rivets by hand in the same time; and the result could not have been so good, as the rivets would not fill the holes so well as those put in by this machine.

Yours faithfully,
(Signed)   Gerald Barker.

From this letter it will be seen that 21 men and 7 boys *would have been* displaced by this machine, if it had not enabled contractors to undertake vast engineering works which could not otherwise have been accomplished.

Mr. Knight, the general secretary of the Boiler Makers' Union, tells me that "almost all boiler work and girder work for iron and steel bridges, and much of the inside work of our vessels, are done by machines; and if all the riveting now done by machinery was done by

---

*This lad must have heated and carried a rivet every twelve seconds for ten hours consecutively!

manual labour it would give employment to 15,000 men more than are now engaged in the work."

In the face of all this evidence of the displacement of hand-labour by machinery, however, it is strange that according to the census tables the number of persons engaged in boiler-making should have doubled between the years 1861 and 1881. (There does not appear to be a separate return for boiler-makers in 1871.)

	For 1861	For 1881
The returns are:	13,020 persons	26,170

In the absence of the tables for 1891 it is unsafe to pass any criticism on the increase of persons employed; but, as before stated, there is no doubt whatever that the introduction of machinery has been absolutely necessary to keep pace with the marvellous developments of shipbuilding.

Still the facts and data here given do not exemplify the course in which hand-labour has been superseded by machinery in iron manufacture as well or correctly as the following letter which I have received from the well-known firm of Tangyes, Limited, Birmingham:—

In reply to your circular letter of 1st inst., we beg to say that while we have for years past been constructing and using machines for the purpose of diminishing hand-labour, the process in our works has been of so gradual a nature that we could hardly give any specific instances of the immediate value of such tools. If we were to make any comparison at all with the present time, we should have to go back many years in order to show the real advantages which have been obtained, although there is no doubt whatever they have been very great. With regard to hours of labour, the only changes that have taken place are the reduction from 59 hours to 54, and the more recent one of leaving at 12 o'clock on Saturday instead of 1. So far as our relations with trades unions are concerned, we have never had any difficulty at all in dealing with workpeople belonging to them; in fact, any question that we have had with them has always been met in a most satisfactory manner.

In another letter Messrs. Tangyes say,—

Our output has largely increased, necessitating improved machinery, and the number of hands has increased also, but we are really unable to say in what proportion.

Leaving now the question of wood and iron manufactures, we must pass on to other industries in which further illustrations will be given of the effects produced by machinery on the employment of manual labour.

41 Fifine versus the Rivet Making Machine
Emile Zola, 1876

This striking passage from Zola's *L'Assomoir*, describes more vividly than any of the documents here the feelings of a skilled worker about the introduction of machines to replace his craft. This Parisian metalworker must have had his British counterpart, proud of his skill in forging rivets, who felt similarly as he contemplated a rivetmaking machine newly arrived in the shop.

Goujet had stopped in front of one of the machines for making rivets. He stood there, wrapped in thought, with bowed head and fixed look. The machine forged rivets of forty millimetres with the quiet ease of a giant. And in truth nothing was simpler. The fireman took the piece of iron from the fire, the striker placed it in the tool-hole, which was moistened by a constant trickling of water to guard against softening the steel, and the thing was done, the screw came down, the rivet jumped to the ground, with its head as round as though it had been cast in a mould. In twelve hours that confounded machine manufactured hundredweights of rivets. Goujet was not spiteful, but at certain moments, it would have delighted him to have taken Fifine (the hammer) and gone and knocked all that machinery about, in his rage at seeing that it possessed arms more powerful than his own. It caused him great vexation, even when he reasoned with himself, and told himself that flesh could not fight against iron. One day certainly, machinery would kill the workman; wages had already fallen from twelve francs to nine francs a day, and there was talk of lowering them still more; in short there was nothing lively in those hulking contrivances which made bolts and rivets just the same as they might have made sausages. He gazed at that one fully three minutes without saying a word, his brow contracted, and his beautiful yellow beard bristled menacingly. Then a look of gentleness and resignation gradually softened the expression of his features. He turned towards Gervaise, who pressed against him, and said with a melancholy smile: "Eh! it makes one feel precious small! But perhaps it will someday help to insure the prosperity of all of us."

Gervaise did not care a fig for universal prosperity. In her opinion, the machine-made bolts were badly forged.

"You understand what I mean," she exclaimed with warmth, "They are too well done. I like yours better. In them one can at least trace the hand of an artist."

In speaking thus, she gave him very great comfort, because he had feared for a moment that she would despise him after seeing the machines. For though he was stronger than Salted Mouth, otherwise known as Drink-without-Thirst, yet the machines were stronger than he was. When he at length parted from her in the court yard, he squeezed her wrists almost to the point of breaking them, because of his great joy.

42 Engineering
J. Swift, 1895

This essay traces from the worker's point of view the history of technical transformation in the engineering industry. It analyses how technical progress over the course of a century had gradually robbed the worker of his skill.

Before proceeding to deal with the engineering industry as it affects the workman, it is necessary that some of the great mechanical inventions that have made the industrial history of the eighteenth and nineteenth centuries so memorable should be briefly touched upon. There is a great absence of reliable information as to the earlier mechanical appliances in use in most industries, the ordinary course being to summarily close all investigations into the early history of manufactures with the remark that "all labour was manual." This was certainly not the case, although up to the time of Elizabeth, at any rate, the mechanical appliances used in production were few, and of a very rude kind. There were water-mills from the time of the Romans, and wind-mills from the time of the Crusades, but of the precise character of the processes performed in these mills, and the extent and nature of the labour-saving appliances which they contained, there is scarcely any information accessible. We may, however, for all general purposes, say that it was in the textile industries that labour-saving machinery was first introduced to any large extent. The first symptoms of that jealousy of machinery which afterwards became a conspicuous feature in the development of English industry, were manifested in 1482, when a complaint was laid before Parliament "that certain articles of clothing, hitherto made with hand and foot, were now being made by the use of tucking and gigge mills," and a statute was enacted forbidding their use. For two centuries later, the statute books contain frequent enactments, forbidding the use of machinery in various industries. In 1543 a machine was invented for making metal pins. In the latter part of the reign of Elizabeth, William Lee invented the stocking frame which he brought to such perfection that it long remained practically as he left it, without receiving any essential improvement. Aware of the national importance of his invention, he took it to court, but the period of his visit was not propitious. Elizabeth was in the last stage of her decline, and her successor, who saw Lee and his brother make a pair of stockings, looked upon the invention rather as a dangerous innovation, likely to deprive the poor of labour and bread, than as a means of multiplying the resources of national industry, and of giving employment to many thousands of men. In spite, however, of kingly hostility and courtly indifference, the stocking frame made steady way, and in time its effect upon the industry reacted upon most of the other textile trades.[1] For over 50 years, indeed, the tide of invention ran almost exclusively in the direction of new and improved machinery for the textile industries, but with the introduction of steam power to manufacture, invention took a wider scope, and has since flowed into every conceivable industry. The whole trend of modern manufacture, indeed, appears now to be in

[1] A full account of the stocking frame will be found in the "History of the Machine-wrought Hosiery and Lace Manufactures," by W. Felkin, London, Longmans & Co, 1867. 21s.

the direction of making machinery do the work formerly done by skilled handicraftsmen. Thus the artisan is reduced to a mere machine-minder, engaged in constant repetitions of a process little more than mechanical, and the results of this change upon his intellectual and economic status have no doubt been often detrimental to the workman, at any rate for a time.

The temporary and immediate loss thus sustained by the workers, has led many to cavil at the introduction of machinery. But we must not allow ourselves to be blind to the fact that, although its immediate effect may be detrimental, yet it must tend ultimately to the advancement of the workers. For the present, however, inventions have poured upon us so rapidly that the powers of organisation possessed by the workers have not been able to keep pace with them, and hence the labourers have been unable to successfully demand their fair share of the increased product resulting from the use of labour-saving machinery.

As the manufacture of labour-saving machinery constitutes so important a part of the engineering industry, it is perhaps desirable that a few words should be here said upon this side of the question. And first a few facts as to the rapid displacement of hand labour by machinery which is actually taking place. In agriculture, machinery is rapidly replacing the farm labourer. According to the census returns, between the years 1861 and 1881, some 110,000 partly skilled and unskilled farm labourers were driven from their usual occupation, and replaced by about 4,000 skilled artisans making machines, which were worked by about 4,500 semi-skilled labourers. In the production of agricultural implements also, new machinery has, during the last 15 or 20 years, displaced fully 50 per cent. of the manual labour formerly employed. There has also been recently introduced a machine worked by a petroleum engine which will with four men fell the same number of trees in the time it would have taken 30 men to accomplish in the old style. Even the humble calling of fire-wood cutting has not escaped, and machines are now in operation which will do both splitting and bundling. Each of these machines will, according to its size do as much work as was formerly done by 12 to 48 men.[1] In boilermaking and iron ship-building, the hydraulic riveting machine will, with one skilled labourer to attend it, do as much work as 9 men under the old system of riveting by hand. Mr. Knight, the General Secretary of the United Society of Boilermakers and Iron Shipbuilders, computes that 15,000 men have, during the last 30 years, been displaced by the introduction of this machine alone. Nevertheless, between 1861 and 1881, the number of boilermakers in the United Kingdom was more than doubled. In the Cleveland iron mines drilling machines have been introduced that will, with one man to attend them, do the work of ten men. We have only to walk round any of the docks to see to what an extent machinery is

---

[1]The inventor of this wood-cutting machine, not content with the suffering thus caused to the poorly paid fire-wood cutters, has placed upon the machine the motto, "Strikers checkmated," which seems quite an unnecessarily cruel way of adding insult to injury.

taking the place of the manual workers there. With the introduction of the elevator, the trimmer, and the hopper, a vessel containing 400 tons of grain which has to be discharged, trucked to the nearest warehouse, weighed and delivered, and would under the old system have employed 108 men, and cost in wages £24 13s. 4d., can now be done by machinery with 36 men, at a cost of £10 12s. 1d. Against this has to be placed the cost of the machinery in the first place, and the wear and tear of the same, but this is no advantage to the men displaced, and only means increasing somewhat the work of the engineers in the manufacture of such machines.

Nor has the engineering trade itself escaped from this tendency to replace hand by machine labour. One often wonders how it would affect the minds of some of the old-time millwrights if they could revisit the scenes of their labours, and closely examine a modern engineer's shop, with its complement of labour-saving machinery. One of Brown & Sharpe's milling machines will do, in a given time, as much work, and finish it quite as accurately, as ten men could in the old style; and it is a common saying amongst mechanics that those machines can do anything but talk.

In the iron and steel industry marvellous improvements have been made since 1856, when Mr. Bessemer introduced his process of directly converting tons of pig iron into wrought iron in a few minutes. Soon afterwards he introduced his method of manufacturing steel, which enormously reduced its cost of production. By this process, from one to thirty-five tons of crude iron may be converted into steel in thirty minutes, while by the old process it took from two to three weeks, and instead of only costing £6 or £7 per ton, its cost was £50 or £60 per ton. Even house painters have not escaped, for at the Chicago Exhibition there was a painting machine used that did nearly the whole of the painting, employing only 300 men, whereas in the usual way it would have taken from 3,000 to 4,000 men; and when visiting Birmingham at the beginning of the year, I was shown a machine called a converting machine, which turned leather into pigskin, alligator skin, or any other fancy hide, by simply passing it through marked rollers,—true Birmingham ware. In the printing and allied trades, the progress of invention and machinery has been so marvellous, and its effects are so patent, that there is no need for me to dwell upon them. In short, there is scarcely a trade or industry in the kingdom in which some machinery which displaces a considerable amount of hand-labour is not now employed.[1]

Side by side with the introduction of improved machinery has grown up the system of subdivision or specialisation of labour. The advantages or otherwise of this system are a matter open to considerable discussion,

[1]Most of the examples quoted are taken from James Samuelson's "Labour-Saving Machinery." London: Kegan, Paul & Co., 1893. 2s. 6d.

but I am compelled to differ very strongly from the opinions expressed by some of the leading political economists in regard to it. Thus, in his *Economics of Industry*, Professor Alfred Marshall says that "the introduction of machinery, with its concomitant subdivision of labour, relieves not only the muscular but the nervous strain of the mechanic, and tends to do away with the monotony of his toil."[1] He further quotes examples, which clearly show how little practical knowledge he possesses on this particular point. After stating, for instance, that the tendency of machinery was in the direction of becoming automatic, he goes on to say that the persons who mind it must have an intelligence and an energetic sense of responsibility, which go a long way towards making a fine character. This reasoning appears to involve a complete contradiction, and how far its conclusion is from the truth, only those who have worked those automatic machines, or watched the effects of such work upon others, can form any idea. Adam Smith and John Stuart Mill wrote much in the same strain as Professor Marshall, and as the subdivision of labour has been carried to a greater extent in the engineering and kindred industries than in almost any other, it is perhaps desirable that a few words should be said upon this subject.

Firstly, then, as to its effects on the skill of the workers. Fifty years ago there existed a class of engineers known as mill-wrights, who, so far as regarded scientific knowledge were no doubt quite uneducated, but who were, nevertheless, men of great intelligence, whose work-boxes contained the tools of nearly every trade, and who could handle these tools with skill and dexterity. Before the days of easy communication, they used to be sent to great distances in charge of works both extensive and intricate, and generally executed them with a thoroughness and intelligence that left nothing to be desired. Through the subdivision of labour, however, this class of highly skilled mechanics has become well-nigh extinct. By all but "dry-as-dust professors" it is generally agreed that it is the monotony of toil that makes life so disagreeable to the workers. Condemned from early morning to late in the afternoon to repeat the same operation hour after hour, day after day, month after month, and year after year, the effect must be disastrous upon the artistic faculties of the workman. Think for a moment of its vulgarising and stultifying influence on human life and conduct. I very well know a certain factory in H. M. Government works at Woolwich, where the introduction of labour-saving machinery and the subdivision of work are carried out to the utmost possible extent. Hundreds of youths are engaged working automatic machines in connection with the production of fuses, cartridges, and bullets. All that they have to do is the merest mechanical work, one operation only, and this operation having to be repeated in some cases thousands of times in one day. There is little or no chance for the men so employed ever to improve their present condition. As the work calls for very little skill or intelligence, what chance have these youths of exercising their artistic

[1] See *The Economics of Industry*, London, Macmillan & Co., 1881, 2s 6d.

190

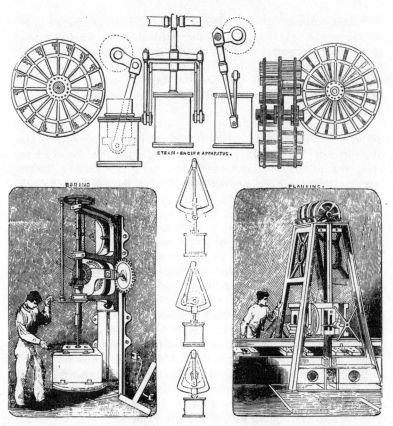

STEAM·ENGINE APPARATUS.

BORING

PLANEING

faculties, or their intellectual energies in the performance of such tasks? Can there be any wonder if they turn their attention, for the sake of a little excitement, to the gin-shop, to gambling or horse-racing, and to all kinds of vice and folly? Noticing one day that only youths were employed on these machines, I inquired what became of them when they grew up to be men. I was told that some were made "examiners." The standard of skill required to be an "examiner" may be gauged from the wages paid to them, *viz.*, from 19s. to 26s. per week. Many others drift into the position of yard labourers, and of the rest, those who are not fortunate enough to die go for soldiers. This, then, is one of the evil effects of that subdivision of labour which is rendered inevitable by the necessities of the age. All mechanics will agree with me that the introduction of machinery has not raised the standard of skill among workmen. Nay, on the contrary, it has enormously increased the monotony of their toil, and limited the scope for the exercise of their ingenuity. It must of necessity dull their artistic perceptions, and tend to reduce them to the mere level of machines capable only of repeating one operation so many times per day. The difficulties in the way of altering this system are many, and where piecework is worked the workers will not be likely to insist upon frequent changes of work, as it would in all

191

probability decrease their earnings. But of this I am certain, that if our workers are to be something more than mere machines, we shall have to give them an opportunity of using their skill and intelligence in their work. The more diversified the work is made, and the less monotonous the toil, the more will the inventive faculties of the workers be quickened, to the ultimate benefit of the state, the workers, and the employers.

It is, perhaps, hardly necessary for me to say that it requires a large outlay of capital to make a modern engineering establishment anything like complete. The tendency is consequently in the direction of eliminating the private employer, and introducing the limited liability company with the board of directors and manager. This, however, is by no means a subject for dissatisfaction to the workmen, as there is frequently much less sweating carried on in large firms, or companies, than in the smaller shops, which are governed directly by the employer, who is often forced through want of proper machinery to work his men at the highest possible tension so as to compete successfully with his better equipped rivals. Another advantage of the "grand industry" is, that the larger factories are generally built with a little regard to the health and comfort of the workmen. As already suggested, the greatest blot on the large factories is the subdivision of labour. This must lessen the interest that the engineer takes in his work, for in proportion as the subdivision of work increases, so the need for skill and intelligence diminishes. I do not mean to imply that the working engineer of to-day is in point of intelligence inferior to the artisan of 50 years ago, for, on the contrary, he is undoubtedly far superior. That, however, is not to be traced to his work, but to increased educational advantages, greater political freedom, and the effects of Trade Unionism.

Of these three main sources to which the superiority of the present-day artisan over his forerunners must be attributed, the first, that of improved educational facilities, is too obvious to call for remark. The second, that of greater political freedom, will not perhaps be quite so generally or readily admitted, although it seems to me to be self-evident that greater powers of self-government, and more political responsibility, have materially assisted in the growth of intelligence and thoughtfulness among the artisan class. Of the third of these three factors, that of the influence of Trade Unionism, more must here be said. It is not my intention to inflict upon you a lengthy history of the Trade Union movement as it has affected the mechanic, from its inception up to the present time, but only to notice a few of its most conspicuous features. Before the repeal of the anti-combination laws in 1824, there were small and more or less local societies in the different branches of engineering industry. The meetings of their members were held, we are credibly told, on lonely heaths or sequestered moors, or more often in some barn or cellar, with a sentinel posted outside, whose duty it was to give an alarm at the approach of any officer of the law. With one or two exceptions, not much reliable information is to be gathered in reference to the Unions connected with the engineering industry during that period.

———

In 1824 the Steam Engine Makers' Society was established, and exists up till to-day, though numerically not very strong, and about the same time all over the country small sectional societies sprang up, each working under different rules and conditions. In 1851 several of the previously existing societies amalgamated, and formed the now well-known and powerful Amalgamated Society of Engineers.[1] In July, 1851, the men employed by Messrs. Hibbert & Platt at Manchester struck against piecework and the practice of putting unskilled labourers on to the machines. This proved to be the preliminary to a great contest. The men won a temporary victory, but the employers formed an association among themselves for mutual defence. In January, 1852, the Amalgamated Society of Engineers, which had been agitating against piecework and systematic overtime, passed resolutions to restrict these two evils in the trade. The employers met this move with a general lock-out of all their men. They refused to negotiate or to re-open their works except upon conditions most humiliating to the workers, including the signing of a "document", which pledged them to abandon their Trade Union, and decline to join any other similar association. The men struggled gallantly against this for four months, but were then practically starved into submission, the whole of their funds being exhausted, and public opinion strongly prejudiced against them. I have spoken to men who went through that fight, and who eventually had to sink their independence, and sign agreements which they never intended to keep, forced to act a lie through starvation. Hundreds drifted out of the trade altogether rather than accept the humiliating conditions. The employers hoped that the Amalgamated Society of Engineers was now crushed out of existence, but, as usual, they entirely under-estimated the strength of the feeling of comradeship among the men, and of their knowledge of the absolute need of a Trade Union to preserve decent conditions of life for themselves and families. In less than two years the Society was stronger than ever before, having 11,000 members and over £20,000, and from that time its record has been one of unbroken progress, both in membership and funds, till it has now 75,000 members, with an accumulated fund of £250,000, and has paid out in benefits during the last 40 years, no less than £4,000,000. The chief objects of the Amalgamated Society of Engineers are to obtain a minimum wage for its members, and to abolish overtime and piecework, but in neither of them has it been completely successful so far. That it has been the means of raising wages few will deny, and where the Society is strongest there wages are highest and conditions of working best. Overtime has to a certain extent been restrained through putting a tax upon it, making

[1] Of these societies, by far the most important was the "Journeymen Steam Engine and Machine Makers' and Millwrights' Friendly Society," established 1826, which had, in 1848, a membership of over 7,000 men, and an accumulated reserve fund of £27,000.

the employers pay time and a quarter or time and a half for all hours worked overtime. On the other hand, this has made the men more ready to accept overtime, because it gives them a higher rate of pay. There is little to say in favour of piecework. If it were beneficial to the men, the employers would not be so ready to force it upon them. Its effect, indeed, is to keep down the rate of wages right throughout the country. To the casual observer, the system of peicework seems to be the proper method of payment. It appears to be simply payment by result. But those who have worked it or thought seriously about it, know that it means much more. Not only does it lead to scamping of work, but it brings into play many of the worst passions of human nature. Men grow suspicious of each other, and envy, jealousy, and distrust are developed under the system. Then it is seldom a question of contract.[1] Foremen or managers fix the price often without consulting the workmen. Some firms, wisely for the men's sake, set a limit to the earnings of the men. Where this is not the case, some men, through special adaptability or greater physical strength, get through their work easier than others, and consequently earn a greater amount. These men are taken as standards, and immediately they earn above a certain percentage more than their ordinary wage, down comes the prices, and they become the whips whereby their fellow-workers are flogged. I need not dilate on the effect it must have on the unemployed. The average earnings of the pieceworker are one-fourth to one-third more than his day-work rate, and no one will be wild enough to imagine for a moment that he gets the extra remuneration without he does at least as much extra work. This means that, on the average, every three or four men working piecework are responsible for keeping one man out of work.

The effects of Trade Unionism in the engineering trade may be briefly summed up as follows. First, it has immensely improved the morals of the workers. By bringing them closer together, and placing them under a system of discipline, they are brought to feel that they are not single units, each fighting for his own hand, but that, within certain limits, each is responsible to his fellow-workers. It inculcates thrift and mutual reliance upon each other's sympathy and assistance in need, while at the same time it breeds a spirit of firm independence, and of strong and united opposition to all forms of industrial oppression,

[1] In the engineering trades, the so-called 'piecework' to which the men are so violently opposed, is not really a pure 'piecework' at all, but rather a form of 'estimate' or 'contract' work. No proper list of prices exists, nor, indeed, would such a list be possible, in view of the constant changes in kinds and qualities of the work performed, and of the enormous variations in methods of production, etc. Piecework, therefore, means that the men so employed must themselves give a price for each job separately. In other words, it involves a complete return to the individual bargain, which is, of course, the very antithesis of the Trade Union or 'collective bargain'. It is against this negation of the Trade Union position that the opposition of the men is so strongly, and rightly, aroused, and their hostility to piecework so-called is not in any way due, as is sometimes supposed, to any theoretical objection to good or quick workmen receiving more wages than others.

among its members. It has raised wages and reduced the hours of toil, and lessened to some extent many of the other evils of workshop life, such as piecework, systematic overtime, and the favouritism or bullying of foremen. That the unions have not been more successful in their objects than is actually the case is due, to some extent, to their conservative tendencies, and their slowness to change and to take advantage to the full of all their opportunities. But still more is it due to the selfishness and desertion of their fellows by the non-unionists, who are content to take all the benefits which the union has obtained, while unwilling to do their share in paying for these privileges.

————

The future of the engineering industry is bound to be a great one, for new sources of employment are opening up in it every day. With the rapid growth of labour-saving machinery on all hands, the engineer is taking the place of the unskilled labourer in all directions. It requires, indeed, no violent stretch of the imagination to conceive that in the near future there will be little work other than machine making and machine minding. Nor is this altogether to be deplored. In spite of the fact that the minding of machinery is a merely mechanical job calling forth little of the better part of a man's nature, it is nevertheless better both morally and intellectually for the worker than is the constant strain of hard physical toil. Indeed, if the workers could secure, either by legislative action or Trade Union control, a fair share of the advantages of labour-saving machinery, especially in the direction of largely diminished hours of labour, its introduction might become an entire blessing, even to the mere machine minder. There can be little doubt that could his day's work be accomplished in a few hours and himself left free to spend the remainder of the day in mental and physical recreation, most, if not even all, the evils induced by his lack of interest in his monotonous employment would quickly disappear. For the maker of machinery much more may be said. His is an occupation in which, if he desires to excel, he must possess a fair knowledge of mathematics, metallurgy, mechanics, and even chemistry. The result is that the genuine mechanic is usually one whose intellect has been sharpened by study, and whose work calls for considerable mental exertion. It is true, of course, that the subdivision of the trade removes to some extent the need and opportunities for the workman to become a thoroughly skilled mechanic. Engineers, so called, are now in reality fitters, or turners, or pattern makers, or smiths, or machinists. But every one of these branches of occupation provides some opportunities for, and gives encouragement to, the workman to exercise some of his faculties, and though it is not possible that every engineer should become a Stephenson or a Watt, yet he may have the satisfaction of feeling that his work is something more than the exercise of mere brute strength.

43 Notes on the Engineering Trades Lockout
Amalgamated Society of Engineers, 1897-98

The Engineering Trade Lock-out was one of the most well known manifestations of the struggle for the eight-hour day and the manning of machine rules. The excerpts included here from a correspondence between employers and trade unionists include some of the arguments put forward on the length of the working day, and on the role of skill.

THE EMPLOYERS' FEDERATION OF ENGINEERING ASSOCIATIONS

29 April 1897

To the President and Members of the Executive Council of the Amalgamated Society of Engineers

Gentlemen,—Conformably with the intention of the Employers' Federation, as expressed by their chairman during the sitting of the recent Conference in London, the Employers desire to add to the statements then made the following remarks, in order, if possible, to make still more clear the position taken up by them in regard to the Machine Question, and in regard to the Local Joint Committees proposed by the representatives of your Society at the Conference.

It may be well to recapitulate the circumstances which brought about the existing condition of affairs. Claims were put forward by your Society in several districts of the United Kingdom for the displacement from machines of men who had been selected and appointed by the Employers as suitable, and who were working the tools to their satisfaction. These claims were resisted by (1) the individual firms concerned; (2) the district associations; and (3) this Federation. In consequence of this resistance aggressive action in support of the claims was taken in more than one district by the delegates of your Society.

————

The arguments brought forward by your representatives at the Conference have not shown to the Employers any sufficient reason why their discretion in the selection of the men to work their machines, and other matters pertaining to the management of their business, should be delegated to any external authority. On the contrary, the more the discussion of these demands was prolonged, the more evident did it become to the Employers that there is no middle course between a concession of them on the one hand and an unqualified refusal of them on the other. The practical issue is to the Employers as simple as it is vital, and they take it to be the preserving or relinquishing of their right to manage their own business.

———

In the matter of discriminating between the men who may work any particular machine or machines or do any particular work, the Employers have a keen appreciation of the services of highly skilled men. It may be pointed out, however, that whatever practice is followed in the different districts or in individual shops such practice has for the most part had its origin in the free and untrammelled exercise of the Employers' discretion in selecting the most suitable men for the work rather than from any deliberate arrangement or understanding between Employers and employed collectively.

———

I have the honour to be,
Yours faithfully,
Henry C. S. Dyer,
*President of the Employers' Federation
of Engineering Associations.*

AMALGAMATED SOCIETY OF ENGINEERS

May 8th, 1897

Employers' Federation of Engineering Associations re Machines.

Dear Sir,—As already advised, your letter of the 29th ult. came duly to hand, and I have now to say that it has been fully discussed here today by Council of above Society.

We regret that you have not been able to offer some counter proposals to those we put forward for the solution of the Machine difficulty, and we cannot accept the suggestion conveyed that we are responsible—by seeking to impose impossible conditions—for the deadlock that has ensued. After carefully noting the points in your recapitulation of the circumstances leading up to, and the arguments put forward at the Conference, we feel compelled to take exception thereto, and to point out that the attitude of your Board in regard to this question of Machines is scarcely consistent with that adopted in regard to trial trips and overtime. The issue is said in yours to be simple and vital, namely, "the preserving or relinquishing of their (the Employers') right to manage their own business." But upon the questions of the restriction of overtime and the payments for out-working and trial trips your Federation has recognised the competence of joint meetings of employers and employed to arrange conditions and make them binding upon employers and employed.

We note your willingness to meet us and, if possible, adjust any question which may arise, as also that your Board is willing to "appoint members to serve on local joint Boards to arrange general rises and falls of wages." But we desire to point out that in view of the increasing proportion of machine to hand labour, and the adaptability of machines to a wider range of work, any "arrangement" of general rises and falls of wages is to us a matter of lessening importance, unless such arrangement covers the question of wages to be paid to machine operatives. And, further, it seems to us that if a local Board is competent to arrange general rises and falls of wages, it should also be competent to settle as to what particular class of work should be affected thereby.

In short, there is no case on record, as far as we know, of objection being raised to a man, whether Unionist or not, who was in receipt of the wage current in the district for the class of work upon which he was engaged; and if we have appeared, in argument, to have put forward any claim for exclusive employment upon machines for our members or for skilled engineers, then it has simply been done because we have thought it necessary to guard ourselves. The plea, therefore, put forward in your letter as to the "necessity laid upon the Employers of considering the large number of men belonging to other trade societies or to no trade society" does not seem to us to have any weight against our proposals, which, subject to wage as agreed upon being paid, would have left the individual employer absolute freedom of choice in the selection of workmen.

I remain, Sir, truly yours,
Geo. N. Barnes,
General Secretary,
Amalgamated Society of Engineers.

Manifestos Issued by Amalgamated Society of Engineers

12th July, 1897

To the Public.—
The lock-out Notices posted at the instigation of the Employers' Federation of Engineering Associations takes effect to-morrow, and thereby a heavy blow is dealt upon the Engineering trade of the country, and untold suffering inflicted upon countless thousands of inoffensive and helpless labourers and their families.

Yet, if actuated only by selfish motives, we, as organised workmen, would find no cause for regret in what has been done, inasmuch as the Eight Hours movement must be immeasurably advanced thereby. The Eight Hours Day is to Trade Unionists a cherished aspiration, having its roots far back in the ever-recurring conflicts which have been co-incidental with the growth of the factory system of industry. Its economic possibility has long been theoretically established, and many of the most enlightened and sympathetic Employers have put it into practice, with immense advantage to their employees and without loss to themselves. Yet there has lurked in the mind of the average man a fear of decreased output, foreign competition and other bogies, a fear which will be dispelled as the publicity now given to the matter has time to do its work. The whole question has been transferred, by the act of the Employers, from the academic to the practical sphere, and the public mind is being familiarised with the beneficial results of the Eight Hours system as worked in the workshops of the Government, as well as in those of Messrs. Mather & Platt's, Salford; Wm. Allan's, of Sunderland; The Thames, Limited, at Blackwall; Johnstone's, of Stratford; Keith's, of Arbroath, Witton Works; Walkers' & King's, Norton Metal Works, Birmingham; Hadfield's of Sheffield; and others too numerous to mention.

We have held our own up till now in spite of the croaking of the pessimists, and we shall continue to do so with an Eight Hours Day. We have it on the authority of a naval expert that the Eight Hours Day, judged by its product, the battleship "Fuji," has been a marked success. In point of workmanship the ship in question was one of the best, if not the best, in the recent Naval Review at Spithead. She was built at the yard of the Thames, Limited, which at this moment has orders on hand amounting to £2,000,000, where the Eight Hours has been in operation four years, and has resulted in placing the firm in a better position than ever before.

It has been successful wherever it has been tried, and there is abundant proof that the fears of foreign competition are groundless. We have reason to believe that such fears do not even exist in the minds of the Employers themselves, as evidenced by the fact of 159 firms in the London district having already conceded. The real object of the Lockout is to crush the Amalgamated Society of Engineers. This has been admitted by Dr. Haswell, one of the Federation Secretaries, who to a Press representative on Saturday said that the Employers had widened the area of the dispute to the utmost limits so as to drain our finances, and because we had pressed upon them a question which had not been discussed at a Conference recently held on other matters. As a matter of fact we had been in friendly negotiation on the Eight Hours question with the Employers outside the Federation and outside the Federation area months before the Conference alluded to had been thought of. Our members inside of the Federation area were working quietly and peacefully up to this week, and the Federated Employers have only themselves to blame for raising discontent where there was none.

We venture, therefore, to place the true position before the public, knowing, as we do, that public opinion is after all the final arbiter in these matters. It is for you to decide whether these pseudo Napoleons of Newcastle are to ruthlessly dislocate the whole trade of the country with impunity in the foolish endeavour to cripple the A.S.E., or whether, on the other hand, the workman is to be allowed quietly, peaceably, and calmly to work his way upward to increased leisure, fuller home life, and greater freedom, with the unfailing concomitants of mental, moral and physical development, which are the true sources of a nation's greatness.

By Order of Executive Council,
Geo. N. Barnes.

The London Position.—Let us briefly re-state the case. For two years Trade has been improving, as have also been the conditions of labour. The London engineer, however, with that moderation which has always characterised him, has refrained from putting forward any claim for higher wages, although wages have in the time been raised elsewhere, and doubtless could have been here. He has, instead, concentrated his attention upon that reduction of the working day which, owing to the peculiar geographical and residential conditions surrounding him, had become an absolute necessity. It should be remembered that the last few years has witnessed a remarkable transformation. Inner London has been beautified and improved by new lighting, by mansions for the well-to-do, by better railway facilities, and a more complete system of transit generally. All this we welcome because it has expedited business and tended to the general good. But it has its harsh side for the workman, who, owing to increased rents, has been pushed further out and away from his work. Starting at the factory at 6 o'clock has necessitated getting up at 4 or 4.30 in the morning, and nine hours in the workshop frequently means twelve to fourteen hours away from home. He has started work on an empty stomach, after a long journey, and therefore unfit to do his best; and he has left it with a sense of wrong rankling in his mind. He has left home at an unreasonable time, without breakfast and before his family were astir, and he has returned to it with a margin of leisure and vitality so small as to debar him from mental culture or participation in public affairs.

Hence the claim in London for an Eight Hours day—a claim which has been recognised by most of the Employers as fair and reasonable—which has been conceded to about 7,000 of our members, and which was in a fair way to being conceded to the others but for the intervention of the Federation before mentioned.

By Order of Executive Council,
Geo. N. Barnes.

19th July, 1897

To The Public.—Since the issue of our last statement organised Engineers to the number of some 18,000 throughout the country, with probably as many more of the allied trades and non-Unionists, have ceased work, and the London Employers, in support of whom the Lock-out was planned, are still coming quietly over to the men's side, fifteen firms, employing about 1,000 men, having conceded during the week.

Time and increased publicity has but served to emphasise the almost criminal recklessness of those who precipitated this conflict. Six firms in Halifax, one at Leeds, one at Leicester, two in London, and one at Belfast, have withdrawn the Lock-out notices, which had apparently never been approved by the leading ship builders and engineers of the country.

It remains now only for the few London Employers who have been inveigled into the Northern Federation of Engineering Employers' Associations to as gracefully as possible extricate themselves from an untenable position.

Conclusion.—We will have further opportunities of addressing you as the struggle continues. Meantime we may say that there has come to us many gratifying assurances of goodwill from the Continent and America, showing that this movement has wider signification than can be expressed in official returns or figures of profit. It voices a world-wide desire not only for fuller life but for a more equitable social adjustment. In spite of machinery and sub-division of labour the life of the people is still absorbed in work, and increased powers of production have not brought that leisure and increased comfort we had a right to expect. Hence the chorus of approval which has greeted the efforts of the Engineering and allied trades, and which has proved that we voice the sentiment of friends of freedom both at home and abroad. The Eight Hours will not create a new heaven or a new earth; unless coupled with a restriction of overtime, it will do but little for the unemployed, but its concession will give new hope to the weary worker everywhere.

By Order of the Executive Council,
Geo. N. Barnes.

44 The Policy of the Engineers
F. W. Hirst, 1898

F. W. Hirst, an established political economist of the period gives his views on the attempts of workers belonging to the Amalgamated Society of Engineers to 'throttle' the introduction of labour saving machinery.

The following is a provincial view of the engineers' policy in the recent dispute. The masters have fought far more against interferences in regard to machinery and the claim of trade unionist officials to "boss" their workshops than against the demand for an eight hours' day. Take a case in Leeds. A firm had two lathes which one good man at 35s. a week was perfectly capable of managing by himself. Possibly a boy only was needed. The trades union official, however, interfered, and insisted that there must be two men at the job, each of whom would be paid say 28s. a week. Another case, which also comes from a non-interested and quite trustworthy source, is equally instructive. A man had a machine to look after which frequently did not need watching for half an hour at a time. During one of these intervals he began sharpening his tools. The foreman came up and told him to put them away. "Why?" "Because this is your own time, and you must sharpen tools in your employer's time." The further development of a system of this sort would of course be ruinous, and one cannot wonder that the masters were alarmed at what seemed to be only the beginning of a new policy.

These recent developments are due to the success of the Independent Labour Party in this particular society; but there is always sure to be *some* discouragement to good workmen, for the trade union must be ruled by a majority, that is by a mediocrity which refuses to allow the best workmen to receive the reward of superiority. Then there are the secretaries. A great deal of unnecessary meddling is done by paid officials who think that they ought to show something for their money. So they fuss about in their district and bully small employers. The local branch of the trade union, and consequently the local policy, is apt to be "bossed" by its own paid secretary, just as a municipality is often controlled and directed by the Town Clerk, who is before the law a paid servant, dismissable at any time by a vote of the Council. The policy of restricting the number of machines which a man may look after might no doubt be defended, if applied in moderation, upon the ground that the mental and physical strain would in the long run be dangerous to health; but unfortunately these restrictions are usually defended by "new" unionists on the fallacious principle that you can increase work, and improve trade from a workman's point of view, by reducing the output. "Lower the productive capacity of labour in order to absorb the unemployed!" is the socialistic idea: and it was a trade unionist of that type who told the Labour Commission that if after the adoption of an eight hours' day there then arose a fresh lot of unemployed, the remedy would be to reduce the day's work to six hours, and if that failed to four. And yet in the same breath these dishonest advocates will tell the public that the same amount of work will be produced in an eight hours' day as in a nine. Either of these opinions *may* be correct, but not both. But the restriction of output, which some try to effect by reducing hours, others aim at by more direct means. Thus the Shoemakers' Union ordered the reduction from eleven dozen pairs to a little over nine dozen pairs of the weekly work to be done by a set of men working certain machines.[1]

It was stated by Mr. Sidney Webb in November, at the London School of Economics and Political Science,[2] that the unions are not

---

[1] *Engineering,* October 29th, 1807.

[2] In the course of an interesting lecture on "The Policy of Trade Unions with regard to New Processes and Machinery".

opposed to the introduction of labour-saving machinery. This may be true in the main, but the conditions of introduction are often so severe that they practically become prohibitive; for it is not worth while for an employer to introduce labour-saving machinery if the machinery is to be "throttled." Moreover, some unions have been almost, if not quite, "captured" by the Independent Labour Party. Mr. Barnes, for example, who was elected secretary of the Amalgamated Society of Engineers, is a declared Socialist, and has given himself up not only to abstract aspirations for a future millennium, but also to the advocacy of the policy involved in the special economic fallacy which we have been discussing. Just about the time of Mr. Webb's lecture an editorial appeared in the monthly journal of the Engineers' Union, which contained the words, "labour-displacing machinery means an ever increasing obstacle to be faced." This monthly journal has proudly enumerated many instances of restrictive policy carried out by administration and legislation (Trade Union bye-law). The "demarcation" of work in order to secure unskilled jobs for skilled workmen, at skilled wages, is one of the commonest methods of attaining the end. No doubt many of the regulations do good; no doubt many of the employers need carefully watching; but that must not prevent us from recognising that the employers have many real grievances, and that trade unionism is doing some harm as well as a great deal of good. Any one can make a rough estimate for himself. I am very far from wishing to overstate the case against the Amalgamated Society of Engineers. Its peculiar constitution subjects its policy and practice to innumerable local variations; and it is certainly true that organised efforts to restrict output have been more serious in some districts than in others.

Nevertheless, so far as the north of England is concerned, I have been reluctantly led by a good deal of independent and perfectly impartial enquiry to the conclusion that the official denials which came from London on this question of the restriction of output are almost worthless. The policy of the Amalgamated Society is the policy of its branches, and at each local branch the idea of increasing employment by restricting output has prevailed to a greater or less extent. Many extraordinary instances have been given by anonymous writers, or accumulated by the Masters' Federation, of the process which is called "throttling the machinery". Let me give another instance, for the accuracy of which I can vouch. A large firm in Leeds purchased four machines (American patents) for sawing steel bars, and turning them into nuts. Their management required no skill, and a boy at fifteen shillings a week was given charge of them. The union interfered, and insisted that the principle of "one man one machine" should be applied. The firm gave way, and just before the lock-out four skilled men were being paid seven pounds a week in wages for doing the work of one unskilled boy. At the beginning of the lock-out the boy was set to work again. Whether the strain is too much for a boy I cannot say. Certainly the work is neither skilled nor heavy. The most general and elaborate mode of wasting the employer's time has been in the sharpening of tools (cf. above), but this ought to have been avoided long ago by the universal adoption of the American system of a separate tool-sharpening department. When the managers are tactful and efficient there is less cause of complaint against the men.

45 The Construction of Machinery Used in Special Trades
Paul de Rousier, 1896

Paul de Rousier, a French social investigator looks at the special case of engineering workers in Platt's textile machinery factories. This firm, the largest engineering works in Britain, had crushed the unions in 1852, and unions were still non-existent in the plant at the end of the century. Workers were bound to the firm by a severe division of labour which had made their skills so plant specific as to prevent any possibility of their finding work elsewhere.

Oldham is one of those manufacturing towns which form an unbroken ring around Manchester, and feed the great textile market. Rochdale and Blackburn are quite near, and the whole country bears witness to almost incredible activity, and gives point to the American epigram which describes England as a town with a few gardens in it. Oldham, however, is not one of the gardens. In this great industrial hive Oldham is specially concerned with the fabrication of the various machines employed in the textile industry. Under the direction of Platt Brothers it has developed enormously. 10,000 men are employed in their workshops. Eight locomotives are busy from six in the morning to eight at night in transporting the finished looms along the special line to Oldham Station, and in bringing back coal and raw material. A network of rails covers the ground floor, so that nearly all the transport is affected by steam, and trucks can load or unload at any point.

The firm has not been content to rely on the wrought and cast iron and steel furnished by iron-founders. Messrs. Platt have started iron-founding to ensure the quality of the material used in the construction of their looms, and mining to supply the coal for their workshops. They own four collieries between Oldham, Manchester, and Rochdale. This important firm, with its complex organisation, is clearly an example of the factory system, from the scale of its workshops, the number of its employés, the magnitude of the capital employed, and the enormous amount of work turned out. The looms made by Platt Brothers are despatched to Europe, Japan, China, India, Australia, Brazil, Mexico, the United States, and, in fact, to all the countries of the world.

But in one way their workshops differ from the most advanced types of the factory system. The work done there is of an extremely delicate and technical kind, and the mounting of the looms in particular requires great care and the most exact finish in all the component parts. Every workman is a specialist. A significant fact in proof of this is that not a single woman is employed by the firm. The young woman who enters a factory to earn her living till she marries would be out of place. There is no room for occasional hands or casuals, who take up any sort of work to-day to drop it for something else to-morrow. Every work-man must be master of his business. Except the porters, who are super-seded as far as possible by lifts and locomotives, almost every individual employed by the firm is a skilled workman.

Here consequently we find apprenticeship flourishing as in trades of the old type, though it is, of course, greatly modified by the different conditions. We have no longer an apprenticeship imposed by a guild jealous of its privileges, and anxious to close its doors on younger men and to regulate their enrolment, but rather an apprenticeship imposed by the conditions of labour and by the demand for technical skill of a high order.

Apprenticeship is thus freed from all artificial restraints. The appren-tices of Platt Brothers are bound by no contract, but are free to go and liable to dismissal. They are retained by the compulsion of circum-stances, and by the advantages which they desire to obtain and which cannot be obtained otherwise. On leaving school at fourteen they are taken on at 5s. a week, with an increase of 1s. a week every year, so that in the last year of apprenticeship they are getting 12s. a week. At twenty-one they are reckoned as workmen, and paid at that rate, as far as possible by the piece, and nearly always with a system of bonuses which increases the minimum salary in proportion to their individual skill.

Now, it is a remarkable fact that these workmen have no Trade Union, and belong to no association for protecting their interests against their employers. In 1851, at the end of an important strike, the Union was entirely crushed, and since then Messrs. Platt have forbidden the form-ation of any such Union among their employés. When the men have any suggestions to make, they send a deputation to their masters, who always hear it with attention. Their demands are examined, and are accepted or refused as seems just, but without discussion. It is the system of grievances of the old régime, while the Union aims rather at the effective representation of the interests of labour.

The absolute position of the masters, so exceptional in the labour world, is explained by the unique position of the firm. Although it is not the only English house of the kind, it is far the most important. It has no rival in the neighbourhood of Oldham, and has, in fact, a mono-poly of this branch of industry, which it has raised to its present importance. Workmen who left would find great difficulty in disposing of their special skill elsewhere on equally favourable terms. It is their highly-specialised character which makes them so dependent on the great firm which directs and employs them.

Thus the exceptional relation between the employés of this firm and the heads of the firm clearly results from the exceptional position of the firm, which is master of the market in a very unusual degree. As a result it can impose its own terms on its men, since it is the only channel through which work can be obtained.

———

We have seen in the small trades that the men are more or less successful in defending the remnants of their industrial monopoly, of which the evolution of industry undoubtedly tends to dispossess them. They still retain some of their old privileges, and though their stronghold is seriously threatened they will continue to hold it until it is definitely overthrown.

The miners are at once the most and least fortunate. On the one hand, they find their ground cut from under their feet, owing to the large and complex scale on which mines have to be worked, requiring large capital as well as technical knowledge far superior to the endowments of an ordinary workman. On the other hand, they have created an organisation which puts at their disposal a force hitherto unknown. Although they cannot rise to the position of employers, they can at least treat with employers on equal terms. They can affect consumers directly by ordering a suspension of work. They have more than a negative share in the direction of this industry, as is shown by the provisions of the treaties signed at the end of the great coal strike.

Here, on the other hand, the influence of the men disappears before the overwhelming importance of the employers. If the latter consent to receive deputations and to hear the grievances of their subordinates, it is clearly stated that it is an act of benevolent condescension, and that their reply will be in accordance with what they think it just to do. No doubt their sense of justice is a very enlightened one, and they are animated by the most praiseworthy sentiments, but nevertheless their men are defenceless and the situation is not unlike a benevolent despotism. Such at least is what, on the face of things, would seem to be the position.

Chapter Six

General Labour

The social and economic split between the skilled and the unskilled or general labourer was partly defined in mid-Victorian Britain as a split between unionized and unorganized labour. Employers too recognized the split and sought through technical and managerial innovations to dispense with the skilled, unionized labourer and to replace him by the easily obtainable and easily replaced unorganized general labourer. By the late nineteenth century, however, the general labourers, whose numbers had also expanded particularly in the gasworks and the docks, also began to organize. After the 1889 dockers' strike, the period of general, or new, unionism came into being to bring about the protection and resistance of the unskilled. The result was in some cases a new phase of mechanization. Now means were sought not to make use of general labour, but to dispense with it. This was especially evident in the wave of technical innovation in the gasworks. The organization of the dockworkers likewise provided incentives for the introduction of mechanical elevators and other lifting devices.

Though not generally grouped with general labour, the special categories of agricultural labour and transport workers had also long experienced the plight of the unorganized. The 1870s was the great age of agricultural trade unionism. The National Agricultural Labourers' Union, which was soon formed out of Joseph Arch's earlier unions, had a membership of over 100,000 by 1873. Farmers responded to this new trade union threat with evictions and harassment, lockouts and concerted efforts to introduce the mechanical contrivances then available for steam ploughing and mechanical reaping. The union successfully resisted these in many places at first. The decline of Arch's union coincided with the collapse of grain prices that came with the introduction of American wheat exports. Investment in land improvement declined and mechanization, though it continued to spread, did so haltingly. In these depressed conditions large numbers of farm labourers simply left the land, seeking better opportunities in nearby towns.

Transport workers formed another new job category created by industrialization and particularly by the steam railway. This was a rapidly growing, but highly regimented and hierarchical group of workers.

Organized by the railway companies under what was effectively a system of military discipline and rank, railway workers did not at first display the militancy and effective organization found among other workers. The men and their unions were known for their 'respectability' throughout the nineteenth century. This was challenged in 1890 when the men of four of the Scottish lines took the initiative and went on strike. Though the men were eventually told by their union to return to work, the incident marked the beginning of a new phase. Railway workers were soon to complement the disciplined nature and organization of their trade union demands.

The results of the emergence of general or 'new' unionism appeared very disappointing by the end of the nineteenth century. Early public support for the organization of the unskilled was followed by a wave of middle class anti-unionism. The strength of the newly formed organizations waned rapidly. By 1901, after the Taff Vale case, trade unions had been stripped of legal rights they had gained as long ago as the 1870s.

46
The Displacement of General Labourers by Machinery
James Samuelson, 1893

This is another selection from James Samuelson's fascinating studies of
the introduction of labour saving machinery. Here he shows particular
interest in the means used to displace general labour, particularly in the
docks. His discussion should be placed in the context of the new unionism in the years just before he produced this collection. Samuelson,
himself, did a great deal of work to promote unionization in the Liverpool docks.

There is one important phase of this question to which we have not yet
directed our attention. In most of the cases hitherto considered,
machinery and improved processes have been necessitated by increased
demand, or by keen competition, or by both; but as having a more
direct bearing on our inquiry, we must now look at those examples
where the action of the labourers themselves has caused employers, in
the first instance at least, to resort to the use of mechanical contrivances, in order to render themselves as independent as possible of hand-
labour. This has been chiefly the case in unskilled trades, and although
I have naturally enough found less readiness on the part of employers
to supply me with data for comparison, quite sufficient have been given
to me, coupled with the results of my own experience and observation,
extending over more than a quarter of a century, to enable me to show
conclusively, that the opposition of employers to strikes is by no means
confined to the displacement of unionists by non-unionists. The secretary of an extensive federation of employers naively tells me that machinery is the answer of the employers to the workmen's demands for
shorter hours and higher wages. To what extent this is so, my readers
will be able to judge for themselves, but it may be at once admitted,
that the facts, as they stand, make it advisable that the leaders of labour
should consider well whether, and to what extent, those who look up
to them for counsel are likely, in case of a strike, to be *permanently*
displaced by mechanical appliances. For in the interest of the men
themselves, I would add that there may be cases, when even from their
point of view it would be better for unionists to work with non-society
men, than to be permanently deprived of the means of earning their
livelihood by the introduction of machinery into their particular
industry. And now to give a few examples in support of this view.

It was last year, I think, that the Directors of the Western Counties
Agricultural Co-operative Association informed their shareholders in
their annual report that much labour-saving apparatus had been erected,
and in reply to inquiries I was told that this had been necessitated by
a strike of piece-work labourers under the direction of what were called

"Union Agitators", and the following details of the changes in working were furnished to me:—

Elevating and distributing machinery, by which grain delivered in bulk into hopper at the quay side is carried to the top of the building and distributed on an endless band into bins in the top loft, and gravitates into bins on the lower floors as may be required for feeding, direct into grinding mills or re-delivering into sacks through shoots. Said grain can be re-delivered into the elevator by means of the conveyor-worm, so as to remove the contents of one part of the warehouse to another without hand-labour, or for cooling grain instead of turning by hand.

In this case, the estimate of labour-saving is as follows:—

This entirely displaces four men, saving in labour 10s. per 100 quarters of grain delivered into warehouse, and 12s. 6d. per 100 quarters on all grain which may be required to be shifted from one part of the warehouse to another, or into the grinding bins. In addition to this there is considerable saving in respect to day-labour when the grain requires to be turned or shifted to keep it cool, for by means of the machinery it is allowed to run from the bins by gravitation into the conveyor-worm which re-delivers it into the elevator, and it is again carried to the top of the building and redistributed into any part of the warehouse required. This process cools the grain far more effectually than is at all possible by hand-power. The contract for fixing our grain elevating and distributing machinery is 670*l*.

There is a little repetition here, which I have intentionally given, in order to show the reader how completely a substance like grain, which is liable to heating, can be handled by automatic machinery; but now I propose to show in detail, on what an enormous scale such machinery is being employed elsewhere, to the disadvantage of the hand-labourer, and the gain of the employer.

Until the year 1880, the Mersey Docks and Harbour Board did not use any of the new elevating machinery at their grain warehouses, but during the great strike in 1879, their regularly employed "bushellers" ceased work in sympathy with other labourers on strike, and were guilty of violence towards imported labourers (probably paupers, &c.) who were set to work to discharge the grain vessels.* As a consequence, the Board fitted up its grain warehouses with grain elevators, patented by Mr. Brice, the superintendent, at the suggestion of Mr. James Spence, a member of the Board, and manufactured by Messrs. S. Stott & Co., Haslingden (of whose labour-saving machinery more will be said here-after). The elevators are of two kinds, fixed and floating, and the latter are also largely employed by some of the leading Liverpool steamship-owners. In addition to the elevator, the grain is shifted by a "trimmer", also Brice's patent, and a galvanised iron hopper for weighing the grain.†

---

*On this occasion the dock labourers were beaten after three weeks' strike (or rather lock-out) against reduced wages, and about a year afterwards they would have struck again, but I induced them to resort to arbitration, and acted as their arbitrator along with the late Mr. R. Lowndes, nominated by the ship-owners, and Lord Derby as umpire. Their wages were restored to them and they have since been further raised.

†For the information of readers who are unacquainted with these appliances, I

The following data will give an idea of the displacement of labour, and the saving of expense by the use of these three contrivances as compared with the old system of hand-labour.

1. The use of an "Elevator" means an average discharge of 400 tons per day, and calls for the employment of 5 men, together with the use of steam or hydraulic power for the working of the "Trimmers". For this work, a tonnage rate of 1¼d. is paid to the men, or say 8s. 4d. per day on the basis of 400 tons per day. The *average* work discharging by hand-labour and the *bushel* would be 200 tons per day, and the gang would consist of 16 to 18 men, 8 of whom would receive 6s. 8d. per day (being piece-work), and the 10 men each 4s. 6d. per day.

2. The "Trimmer" is used for moving the grain in the hold of a vessel to the foot of the "Elevator", and needs, as before stated, 5 men. Should it be attempted to do the same work without the aid of the "Trimmer", i.e. by the use of corn-shovels, the employment of 12 to 20 men would be necessary at 4s. 6d. per day each.

For the storing of grain in the warehouse rooms, turning by machinery, weighing over, and delivery to craft, 3 men and a "Trimmer" do the work which otherwise would call for the services of at least 8 men (3 men at 4s. 11d. each, instead of 8 men at 4s. 3d.).

3. The "Hopper" for weighing grain in bulk is used for effecting deliveries to carts and to craft, in the former instance by means of a platform which is made on the quay and stands to the height of the cart. The "Trimmer" and "Hopper" combined require a gang of 6 men (at 4s. 3d. each), and deliver to carts, say 1000 sacks, and to craft 1200 sacks per day. Similar work performed without these two inventions would require 12 men at least: i.e. 10 men at 4s. 3d., and 2 men at 8s. 8d. per day.

To put this calculation before the reader in a more concrete form, we will suppose a vessel to have entered the dock with 400 tons of grain, which had to be discharged, trucked to the nearest warehouse, handled in warehouse, weighed and delivered, all by hand-labour; and the same operations to be performed with the aid of machinery. And inasmuch as the work is done under the new system in one day whilst it formerly occupied two, the number of men and the wages under the old system must be doubled.

Under the old system there were employed:—

On Ship	Wages	Truckers	Wages
36 men	£9 14 8	24 men	£5 2 0

Handling in Warehouse	Wages	Weighing and Delivering	Wages
16 men	£3 8 0	32 men	£6 8 8

may mention that grain is lifted *perpendicularly* by 'buckets' running upon an endless strap or chain; that it is conveyed *horizontally* by broad endless belts on which it settles; and that it is *trimmed* by a large scoop which is hauled along by machinery, when full, and guided by a man who drags it back empty for refilling.

With modern machinery:—

Trimming Machine in Hold	Wages	Working Elevator	Wages
5 men	£2 18 0	4 men	£0 18 4

Handling in Warehouse	Wages	Weighing and Delivering	Wages
3 men	£0 13 9	24 men	£6 2 0

Or, all operations:—

Under the old system	108 men	£24 13 4
Under the new system	36 men	10 12 1
Equal to men saved	72* Wages saved	14 1 3

*Perhaps it would be more correct to say that 36 men are displaced for 2 days.

Although it is of no advantage to the men displaced, there must be put against this gain to the Board, the cost of hydraulic power, and the interest, and wear and tear of the machinery. It will be remembered that the cost of the machinery in the case first cited was 670*l.* From other data which I have received, I estimate that the proportion of first cost of machinery doing 400 tons per day would be about 1280*l.*

The following are particulars of the number of elevators in use on the Mersey, which have enabled the Board to reduce the charge for handling grain 20 per cent.:—

Stationary	belonging to the M.D. and H. Board	3
Stationary	belonging to the Grain Storage Company	4
Portable	belonging to the Liverpool Grain Elevator Company	15
Floating	belonging to the Liverpool Grain Elevator Company	3
Floating	belonging to Mr. McCabe	1
New Portable	belonging to S. S. Stott & Co., Haslingden	1
		27

But whilst it is an undeniable fact that the men themselves were the cause of the introduction of this labour-saving machinery, it would not be fair to them to omit saying that sooner or later something of the kind would have happened.

———

I have already referred to the labour-saving apparatus in a great west of England store, and similar appliances are to be found in oil mills, sugar-refineries, flour-mills, &c. One large seed-crushing firm writes me that their machinery is for "saving of labour generally, and making our manufacture as much automatic as possible" to reduce working expenses. In that mill the seed is largely handled by machinery in all but the hydraulic pressing. Another seed-crusher gives an estimate of labour saved by recent improvements in machinery whereby the work of 19 men is now performed by 10, a little over 50 per cent., and this was mainly caused by the necessity for expediting work and economising labour in competition with foreign seed-crushers.

The well-known firm of Aveling & Porter makes road and street rollers, and supplants thereby another form of pauper labour. The necessity for this labour-saving appliance no one will deny, both to prevent the cruelty of compelling horses to trample down the sharpened stones in what is mis-named macadamising, and to save wear and tear of the wheels of every kind of conveyance. These steam-rollers are in use over the whole civilised world and the testimony to their efficiency is universal. The users all speak of their economical working, the surveyor of the Stirlingshire roads saying, "The saving of material in a rolled road is at least 30 per cent. and that in surface-labour still more"; whilst the street superintendent of an important town in Massachusetts says, "I estimate that the steam-roller, with the pick attachment, and two men with hand-picks, will do the work of from 20 to 40 men with hand-picks alone, according to the hardness of the road-bed". As to their own work Messrs. Aveling & Porter tell me, "Our plant, i.e. the tools and machines we have from time to time bought, have been of a general character. The number of men has gradually increased, but there has been no decrease of hours".

Again, one of the most important branches of civil engineering in which powerful machinery has largely supplanted manual labour is the excavation of docks, canals, &c. This has been accomplished chiefly by the "Steam Navvy", the operation of which I have had frequent opportunities to observe, notably in the works of the Manchester ship-canal, and the new works at the Canada Docks, Liverpool. In both these great works the "Steam Navvy" of Messrs. Ruston, Proctor & Co. has been found the most efficient, and the following is an estimate of the difference between its working and hand-labour. The weight of the machine is 34 tons, and the bucket for excavating and lifting holds 1½ cubic yards. At the Canada Dock works I was told that the average quantity of "soft muck" excavated in a day of ten hours is 1000 cubic yards; but the engineer of the Manchester Ship Canal (Mr. Leader Williams), in a testimonial which he has given to Messrs. Ruston, Proctor & Co., says that about 2000 yards of good material has been excavated in 10 hours.*

To be quite within the mark, however, it will be as well to estimate the quantity worked at 1000 cubic yards, which gives the following results: *Men employed and Wages per Diem with Steam Navvy:*

Engine driver, 7s. 6d.; 3 labourers, 4s. 3d. each, together:	£1	0	3
Men laying rails and working about the machine, 12 at 4s. 3d.:	2	11	0
	£3	11	3
The same work done by hand-labour would require 50 men at 3s. 10d.:	9	11	8
Men displaced, 34. Wages saved:	£6	0	5

*In 1891, there were 58 of these machines in use on the works of the ship canal, and I believe more were added at a later period, and the engineer speaks of Messrs. Ruston & Proctor's machine as being the best for removing hard materials.

Against this must be placed cost of coal, interest, and wear and tear of machinery, as the hand-labourers find their own tools.

I have already spoken of the labour-saving machinery in the works of Messrs. Tangye Brothers, Birmingham, and amongst the appliances made by that firm are hydraulic jacks for moving large objects. This is the quaint advertisement which they have forwarded to me, and, whilst they are responsible for its absolute historical accuracy, it exhibits in a striking manner what changes have taken place through the introduction of labour-saving appliances.

How Obelisks have been Raised

A.D. 1586.	Fontana raised an obelisk at Rome with 40 capstans worked by 960 men and 75 horses.
A.D. 1836.	Le Bas raised the Luxor obelisk at Paris with ten capstans worked by 480 men.
A.D. 1878.	John Dixon raised Cleopatra's needle in London with 4 of Tangye's patent hydraulic jacks worked by 4 men.

All kinds of unskilled labour have been superseded in a greater or lesser degree by machinery. Messrs. S. Stott & Co., of Haslingden, the manufacturers of the grain elevators, also make elevators and conveyors for supplying coal to stoked boilers, for transferring bundles of cloth from one part of a manufactory to another, for removing barrels and boxes either from warehouse to warehouse, from warehouse to trucks, or even from the ground over a line of railway with its waggons into the upper stories of a warehouse. It would be possible to mention a variety of other labour-saving contrivances made by that and other firms, but enough has been said to show how such appliances, actuated by steam or hydraulic power, are gradually superseding hand-labour.

As regards the statistics of unskilled labour, it must be mentioned that the Census tables are an unsafe guide, first, on account of the uncertain and changing methods adopted in successive enumerations, and secondly on account of the much larger and indefinite number of unemployed. With these reservations the following may be taken as the statistics of England and Wales:—

	1861	1871	1881
Labourers: Dock, Dock-yard, Road, Cotton-porter, Coal-heaver, and "General".	375,783	565,234	685,077

In each of these three enumerations the labourers are differently classified in the Census tables, but I have endeavoured to reduce them, as far as possible, to uniformity, and before passing on to the conclusions to be drawn from this and the preceding chapters, and discussing the general situation, it is right once more to mention the fact that in the numbers of labourers given above there must be included a large percentage of those who were divorced from the soil, and who migrated into our large cities and seaports.

214

BELL'S IMPROVED REAPING MACHINE BY CROSSKILL

47 The Displacement of Hand Labour in Agriculture
James Samuelson, 1893

In this essay James Samuelson discusses the means which used to displace agricultural labour, and estimates their effect. In fact the rate of technical progress in agriculture was retarded, as was general agricultural improvement, by the agricultural depression of these years. The depression was probably more responsible than technical progress for the numbers who left the land.

It is difficult to point to any one of our industries, and to say, that particular branch has been the most largely affected by the introduction of machinery as a substitute for hand-labour; but for various reasons the one which appears to be the most striking and important is agriculture. Of the vast number of men who have been displaced by machinery, a certain proportion figure in the emigration records, but the change has made itself more sensibly felt in the immigration of farm labourers into our large towns, where they overcrowd the labour market, and add largely to the tale of the semi-employed or the entirely unemployed. Every branch of agriculture has been revolutionised by the introduction of machinery, which has largely displaced hand-labour, and the very manufacture of the machinery itself has undergone great changes from the same cause. For this reason alone, it is necessary to limit our inquiry as much as possible, and to select one or two striking illustrations of the changes that have affected our labouring community.

Thrashing machines probably first superseded the flail in Scotland

about the end of the last century; improved ploughs were first introduced by the Ransomes at the beginning of the present one; reaping
and mowing machines came largely into use between 1860 and 1874
(their introduction being stimulated by the prosperity of farmers, and
the universal demand for labour about that period) with what effect on
hand-labour we shall see presently. Added to the mere reaping operations, we have now the so-called "binders", which reap, collect and
bind the grain; we have the steam plough, the mechanical drill, the
horse-rake, a substitute for the hand-rake, winnowing machines worked
by steam, chaff-cutters, turnip-cutters, cake-breakers, and a variety of
other appliances in the field, the dairy, and the farmyard.

Let us take, first, as an illustration of the displacement of hand-
labour, the effect of the introduction of machinery in the cultivation
of grass and cereals.*

Comparison between the labour employed in Agriculture, when work is done by
machinery and by hand-power only.

A full day's work.	In acres	Men employed	Same work done by manual labour	Number of men displaced by machinery
2. H.P. grass-mower	12 acres	2 men	9 men	7 men gained
2 H.P. reaper	16 acres	3 men	12 men	9 men gained
Binder	12 acres	2½ men	12 men	9½ men gained
Hay-rake or corn-rake	16 acres	1 man	2 men	1 man gained
Seed-drill (small seeds)	20acres	2 men	1 man	1 man lost

In this estimate, all preliminary and subsequent work is considered,
and it must be mentioned that the work done by mechanical drill is
superior to that by hand-labour. An immense gain to the agriculturist is
the speed with which farming operations can be carried on by machinery, rendering him less dependent upon the weather, and, to some
extent, more independent of trades unions. This is, of course, looking
at the question from what is called the "economic" point of view alone*.

Let us now turn from this limited aspect of the question to the
wider one of the general divorcement of a great mass of labourers from
the soil; bearing in mind that the years when reaping and mowing machinery most largely superseded hand-labour were from 1860 to 1874.

Agricultural labourers reported as employed, in the Census Tables.†

	Men	Women	Total
In 1861	914,301	43,964	958,265
In 1871	764,574	33,513	798,087
In 1881	807,608	40,340	847,948
	Decrease, 1861 – 1881, 110,317		

*The estimate which follows, and other valuable information, has been given me
by F. C. Marshall, Esq., of Riseholme Grange, Lincoln.
*It will be found from the sequel that this "expedition" is a necessity which,
in one way or another, affects every department of industry.
† Vol. III. 'Occupations of the People.' The volume for 1891 is not yet completed.

More than 110,000 persons, therefore, have been displaced, largely by the introduction of machinery. It is necessary to qualify this state-ment, because during some of those years considerable changes were made in the nature of the crops cultivated. The agricultural returns are imperfect in this respect until the year 1871, but it will be found that out of every 1000 acres of arable and pasture land in Great Britain—

	In 1871	In 1881	In 1891	1871 to 1891.
The total permanent pasture was	403	455	499	+ nearly 10 p.c.
The total of arable was	597	545	501	- nearly 16 p.c.

involving a considerable diminution of field labour.

But we are also enabled to judge of the increase in the use of mac-hinery as a substitute for manual labour by the growth of the imple-ment manufacture. According to the census returns there were em-ployed in this industry:—

	In 1861	In 1871	In 1881	Increase be-tween 1861 & 1881.
Artisans and dealers in implements	1034	3617	4119	2583
Labourers *with* implements	1205	2152	4260	3055

Thus we find that between 1861 and 1881 more than 110,000 com-paratively skilled and unskilled farm labourers have given place to about 4000 skilled artisans making machines, which were worked by 4260 semi-skilled labourers. And it must not be forgotten that a very large number of additional machines of various kinds have been annually im-ported from the United States, a fact which probably accounts for the comparatively greater increase of labourers using implements over that of the artisans making them.

———

The general effects of the introduction of machinery into agriculture in this country have been, as already stated, to shorten the time for farming operations; to enable the British agriculturist to meet to some extent the grave competition of distant lands which send their pro-ducts into our markets; to displace vast numbers of hand-labourers in the fields, thereby diminishing the periodical immigration of Irish im-migrants during harvest; of driving English labourers into our large towns or compelling them to emigrate. On the other hand, it has created a new and rapidly increasing industry, that of agricultural implement making, which is calling into existence a new class of skilled artisans, and perhaps a higher class of labourers in field and farm. I hear also that it is causing a growing disinclination in women to take part in field-labour; is making the male agricultural population dissatisfied with the prevalent dulness of village life and their surrounding ignorance, and thus calling for higher education and a more rational existence than that which begins with the taproom and ends in the workhouse; and generally that it is raising the whole class. To put it tersely, as my friend Joseph Arch has done on the back of a post-card which I have recieved from him:— "No doubt but the introduction of machinery woke the rural labourers and set them thinking and did, I believe, a great deal towards their combination."

48 The Scottish Railway Strike
James Mavor, 1891

James Mavor wrote widely on many topics of political economy. While teaching in Glasgow he was assistant editor of *Industries*, and did several studies on railways. His interest in labour is also seen in two substantial works, *Wages Theories and Statistics*, 1888, *and Labour Colonies in Germany*, 1893.

This extract is an analysis by Mavor of the great Scottish railway strike of 1890, when railway workers on four of the Scottish lines abandoned their respectability and engaged in violent demonstrations. Mavor attempts here to explain the positions and grievances of both the men and the companies.

Perhaps the most serious labour struggle which Scotland has experienced in this generation culminated on December 21, 1890, in a strike of a large number of men, employed chiefly in the traffic departments of the three leading Scottish railway companies.[1] The Immediate consequence was paralysis of the system of internal transport in the industrial districts of Scotland. This paralysis in its acute form lasted merely a few days; but during the six weeks of the strike, only a partial passenger and merchandise service was carried on, while the mineral traffic was almost entirely suspended. The effect upon the industries of Scotland of this arrest of the means of railway communication was prompt and serious. The coal supply, by which the wheels of industry are fed, was curtailed almost to the quantity that could be carted into the towns from neighbouring pits, for stocks were speedily exhausted. Shipbuilding yards, engineering works and factories closed their doors. At one time probably a hundred thousand persons were idle from causes directly or indirectly due to the strike. Some commodities, coals, for example, reached famine prices.[2] Ships were laid up in all the Scottish

1. The North British, the Caledonian, and the Glasgow and South Western Railways. The companies suffered in the order mentioned. The strike on the N.B. Co. ended on the 29th January, 1891, that on the Caledonian on the 31st January, and that on the G. and S. Western on the 31st December, 1890. It is very difficult to form an accurate estimate of the number of men out at any one time, and the number varied during the strike, but the maximum number was probably over 8,600.
2. Coals sold in the streets retail at 9*d*. per cwt. prior to the strike were during its course sold at 1*s*. 6*d*. to 3*s*., and isolated cases occured of higher prices up to even

ports for want of cargo due by rail, and for want of steam coal. Some business was no doubt deferred, much was altogether lost.

The strike was in the making for a long time. Discontent with the conditions of employment had existed on at least two of the lines for years, and had month by month become more acute; representations had repeatedly been made to the companies, both through ordinary departmental channels and through the secretary of the Railway Servants' Association without substantial result, and a feeling had been growing among the men and among those interested in railway administration that a strike had become inevitable. Fatalism, to which masses of people are often prone, prepared the way for the contagion by which the strike-fever spread from centre to centre.

Each side obstinately fought for its own assumed interests, and each appealed for sympathy and support to a different public. One appealed to the traders and the other to the trades. The men could not have held out for six weeks without substantial help from the trades unions. The directors would have collapsed in a few days but for the support and forbearance of the trading community. The hypothesis frequently stated during the course of the strike, that had the men given in their notice in proper form, and then engaged in a strike, the sympathy of the commercial public would have been with them is probably groundless. The working-class public was in sympathy with the men in spite of the breach of contract. The sympathy of the commercial public would probably have been with the companies under any circumstances. The view of the commercial class was that the spirit of the men must be broken, and that whatever concessions might have to be made afterwards, the men must be driven to surrender in order that the concessions might not appear to be the outcome of the strike. It was felt that, at all costs, the working classes must not be allowed to 'taste' power. The view was widely prevalent that the strike was an attempt to carry the labour war into Scotland, that it was one of a series, and that the railway companies should be encouraged to fight the battle of the general body of employers. It was thought that if the demands of the railway men were granted, employees in other industries would make similar demands, and that the New Unionism[3] would break down the

7s. 6d. per cwt. having been paid. For quantities the price rose from 15s. to 40s. per ton.

3. Although Mr. John Burns went to Scotland to render assistance during the later weeks of the strike, there is nothing to show that he or any of the leaders of what is called the New Unionism had anything to do with the promotion of the strike. The dread of the New Unionism was rather an ignorant dread, since the railway servants were not even organised up to the level of the Old Unionism, and had neither knowledge of nor sympathy with the New Unionism. The essential feature of the New Unionism, the concerted action of different trades, was altogether absent from the railway strike. An attempt was made by a section of the carters, it is said spontaneously, to promote a sympathetic strike in their ranks, but it did not succeed. To connect the railway strike save in the most distant way

influence of the commercial classes and assume a share in the control of the industry. The specific causes of the strike, the alleged intolerable length of the hours of labour,[4] the strength of the combination of the men, and their determination to effect a change in their conditions of work were wholly ignored in this view.

The Views and Proceedings of the Railway Boards.—In view of the directors, the men were guilty of breach of contract, and they there-fore refused to treat with them until they surrendered. The companies availed themselves of all the resources which the law allowed them; they evicted strikers from their houses;[5] they arrested funds supplied by the public for the maintenance of the men on strike;[6] they sued hundreds of the men for damages for breach of contract, and instituted proceedings under the Conspiracy Act with the object of proving that in leaving their employment without notice, the men had infringed Section 5 of that Act.[7]

———

The Views and Proceedings of the Men on Strike.—Throughout the controversy prior to the strike, and during the whole of its course, the men insisted that their leading grievance was the excessive amount of overtime, and proposed, with a view to check this, that wages as for time and a quarter should be paid for overtime. The railway managers affected to treat the whole question as one involving a demand for increased wages. The men warmly repudiated this, and there is no

with the recent labour movements in London or elsewhere, were simply to mis-understand it. Even the important gain made by the servants in the North Eastern Railway came only to encourage the men after their resolution to strike. The threatened general strike of railway servants does not seem to have had any serious meaning.

4. The often repeated statement that hours on duty do not mean hours of labour explains nothing. The strike was not made by the porters at sleepy country stations, but by men who alleged that they were suffering severe strain from spells of duty from twelve to eighteen, and even up to thirty hours at a stretch. It is quite obvious that the number of hours of duty must be considered in relation to the strain. The men allege that while this aspect of their work has been so considered as regards some grades of servants, it has not been sufficiently considered as regards others. From three to four hours of duty at a time is regarded as quite enough for express drivers, but in those grades whose work involves relatively less severe strain, it is alleged that there is a total disregard of strain. The men among whom discontent chiefly existed, were goods-drivers. The work of these men requires more skill and involves less strain than that of passenger trains. More skill is required in one case than in the other on account of the use of inferior brake power on goods trains, and less strain is involved owing to the speed being less and hours of actual waiting being longer. The danger of overstraining passenger-drivers is obvious enough to have secured attention to their claims, while the claims of the relatively less highly strained goods-drivers have been neglected. The details of the conditions of railway employment will doubtless be brought out fully in evidence before the Select Committee on the Hours of Railway Servants.

5. The Caledonian Railway Company at Motherwell, 5th January, 1891.

6. The North British Railway Company, see *Scotsman*, 24th January, 1891. Cf. *Scottish Railway Strike.*, p.36.

7. See case tried by Sheriff Buntine, at Stirling, and found 'not proven'. See *Scottish Leader*, 7th January, 1891.

reason to doubt the sincerity of their desire to reduce the number of hours of work, rather than to increase wages. The men again and again, before and during the strike, pleaded for arbitration. but this was consistently refused by the companies.

The Causes of the Strike.—1. As regards the railway companies:—(a) The leading cause of the strike was the mere fact of growth in dimensions without accompanying growth in administrative skill, personnel, and means. Rapidly growing corporations, like rapidly growing organisms of all kinds, pass through periods of delicacy and danger. These periods mark their transition from one place of organization to another, function preceding organization on each plane. The dangers attending sudden expansion necessarily diminish as the corporation grows larger, since under normal circumstances each increment bears a lessening proportion to the whole, and steps become easier from one plane of organization to another. Thus, although a huge corporation like the London and North-Western Railway, for example, is subject to the class of dangers to which bureaucratic governments are liable, it is worth its while to secure an abler body of administrators than a smaller corporation, and, having altogether larger interests, can as a whole secure more adequate administration of details.[1] The Scottish railways, especially the North British Railway, have grown too fast from insignificant into considerable corporations.[2] They are at once too large and not large enough. Their development has been lop-sided. They have, in relation both to their mileage and their vehicles, only about one-half the engine power of the English lines.[3] The rolling-stock and the station accommodation are alleged to be alike inadequate, especially on the North British and on the Caledonian lines. The three railway systems suffered from the strike directly as the rapidity of their expansion in recent years, and inversely as the proportions of plant to work.[4] (b) The second cause as regards the companies was the keenness of the competition, especially between the Caledonian and the North British companies. This competition has manifested itself not so much in reduced rates either for passengers or for goods, as in securing main routes and access to large towns. The practical monopoly of the carrying trade in Fifeshire and the hold upon the North traffic secured by the North British Railway in its Forth and Tay Bridge schemes and connections, rank really among the great exploits of railway tacticians, but they have their evil side for all that. These enterprises were pro-

1. The Scottish railways have, *e.g.*, no separate signal department and no uniform signal system.
2. On the development of the Scottish Railways, see Acworth, *The Railways of Scotland*.
3. It is to be noted, however, that the proportion of single lines to double lines, and lines more than double is in Scotland 9 to 4; in England it is as 5 to 9. See Parly. Paper, C. 6118.
4. See tables in *The Scottish Railway Strike*, pp. 65, 66. The congestion of traffic upon the Scottish railway lines during thesummer of 1890 was notorious.

moted for purely competitive reasons. They may pay future generations of shareholders; at present they can only be maintained by the company at the cost of parsimony in other directions. The extensive schemes securing access to Glasgow, in which the Caledonian Railway have embarked several millions, and the rival schemes now before Parliament involving access to Edinburgh, also mean immense capital expenditure for merely competitive reasons. In consequence of competition, too, trains are run on many routes half empty in order to give a delusively attractive service—delusively attractive because trains start at the same hour from each station, whereas the public convenience would demand that they should be so arranged as to give the maximum number of opportunities for travel.

2. As regards the men:—The lop-sided development of the railway systems described above affected the men (a) by increasing their hours of labour, and, in doing so, breaking in upon their established personal customs;[5] (b) by unskilful arrangement of conditions of work, and want of obvious provisions for comfort of employees;[6] (c) by pettily autocratic treatment of men by unpractical subordinate officials, involving ignorance by departmental heads of the existence of grievances, and consequent accumulation of these grievances, and arbitrary punishment of men for trifling offences. The specific grievances arising out of those conditions were these:—

1. The 'booking' and the 'trip' systems, by which it is alleged the men were paid for a number of hours less than those actually spent on duty.

2. Systematic overtime working.

3. Degradation or dismissal on trifling pretexts of men who presumed to complain on behalf of themselves or their fellows.

The evidence on all of these points offered by the men is abundant but unauthoritative. Although the returns of the companies to the Board of Trade sustain the men's complaints of systematic over-working, only an inquiry like that undertaken by Sir Michael Hicks Beach's Committee can secure full disclosure of the facts.

———

Summary. — The plain statement of the case is, then, that the men were overworked or thought they were, that they left the service, or remained discontented, and that the places of those who did leave were filled by others who had by disposition or custom less inclination to adopt the dignified method customary in the higher grades of labour, viz., withdrawal from irksome employment. Railway employment became less desirable, and less desirable men undertook it. This was the reason for the occurrence of the strike, and for its occurrence without

5. That working men are extremely conservative as regards their personal habits is apt to be ignored by employers. Nearly every strike might be traced to be due to some invasion or attempted invasion of custom. The Indian Mutiny was due to the unwonted greasing of cartridges.

6. As, for example, want of barracks at great centres. Such barracks are universal on the English lines.

notice.

If the theory of the strike advanced above is a sound one, it is quite clear that in the nature of things, the administrators of the Scottish railways must take a rather larger view of their functions than they have hitherto done. If adminstrative skill adequate to deal with rapidly growing organizations is not forthcoming, retribution, which has overtaken the companies once, must overtake them again.

Conclusions

Study of the Scottish railway strike suggests the following:

1. Huge combinations of capital so employed as to involve the administration of great masses of men are liable to the same evils as bureaucratic governments, and are subject to eruptions analogous to revolutions. Large numbers of subordinate officials with nominally limited but really extensive powers in the management of men tend to abuse these. When the combinations are employed in socially necessary functions, this mal-administration results in public crises in which the public must bear the brunt of the loss.

2. The growth of large businesses is attended by periodical friction, owing partly to the want of adaptability of men (manual and administrative workers) to changing conditions, and to want of provision of adequate material resources on capital account during periods of transition.

3. There is not an unlimited number of highly skilled artizans from which efficient workmen may promptly be drawn. The artizan class has come to consist of a great number of strata, skill being specialized highly and even localized on each plane. This gives an increasing amount of power to certain strata of artizans. Thus, the strike of a score or so of signalmen on one part of the N.B. system rendered that part of it useless;[8] traffic upon it was therefore entirely closed during the strike. The widely extended paralysis caused by the strike of at most 9,000 men was a significant and serious circumstance.[9]

4. The increase of comfort, education, political power, and independence of feeling of the upper grades of the artizan class has rendered the dictatorial method of dealing with them customary in the earlier years of the century, and now surviving among railway officials, at once absurd and dangerous.

5. Although the railway strike might be classed among the conflicts between capital and labour, it would be more accurate to describe it as

---

8. The Glasgow City and District Railway (underground), was closed for traffic for five weeks during the strike.

9. The railway companies found it quite impossible promptly to replace the men who had struck by equally efficient servants, not so much because of the possession by the men of an unusually high degree of skill, but because a peculiar kind of skill was required by the nature of the employment. This skill could be acquired but it took time to acquire it. Thus the number of men left 'out' at the termination of the strike was insignificant. The numbers were approximately, Caledonian 300; North British 200; G. and S.-W. 30 of all grades.

a revolt of labourers against inefficient organization of their industry. The charge against the railway companies is not that they have secured enormous gains by overworking their employees; but that having undertaken the function of public carriers, they have exercised this function inefficiently. They have organised their labourers badly, and their labourers have revolted.

6. The full effect of the strike cannot yet be seen, but even so far as may be discerned, it is fairly clear that it indicates that combined action among workmen is by no means ineffective in limiting the hours of labour in certain skilled industries, and that thus from the point of view of the labourer, resort to legislation is not always necessary for this purpose.

Chapter Seven

The Sweating System and Working Women

The mechanization and heavy industrialization that characterized so much of the late Victorian economy was matched in its rapid progress by the growth of the sweated consumer trades, carried on for the most part at home, or in small workshops, by women. Low overheads and even lower limits on wages, made sweating a viable alternative to mechanization. As a means of exploiting labour and achieving high profit margins, it seemed unsurpassed in the ever-expanding labour markets of the major cities and smaller industrial towns. Tailoring, dressmaking, nail and chain making, cabinet making, paper box making, cigar and match making and myriad other consumer trades were all sweated trades organized in complex hierarchies of subcontracting, and requiring extremely long hours of labour at menial and repetitive processes to gain the barest of subsistence.

It was the tailoring and dressmaking trades in London which developed sweating most extensively. The system started on the basis of hand sewing in the late 1830s. But it was the sewing machine that was to greatly extend the system in the later nineteenth century. The sewing machine was, perhaps, the most powerful innovation in the production of consumer goods since the power loom. It made the needle and thread obsolete, but allowed for the great extension of exploitation and sweating in the clothing trades. The large sweatshop and putting-out arrangements increasingly replaced craft seamstresses and tailors' shops. The clothing industry drew on women workers and immigrant labour from central and eastern Europe. Subcontracting and piecework were highly developed. The technical attributes of the sewing machine were also crucial in the transformation of machine processes in other industries. Conceived as a consumer good to be worked in the home, the sewing machine was sturdy and ran smoothly and quietly. It demanded precision manufacture and interchangeable parts, attributes which spread rapidly through other industrial processes.

The expansive labour market drawn upon by the clothing and other sweated trades consisted largely of women, and was swelled by large numbers of immigrants. As sweated work did not require great physical strength and was easily carried on at home, it could be done by women tied to the home by family needs or by social expectations. It was labour 'hidden away', not subject to the Factory Acts, nor later even to the 'Workshop Acts'. It was unskilled, unorganized, degraded and underpaid—labour for women and outcasts. Sweating was one of the many alternatives of the rationalized and sophisticated methods of exploiting labour which had developed through Britain's industrialization. Combined with sexism, it created and has sustained into the twentieth century, some of the cruellest working conditions possible.

49 The Sewing Machine
Alexander Hay, 1880

Alexander Hay here analyses the history of the sewing machine, and its social and economic impact. He demonstrates that though the sewing machine did away with a great deal of exhausting and tedious hand labour, it did not do away by any means with the spread of sweated outwork. In fact, it provided the basis for an immense expansion of subcontracting and piece work in the clothing industry.

The Sewing Machine trade had now been placed on a firm basis, and business went on smoothly. Up to 1854 sales were almost entirely confined to manufacturers, but at this time the Wheeler and Wilson Company first conceived the idea of introducing their machines into households, and for this purpose secured agents throughout England as well as France. The step met with marked success. Other manufacturers adopted the same method. Sales were at first made for cash, but a scarcity of ready money in certain districts caused the inauguration of a credit system by means of notes. This trade was fully pushed, until the people of means were supplied with machines.

The renting system was the next innovation, intended to reach the poorest class of people, who had no property in any shape, and no credit. From this sprang the instalment plan, which has of late years occasioned so much annoyance and loss to the companies, that it is a question whether it has proved profitable to those who have adopted it. This method was usually in the form of a lease, with payment of 5 dols. per month, the company reserving the right of replevin in case of failure to pay the instalments. This plan has been fruitful of abuses. A number of unprincipled second-hand dealers have taken advantage of the system to palm off their wares on the poor people, always retaking the machines, in a summary and brutal way, whenever any of the instalments fell due and were not paid.

Although the instalment plan has its evils, there is no doubt whatever, that it has been of incalculable benefit to the poorer class of working women, whose condition in life it has done much to alleviate. Thousands of girls in our large towns can testify that they directly owe their elevation to happy and comfortable homes from a state of degraded poverty to the liberality of the companies, who trusted valuable Sewing Machines to their hands when they could not get credit for bread. It it noteworthy that while the inventions which supplanted the spinning-wheel and hand-loom were controlled by capitalists, who built enormous factories and monopolised profits, in the case of the Sewing Machine no one has stood between the woman and her work. The net profits were hers.

Under the instalment plan, the competition in the Sewing Machine business has probably been greater than in any other branch of the trade. So great has been the cost of carrying on the business that all, or nearly all, the profits have been absorbed. This has compelled the retail prices to be kept up from sheer necessity.

———

The Sewing Machine is thus quite familiar to all persons nowadays. It was not, however, until the year 1860, when Mr. Thomas's patent rights expired, that the public in England became fully aware that such a Robin Goodfellow was in our land. Mr Thomas kept the instrument entirely in his own hands, granting no licences to others to use the invention, and giving no publicity to the fact of its being in use in his own trade. Some years after Howe received his £250 for that invention, Thomas paid upwards of £2000 to another person for a very simple improvement in its feed apparatus.

Since the patent became open in this country, enterprising American firms possessing patent Sewing Machines have established themselves among us. They were all, as we have seen, founded upon the principle of Howe's original instrument, and paid him a royalty; but they are, by no means all equally valuable as Sewing Machines. The worst, however, is immeasurably superior in its work, and the speed with which it is performed, to the old hand-sewing. Thirty stitches a minute is the average speed a good sempstress makes: a Wheeler and Wilson machine, or one of the Howe machines, will make five hundred in the same time. It is, in fact, to the ordinary hand-sewing what the spinning-jenny was to the spinning-wheel; and it does everything a good needle-woman can do — hem, tuck, gather, braid, and bind, with a celerity and neatness the human hand cannot approach. Manufacturers have for some time been steadily availing themselves of its use in all matters in which the old needle was used, and contrary to all anticipations on the part of the workers, they have, with one or two exceptions, been the means of advancing wages instead of lowering them. In the shoe-making trade, for certain parts of the work, they have entirely superseded the old needle. Almost all machines, with many wonderful modifications, are adapted for what is called waxed-thread work, and nearly all shoe uppers are now sewn by them. A Sole-sewing Machine, patented by Messrs Pearson and Co., of Leeds, in 1879, is coming into general use. All the uppers of shoes and boots are now therefore done by the Sewing Machine, and before long the soles promise to be so. When upper Sewing Machines were first introduced into Northampton, twenty years ago, a thousand men in the trade struck work, and left the town rather than use them. Now, you cannot go near a cottage in the neighbourhood of the town without hearing the click of the machine, and in large factories big rooms are occupied by sewers and cutters out of uppers. In Northampton it is the custom for the workman to buy his own machine, and work at home. This home-work has an admirable effect upon the habits of the people, and a pleasanter picture of labour would not well be found than the interior of one of these Northampton cottages, in which the Sewing Machine finds employment for all the members of the family, even down to the children. One machine is calculated to give employment for four persons, in preparing the work for the final process of sewing. In Stafford, where women's shoes are made, the machine finds work for more hands than could for a long time be found — indeed the cry was everywhere for women to work these machines; and yet, when the agent for Howe's patent went into the market-place, and, in the presence of ten thousand women, sewed before their eyes, as they had never sewn, they were ready to tear him to pieces, and did, in fact, drum him out of the town. If he were to return, he would meet with a very different reception, for not only is there more work than there are hands for, but the pay is far better than of old. In towns, as a rule, it is not so much the fashion to find the workman working his own machine. Large capitalists supply them to their workers in large well-ventilated rooms, as different from Hood's wretched garret as light is from darkness. We inspected on one occasion a factory in which five hundred young girls were employed in shirt-making by these machines, and a greater contrast to the poet's wretched figure, with "fingers weary and worn," could not have been afforded than by these merry bright-cheeked girls. There is a dark side to every picture, however, and we are sorry to find that there is a class of masters in London, and there only, who, totally regardless of this new means of bettering the condition of their needle-women, have adopted measures which defeat its value to them, and tend to grind them to the earth as of old. The great ready-made clothiers, instead of employing women in factories under their own eye, buy machines and let them out to *middlemen*; these again employ women, and deprive them of all the advantages of the invention. This abominable employment of middlemen is only resorted to by three or four well-known firms, but their example will do an enormous amount of damage if they cannot be persuaded to work like other manufacturers.

———

In the beginning of 1878, an ingenious gentleman patented an invention by which electricity was used as a motive power for the purpose before us. It was claimed for the beautiful little engine he produced that it could be put in any place without in any way impairing its usefulness. It might be attached to the smallest Sewing Machine, and do the work of the stoutest feet and limbs, at an insignificant cost. When attached to a Sewing Machine it does not interfere with the treadle or footpower, but enables the operator to make use of either, without his being in any way inconvenienced. The battery can be placed in a cellar, or in any room or position desired, from whence two wires convey the electric current to the motor. By touching the switch the machine may be put in motion, or instantaneously stopped, and the speed regulated at will. But we are not aware that this convenient contrivance has yet found a general acceptance amongst housewives.

This application of electricity does indeed make us think of the Trolls or lubber-dwarfs of Scandinavian folk-lore—the willing and serviceables slaves who, by night and day, did their silent service, and sought no rest or material reward. The figure recalls to us some admirable words of the great and philanthropic Horace Greeley, which we must crave leave to quote:

"Women can no longer be sent to the loom and the wheel, as in days when the garments of the household were woven and spun by the loom and spindle at home, for our spinning-jennies have taken the labour out of their hands years ago. New modes of labour opened with the opening resources of the country. Women found more leisure for mental improvement, with the disuse of the spindle and loom. Still there remained her servitude to the needle; side-stitch, hem, fell, 'seam and gusset, and band,' 'band, and gusset, and seam,' from matins to vespers; wife, maid, and servant; lady and working-woman — all of the feminine class, were to be occupied for ever and for ever, to all eternity in futurity, to gather breadths of linen for a household.

"As a last relief came the Sewing Machine. We saw in it another step in the emancipation of women. We saw that she would be exonerated from much that was monotonous, wearisome, and belittling in her lot. We saw that the machine would save numberless eyes, myriads of nerves, and that households must, through this invention, become more intelligent, more genial, and altogether help a better development in society. The solitary needle will pass into disuse. The Sewing Machine does all that was fatiguing and wearisome in the manufacture of garments, and now women have taken another step towards freedom. It will force the industry of women into a thousand new channels, and emancipate them from the cramped posture and slow starvation of needlework.

"Ultimately, nearly every comfortable household will have its Sewing Machine. There are seamstresses in our city who first borrowed the money to buy one, and now own two or three, having other seamstresses to work those for which their own hands do not suffice. The time is rapidly approaching when at least three-fourths of the sewing in our city will be done by machines. Let us hope that the blessings of the industrial progress which is opening a new era of mankind, will be enjoyed by the many. Woman's brain will soon do its office in the world, as she has opportunities to use it. The thraldom of the needle has been her greatest trial in the civilised society."

———

The working woman will now work fewer hours, and receive greater remuneration. People will have more work done, will dress better, change oftener, and altogether grow better looking, as well as nicer looking. The more work can be done, the cheaper it can be done by means of machinery, *the greater will be the demand*. Men and women will disdain the soupçon of a nice worn garment, and gradually we shall become a nation without spot or blemish.

A word or two more on the great social benefit of the invention or series of inventions. The machine at one blow emancipates the sempstress from the fatiguing position, and the contracted chest, that oppressed her of old. There can be no doubt that the needle killed far more than the sword ever did. And we trust we may hear no more of young girls done to death by the excessive fatigue caused to poor milliners during the London season.

What the committees of the House of Lords have failed to accomplish, the American machine will inevitably bring about. Although human muscles break down under the inhuman stress put upon them, the iron fingers of the Sewing Machine are all-enduring. We are told that whilst a hand-made silk dress occupies eight hours and twenty-seven minutes in making, the machine-made dress only occupies one hour and thirteen minutes; it is true that lace cannot be sewn on by the machine, therefore the trimmings would still have to be sewn by hand. But the main part of the work can now be done in an incredibly short time, and there can be no longer need of poor girls sitting up the whole of the night for six nights in succession in order that "my lady" may flutter for an hour or so in the ball-room.

The cry on every hand is still for more educated labour. All the unemployed sempstresses in London would be engaged in a week if they but thoroughly knew the manner of using the Sewing Machine. Here is an admirable opening for philanthropic persons bent upon ameliorating their hitherto forlorn condition. If a few of those individuals who are going about seeking those to whom they may do good were to hire a large room, obtain the loan of a score of machines — they would be lent gratuitously by the different patentees, we have reason to know — and employ half-a-dozen instructresses in their use for all poor women applying, they would be aiming a great blow at the "social evil", and doing more for the surplus female labour of this country than all that has been done heretofore. Ladies who have themselves acquired a general notion of the working of the machine could impart the knowledge to their poorer sisters. Congregations, we believe, could effect great changes for the better by raising collections or subscriptions to aid a number of struggling needle-women to get a machine of their own. Thousands of women are starving for want of work, on the other hand hundreds of masters are crying out for workers — all that is wanted is the little preliminary education with the machine which neither the poor women nor the masters can afford to give; and this instruction can easily be acquired by active intelligent women in the short period of a week. We have shown how this aid may be afforded, and, we may add that the machines of one of the largest patentees have been offered free of charge, and, we regret to say, declined. The thing is to be done, however, and we only desire to make it widely known, sure that help is at hand.

50 Dressmakers and Tailoresses
Frances Hicks, 1895

This selection depicts the depressing conditions of women clothing workers, their exploitation through sweatshops, piece and home work, and internal competition in the trade. The writer shows that these very factors make unionization difficult, but nevertheless sees this as the only solution.

An apprentice or improver is generally very glad to leave this work and try her hand in the West End. If she has made good use of her time, and applies for work at the right season, that is the end of March or the beginning of April, she can almost certainly get taken on as a season hand at one of the large dressmaking firms in the neighbourhood of Oxford Street, starting with wages of about 8s. per week.

———

This is a time that tests a girl's character very severely. There is a greater amount of a kind of freedom in this life, for, except in the matter of wages, every one is on terms of perfect equality. Individuality is completely lost sight of, and each one becomes part of a collective machine. It is soon discovered for what branch of the work a girl is most adapted. If she has the knack of doing small trimmings she becomes a sleeve hand, while if her fingers are light enough she arranges lace and soft silks so gracefully that they look as if they had fallen from the wand of a fairy. A costume with an immense amount of work in it, must, when all is finished, look as if hands had never touched it.

The fitter of the costumes is the forewoman, and is seldom a woman who has risen from the ranks of the workroom. She belongs often to the class of showroom ladies who have paid a premium to walk about in the front shop exhibiting a good figure and making themselves agreeable. But a West End fitter must have in addition great skill and immeasurable patience. Her salary ranges from two to seven or even eight guineas a week, and raises her far above the level of ordinary dressmakers. The wages of these latter rarely reach one pound, the average for a skilled workwoman being 15s. or 16s. per week. It is, however, impossible to get an average for the year except from an employer's wage-book, and this is not available to me. But even that would only show the wages of the most fortunate few who are kept at work all the year round.

The majority of the workers are simply season hands, and if they begin work at the end of March they will perhaps be kept busy until August. Then, if the firm is large enough to have more than one workroom, each room is closed in turn for a few weeks and all the superfluous workers discharged. They may get a few more weeks' work from October to December, but this is not to be relied upon. What they do until the season begins again cannot be said. I know that some will be able to get enough needlework to do at home to keep themselves, but are obliged to let their rent run into arrears. Some get temporary work at the homes of people with families where they make up school dresses and children's clothes, and do the general repairs of a lady's wardrobe, being paid 2s. or 2s. 6d. a day and their meals. Others, like myself, live with a family who all share the pinch of slack times. But in addition to these, there are a large number unaccounted for, who, from pride or some other cause, are very reticent as to their mode of existence during the winter months.

———

In this description I have endeavoured to generalise the chief features of the main groups into which the trade is divided, and to avoid all extremes and exceptions. The chief things necessary to a successful dress-maker may be summed up as considerable manual skill, and delicate fingers; a good knowledge of fabrics and of what can be done with them; the instinct of an artist to grasp the idea of a costume, and to work out the details without having everything got down in black and white; and a quick perception of, and adaptability to, the frequent changes of style and fashion.

So far I have dealt only with the hand dressmaker. I must now turn to the machinist. This is a very large industry, and in some directions it supplants all varieties of hand needlework. Machinists who work with the best dressmakers are paid daily or weekly wages, which average from 16s. to 24s. per week. They must, however, be exact and quick workers and know their trade and machine well to earn these sums. A false stitch by the machine will irretrievably ruin some of the fine fabrics, and often one might as well be a foot out of line as an eighth of an inch. The heavier machine work, such as cloth mantles and tailoring, when paid for by the day or week, brings in from 18s. to 30s. weekly. This comparatively high wage attracts many to the work, but very few women can stand more than four or five years constant employment in this branch without their health being ruined. A great difference is made if only half the time is spent at the machine and the other half at hand work, and this is often arranged.

Apart from the best work, when garments are entirely, or almost entirely, made by the machine, piecework is the usual method of payment. There are many factories in London and elsewhere for this class of trade. In some of them steam-power is used to drive the machine, and affords a great advantage so far as the health of the worker is concerned. The earnings at this work vary considerably according to the strength of the woman working the machine, and the class of work done. I know one factory where there are two young women who can earn from 18s. to 25s. a week each, at the piecework prices they are paid for the work. But among thirty to forty others employed in the same shop, on similar work, and at the same piecework prices, there is not one who can drive the machine fast enough to earn more than 16s. a week. It seems almost an inevitable law of this kind of work, that the coarsest and heaviest is the worst paid. I am told, that where corduroy trousers are machined and made, many of the women have to leave the work after a short time, stricken with paralysis or other nervous disorders, caused through driving the heavy machines fast enough to earn only 10s. or 12s. weekly.

There are many machinists who prefer to work at home, because they are not then bound by the hours of a factory or workshop. Some factories also have a system of giving out garments by the dozen to a machinist, paying her the whole price of the work when finished. She thus becomes a sort of sub-contractor, paying as many assistants as she can keep employed to prepare and finish off the work. Some of such sub-contractors can keep three or four women at work constantly.

Work of this kind which is given out to be done, either direct from the employers or through such a sub-contractor, is almost always badly paid, and any woman who has to live by it must work long and irregular hours. All kinds of articles, from handkerchiefs and pinafores to greatcoats and horse-cloths, are cut and given out from East End and City warehouses, by employers who are glad to get their work done cheaply, and to save the cost and trouble of workrooms and foremen. Anyone who can work a machine can get this work, a pattern garment to copy from being given out with the first order, and none of the workers know the cheapest price for which it is being done.

—————

Women who work at home as an additional source of income are making it possible for their husbands to accept a lower wage than is necessary to support a family upon, and, in addition, compelling them to seek elsewhere for the comfort and rest they should find at home. I do not know the husband who likes to come home and find work about. Women who are too proud to go out to work should be compelled to live and die upon what their pride could obtain. Gentlewomen, who eke out small private incomes by taking fine needlework at starvation prices, deserve the severest censure, because they compel other women without the small incomes to work and to starve at the same prices. Working in a workshop together they could combine. A living wage could then be made on the basis of pay, and the small income would form an additional comfort.

Those who work in the cheap clothing factories suffer very keenly from the competition of the home workers, whom it is quite impossible to organise for a decent minimum wage. When they have reached so low a level that the smallest comforts, sometimes even the barest necessities, are beyond their reach, wages of any amount, high or low, must ever be their first consideration. Some will say that they prefer to see girls working long irregular hours amongst families, rather than that they should be exposed to the temptations I have described as occurring in dressmakers' shops. But to these I would reply that the temptation is incidental to the class of work, and is increased, rather than diminished, in the smaller workshops, because the employment is more personal and not so mechanical. I am confident that if it were possible to compare the morality of women in workshops with that of women working in homes, those in the workshops would not suffer by the comparison.

The question of what can be done to improve the condition of women workers is a very complex one, and even healthier and improved workshops would not entirely answer it. There are so large a number of girls and women who are only partially dependent on themselves, and who do not expect to make their earnings the sole means of their support. Thoughtlessly they accept just what is offered to them, to the serious injury of the remainder. Education in simple economics is the best remedy for this, though the process is a very slow one, and in the meantime, men are very jealous of allowing women any new openings in other industries. Meanwhile the few in which they have already entered become more and more crowded every day. From the very nature of the difficulties presented voluntary effort on the part of the women is only practical in a very limited degree. The most that can be done is to form Trade Unions in the skilled trades where the workers are not easily replaced. This is being tried, and men, finding that it is impossible to stop the current which has once set in, and that the better way is to direct it in the right channel, are beginning to assist instead of to obstruct the organisation of women.

51 Women in the Cigar Trade in London
Grace Oakeshott, 1900

At the end of the nineteenth century women were increasingly entering trades formerly dominated by men, but these trades had already been degraded, and women were paid at much lower rates than men. Grace Oakeshott describes the inequality of women cigar makers. She ascribes part of their inequality to an inherent lower productivity among women, yet fails to enquire into the social conditions condemning women to worse jobs with few incentives or opportunities for advancement.

The cigar trade was at one time the monopoly of men aided by children whose employment brought the trade within the scope of the enquiry of the first Children's Employment Commission of 1843. The Commissioners reported that the men made the cigars, each journeyman himself employing three or four boys or girls of from 8 to 13 years of age to wait on him. The children's work was to prepare the tobacco for the outside cover of the cigar, to strip the leaves, and fetch the material, and as they grew older they were taught to make the "bunch" or inside of the cigar. The boys, if promising, were after a time apprenticed to the trade. The usual hours were 11 or 12 per day, with one hour deducted for dinner; there was occasional overtime, when the hours were 15 or 16 per day.

This was the state of the industry in 1843, in London and in those towns in the kingdom in which the trade was carried on. By the time of the Commissioners' Second Report, in 1865, women were employed in two important cigar factories in Liverpool; one factory having 200 females over 18 years of age, as compared with 90 males; another employing 90 or 100 girls and women, but no men, with the exception of a foreman to manage them, and a lad to do the heavy work. Mr. Steel, the master of the latter factory, was the first to apprentice girls in 1850, and the fact of his having only women in his employ by 1865 shows with what success his attempt was attended.

As in many other trades, women came in by the back stairs. They were at first used chiefly for the less skilled branches; a small number only were employed in the more skilled work; but in both divisions alike they worked for a lower rate than the men. For a period of 20 years they were an unorganised body. The men had formed a Union in 1835, but it was not until 1887 that a Union for women was established. After its establishment they still continued to undersell men; and the men who at first were hostile to women in the trade, saw that it was hopeless to try to keep them out, and that for their own sakes it would be wiser to amalgamate the Unions. Accordingly, five years ago, men and women joined in the same Union. The question of wages formed the chief difficulty at the time of amalgamation. Union hours were already limited to 50 a week, overtime only being permitted by consent of a board of management; but the difference between men's and women's wages proved a great stumbling block.

To raise the scale of women's wages to the same scale as men's would probably have meant to drive women from the trade and to alienate public sympathy; to leave them at a lower scale would mean to let women continue to undersell men. It was finally decided to take the highest rate of pay for women then existing and make that the basis of the scale of women's wages. Since the amalgamation, women's wages have risen 25 per cent., and it is a recognised policy of the Union to raise the scale still further by making advantageous terms with each employer opening a new factory. But even so, the women's scale is 25 per cent. lower than the men's, and this fact has been of material assistance in helping them to gain a firm foothold in the trade.

———

Other firms, which are not "fair" shops, because they desire to get cheap labour, exploit their employees in either of two ways:—they pay less—in some cases far less—than the Union scale of charges; or they run their factories by means of apprentice labour;—that is to say, they employ two or three journeywomen to a large number of girl apprentices. The journeywomen do the really skilled work, and are paid good wages; the apprentices learn enough to enable them to make an inferior cigar, and before their five years have ended, they have become quick hands. ———

The work of women in cigar factories is chiefly the actual making of cigars. A few, however, are employed in what is called "stripping", which consists in tearing the middle fibre from the tobacco leaf. It is not a very skilled process, and is easily learned in a fortnight. "Strippers" usually earn 12s. or 14s. a week, timework. Others are "Sorters," i.e., they sort the cigars according to shades of colour. For this they are paid by piece-work, and their earnings are about 24s. to 28s. a week. Others again are bundlers or packers, and can earn a weekly wage of 14s.

Most, however, are cigar-makers. Young girls, as soon as they leave school, are apprenticed for a period of 5 years to a manufacturer of cigars. For the first two or three months of their apprenticeship they are known as "runners," — they run errands, weigh out tobacco, and wait on the journeywomen. They then are taught to case or cover the cigar, and this is the most difficult and skilful process in cigar-making.

There are two sorts of cigars made; the machine, or moulded, cigar, and the handmade cigar. The former requires far less skill and length of training than the latter; it is an inferior and cheaper cigar, and allows of inferior work. A connoisseur speaks with the affection of an artist of the handmade cigar, declaring that it requires years of practice to learn to make it well in its various shapes. The difference in manufacture is simply that in mouldwork as soon as the "bunch" is made, it is put into a wooden mould which is shaped like a cigar, and subjected to pressure, thus being forced into its right shape. It is then taken out, and cased with strips of tobacco leaf. In handwork the cigar is made entirely by hand, and to make the "bunch" a perfect shape and to case it firmly and neatly without artificial pressure requires great skill. It is evident that the learning of the two processes might be included in a 5 years' training, and it is to a girl's advantage that she should learn both. A handworker commands a higher wage than a mouldworker, and has besides two strings to her bow. She can turn to mouldwork if handwork should fail her, whereas a mouldworker cannot make a handmade cigar. This two-fold training, however, is not always given. Sometimes a girl does not want to learn handwork; sometimes she is not given the opportunity. As the trade is organised at present women are required more for mouldwork than handwork, and it is therefore, from the employer's point of view, a waste of time to give a girl training in both, when it will be mouldwork only he will want of her; but the training a girl gets depends largely on the kind of factory to which she is apprenticed.

In the first place, women's wages for the same work are 25 per cent. lower than men's according to the scale of wages agreed upon by the masters and the Union, but this does not altogether account for the lower wage. Secondly, they are on the whole less valuable than men. This is partly because they are slower workers. But what makes the women slower, and why are they less valuable in other ways? The answers to these two questions are closely connected. The employer will tell you that women cannot do such good work as men. You point to a case he has mentioned of a woman who does as good work. "Yes," he says, "an isolated case." Pressed for a reason, he will vaguely shake his head. He will admit, that on the face of it, there is nothing ro prevent women from doing the most skilled work, that the trade requires merely the deftness and skill in manipulation which women's fingeis are supposed to possess to a larger degree than men's; and he will even go so far as to say that some women are as good as men, but—and here comes in the bugbear of the employer.

———

The investigator who is interested in the position of women in industry, cannot resist an attempt to forecast the future, and to hazard some guess as to the developments awaiting this trade. Here is a trade which in itself appears to be essentially a woman's trade. It is healthy; the work itself is light, there is no heavy work in the way of lifting or moving; there is no machinery, and the rush and whirr and nervous strain that this involves is thereby avoided; the hours are short and there is no overtime. There is no opposition to women on the part of men; the women belong to the same Union, work in the same shops, and have a foothold in factories where the best work is done: they even undersell men; and since each individual in a factory works entirely by himself, there is nothing to prevent a woman who shows herself capable of it from doing the same work as men. Every year there are fewer boys apprenticed to the trade, while more firms employ women, and others express their desire to do so if their premises admitted of it. At the first glance it seems inevitable that the trade should fall entirely into the hands of women — mouldwork is rapidly so doing — and in Liverpool, where a great deal of mouldwork and very little handwork is done, the whole of the trade appears to have passed into their hands. But even there, where there are no male cigar-makers whose work can be compared to the women's, the same complaint of unpunctuality and "slackness" is made. Insistence on fixed hours and regularity, as in other trades, would no doubt help to overcome this fault; but until women can surmount the obstacles which are in their character and their lives, and can realise the importance of regarding their industry as a career, and applying the whole of their powers to it, it seems probable that there will always be an aristocracy of male workers at the head.

Grace Oakeshott

52 Sufferings of the Lucifer Match-makers
Dr. Wynter, 1870

Dr. Wynter's study of the Lucifer match-makers shows the hazards and diseases many women worked under in match-making, one of the classic factory industries employing women in the East End of London.

Whilst it is difficult to over-estimate the gain to the community, both in temper, trouble, and time, by the invention of that inconsiderable article, the lucifer match, it has of late years come to the knowledge of medical men that this valuable invention has also brought with it a class of disease never before observed, namely, the destruction in many cases of the jawbone of the workers employed in the lucifer-match manufacture. It must be remembered that nearly the whole of the phosphorus produced in the country is used by these match-makers, and that, in the process of melting this material, fumes of phosphoric acid are continually being given off, and that the same exhalations escape in the process of drying the dipped matches. Now, as it is well ascertained that it is the fumes which destroy the bone and cause ill-health among the artisans employed in the manufacture, we can readily understand the sad frequency of this disfiguring disease in the workshops of the match-makers. The affection was observed on the Continent before it attracted the notice of our own medical men, for the reason, probably, that Vienna and Hamburg are great centres of the trade; but the frequency with which cases of this kind came before the surgeons in our hospitals led Mr. Simon to direct a special inquiry into the condition of the English lucifer match-makers, and the report of Dr. Bristowe on the subject is printed in the fifth Report of the Medical Officer of Health. The report goes into the whole process of match-making with great minuteness. The factories in which it is carried on vary in size from that of the largest London maker, who employs 500 hands, and makes 10,000,000 congreve matches and 3,000,000 wax vestas per diem, to the small makers who make no more than between 70 and 100 gross of boxes per week. In the large factories, in consequence of the magnitude on which their operations are conducted, the rooms are so large and well ventilated, and such care is taken to separate those portions of the manufacture in which phosphorus fumes are given off from the workers employed in other departments, that a much smaller per-centage of the artisans are affected than in the smaller shops, where the whole process is carried on by the family in one room, without any precaution being taken to separate the noxious from the innoxious process. The phosphorus fumes affect the jaw by attacking it in some weak and exposed place—a rotten tooth, for instance, gives access to the fume, which speedily kills the periosteum, or investing membrane of the jawbone, and which nourishes and supports it; this destroyed, the bone dies, and in the large majority of cases in this manner a large portion of the jaw, generally the under one, decays and comes away, leaving a frightful deformity in the appearance of the person who is the subject of the disease, and sometimes causing death. It was at first thought by many observers that this necrosis was due to the action of mercury, or to that of a certain disease; but that phosphorus fumes were the real delinquents was proved by Dr. Van Bibra, a German physician, who exposed rabbits to these fumes for a considerable length of time, and the jaw of one of them having been accidentally fractured, just the same disease was set up as we have seen in the human subject. Some of the German Governments, noting the conditions which are likely to lead to the affection, prohibit all persons suffering from decayed teeth from working in these factories; and, indeed, the occupation is considered so dangerous in others that convicts are alone employed in them. Dr. Bristowe records sixty-one cases of this terrible disease that have come under his notice in England, and these, of course, do not give us a complete picture of the ravages this new scourge has committed among the match-makers. An extract from one of these cases, taken at random from those given in the Report, will show very graphically the serious nature of this disease.

Mr. Cooke, a manufacturer of congreves at Nottingham, employed at times twenty hands, and making both bundle and frame dips (matches). He used to mix and dip (the most dangerous processes). About fifteen years ago, having then worked for eight years on his own account as a dipper and mixer, he was attacked with severe pains in his upper teeth (one or two of the back ones were carious). Much swelling and discharge ensued, and at the end of two years he had lost, bit by bit, all of his upper teeth, with their sockets, and portions of the superior maxillary bones reaching up to the nose in front. The roof of the mouth remained. The disease during this time attacked also the lower jaw, and about twelve months later the teeth and alveolar processes of the jaw also came away.

We question if the humane portion of the public would be content to accept the lucifer match, however great the boon, on the condition that its production should cause such horrible suffering, deformity, and disability as this to the poor operative engaged in the manufacture.

But happily there is no necessity whatever for this suffering. As we have shown, the larger factories are tolerably free from the disease; and the cases mainly arise from the small makers, who have neither room nor inclination to attend even to their own health. As the Legislature cannot do away with this class of producers, the only other course left it is to prohibit the use of the common phosphorus altogether, and to substitute in its place amorphous phosphorus. This singular substance is nothing more than common phosphorus subjected for a month or six weeks to a temperature of 500°, which has the effect of entirely altering its nature, and particularly so as to its ignitability; for whilst the common white phosphorus will fire by the slightest friction, and even sometimes spontaneously, the red amorphous phosphorus will not ignite under a temperature of 500°, and, moreover, it gives off no fumes while being manufactured into matches. The application of this modified material has been more than once adopted by match-makers; but, in consequence of the cheaper method of producing matches by the old and dangerous process, it has never been brought into general use. The testimony of Mr. Albright, one of the largest manufacturers of phosphorus in the kingdom, is conclusive on this point. He says—"I am certain, from the countless experiments I have made myself, and from those of others I am acquainted with, that the difficulties which stand in the way of realising this result (the adoption of amorphous phosphorus) would all yield to a determined effort to insure success; and I am convinced, beyond all doubt, that if the use of common phosphorus could be prohibited, the end would be obtained completely in six months, to the satisfaction of the manufacturer and the public advantage." Whilst the Legislature is pausing, however, ere it pronounces the word "prohibition," a private firm has introduced a match which bids fair to supersede the use of the common congreve in all better-class dwellings, and with every person, in fact, who has any care for the artisan. These are the matches patented by Messrs. Bryant and May. These lucifers do not, it is true, settle the question as to the practicability of employing amorphous phosphorus alone in the production of matches; but this material is used in combination with chlorate of potass in a manner which possesses many great advantages. The match itself is charged with chlorate of potass alone, and the box, instead of the old sand-paper, is smeared on one side with amorphous phosphorus. The match is rubbed on this prepared surface, and an instant light is the result. But the match will not light by mere friction; hence the box is as necessary to ignition as the match. The value of this combination before a light can be struck must be manifest. Their general adoption would do away with a large per-centage of fires, which arise from the accidental ignition of common matches. Fire offices are well aware how severe their losses are from this source alone; and, indeed, one office, the Imperial, makes it a condition that the farm labourers on the farm they insure shall not be allowed to carry them loose in their pockets. The mere act of stepping on a congreve is sufficient to set it on fire, and many women have been burnt to death from this cause alone. In addition to these sources of danger from the common match, there is its constant liability to spontaneous combustion, which is very great indeed. The patent matches of Messrs. Bryant and May preclude the possibility of loss from these causes, and they require the deliberate action of a human being to make them strike fire; whilst their production is perfectly free from all danger.

In all probability the great and growing fame of this new match, which obtained a prize at the International Exhibition, will be of itself sufficient to drive the use of the common congreve match out of the field, inasmuch as the manufacturers, not being able to infringe the patent right, will be forced to perfect the manufacture of matches prepared with the amorphous phosphorus. If such a result shall take place, it will be a thousand times better than any intervention on the part of the Legislature. If, however, the small additional expense of the patent match should prevent its universal adoption, we hope the poor matchmaker will be considered worthy of the attention of Government, so that such precautions shall be insisted upon with respect to the process of manufacture as to preclude the possibility of rotting people's jaws, and thus depriving, and to a certain degree disabling, them for life. Public opinion, in the majority of cases, is quite sufficient to deal with the noxious conditions under which so many of our handicrafts are carried on; and in order to call forth its potential force it is only necessary that Government commissioners, such as those we have been referring to, should clearly point out the evil and propose a proper remedy. Assuredly there is no difficulty so stubborn as that which artisans themselves place in the way of those who endeavour to save them, and yet they are easily displaced if determinedly combated. For half a century the dry grinders of Sheffield were not only content to destroy themselves at the average age of twenty-nine years, but they actually declared that early mortality was an advantage to the trade, as it kept up the rate of wages. The mere introduction of a fan to blow away the dust at once removed the cause of a most fatal disease. The introduction of sweeping-machines, again, has abolished the cruelties inflicted upon climbing-boys; and there is scarcely a trade, however unhealthy, that may not be rendered safe by the introduction of proper precautions. To a country like England, swarming with artisans, it is a matter of the first importance that they should not toil under unnecessarily unhealthy conditions; and we trust that in the manufacture of lucifer-matches, as in the dry-steel grinding and in shoddy-grinding, we may speedily see an end put to all unnecessary suffering brought about by sheer ignorance and neglect.

Bibliography of Documents

Amalgamated Society of Engineers
43. 'Notes on the Engineering Trades Lockout', London, 1897-8.
Babbage, Charles
5. *On the Economy of Machinery and Manufactures*, third edition, London, 1835.
Brougham, Henry
10. 'An Address to the Labourers on the Subject of Destroying Machinery', London, 1830.
Burges, George
11. 'Plain Sense and Reason: Letters Addressed to the Present Generation on the Unrestrained Use of Machinery', Norwich, 1831?
Callis, Frederick
31. 'The Cutlery Trade of Sheffield', Harold Cox, ed., *British Industries Under Free Trade*, London, 1903.
Chamber of Commerce, Manchester
2. 'Address on the Export of Machinery', *Sixth Annual Report of the Board of Directors*, Manchester, 1826.
Coal and Coal Mining [Anon.]
36. 'Holing', and 'A Coal-Cutting Machine', London, 1873.
Colley, G. and Thomson, J.
32. 'Testimony on the Sheffield Outrages', *Report to the Trades Union Commissioners on the Sheffield Outrages*, Parliamentary Papers, vol. 32, 1867.
Committee of Machine Makers, Manchester
3. 'Facts and Observations Illustrative of the Evils of the Law which Prohibits the Export of Machinery', Manchester, 1841.
Crory, W. Glenny
25. 'The Paper Trade and Printing', and
38. 'Iron Shipbuilding', *East London Industries*, London, 1876.
Day, John T.
37. 'The Boot and Shoe Trade', Harold Cox, ed., *British Industries Under Free Trade*, London, 1903.
Dodd, George
4. 'Block Machinery', *Dictionary of Manufactures*, London, 1869.
6. 'A Day at a Copper and Lead Factory', *Days at the Factories*, London, 1843.
24. '*The Times* Printing Machine', *Curiosities of Industry*, London, 1858.
28. 'Saw Mills and Wood Working', *Where do we get it and how is it made?* London, 1862.
29. 'Brickmaking', *Dictionary of Manufactures*, London, 1869.
Hay, Alexander
49. 'The Sewing Machine', *Industrial Curiosities*, London, 1880.
Hicks, Frances
50. 'Dressmakers and Tailoresses', F. W. Galton, ed., *Workers and their Industries*, London, 1895.

Hirst, F. W.

44. 'The Policy of the Engineers', *Economic Journal*, 1898.

Oakeshott, Grace

51. 'Women in the Cigar Trade in London', *Economic Journal*, 1900.

Oastler, Richard, and others

12. 'Political Economy versus the Handloom Weavers', Bradford, 1835.

Official Gazette of the Trades Union

14. 'The Well Paid Artizan and the Half Starved Labourer', London, 2 August, 1834.

Owen, Robert

8. 'To the Superintendents of Manufactories', *A New View of Society: or Essays on the Principle of the Formation of Human Character*, 1813.

The Pioneer, Birmingham

16. 'To the Working Builders of Great Britain and Ireland, 28 September, 1833.

17. 'Machinery', 28 September, 1833.

18. 'Science and Labour', 22 February, 1834.

21. 'The Women's Page', 22 March, 1834.

22. 'To the Straw Bonnet Makers', 24 May, 1834.

Price, John

39. 'Testimony on the Shipbuilding Trades', *Royal Commission on Labour*, Parliamentary Papers, 1893-4.

Roll, Eric

1. *An Early Experiment in Industrial Organisation, being a history of the firm of Boulton and Watt*, London, 1930.

Rousiers, Paul de

45. 'The Construction of Machinery Used in Special Trades', *The Labour Question in Great Britain*, trans. F. L. Herbertson, London, 1896.

Samuelson, James

40. 'Displacement of Hand Labour in Wood and Iron Manufactures',

46. 'Displacement of General Labourers by Machinery', and

47. 'Displacement of Hand Labour in Agriculture', *Labour Saving Machinery*, London, 1893.

Swift, J.

42. 'Engineering', F. W. Galton, ed., *Workers and their Industries*, London, 1895.

Taunton, George

30. 'Testimony on the Manchester Outrages', Inquiry into the Manchester Outrages, *Royal Commission on Trade Unions*, Parliamentary Papers, vol. 29, 1867-8.

A Traveller Underground

35. 'Putters and Hewers', *Our Coal and Our Coal Pits*, 1853.

Ure, Andrew

9. *The Philosophy of Manufactures*, London, 1835.

A Working Man

26. 'The Unskilled Labourer', *Working Men and Women*, London, 1879.

Wright, Thomas

27. 'On the Inner and Social Life of the Workshop', *Some Habits and Customs of the Working Classes*, London, 1867.

Wynter, Dr. Andrew

33. 'Special Diseases of Artisans', and

52. 'Sufferings of the Lucifer Matchmakers', *Curiosities of Civilisation*, London, 1870.

Zola, Emile

41. 'Fifine versus the Rivet Making Machine', *L'Assomoir*, (1870), trans. from the French edition, London, 1884.

Hodgskin, Thomas

13. *Popular Political Economy*, London, 1827. The Journeymen Bookbinders.

15. 'Reply of the Journeymen Bookbinders to Remarks on a Memorial Addressed to their Employers on the Effects of a Machine Introduced to Supersede Manual Labour', London, 1831. Lardner, Dr. Dionysius.

23. 'The Workshop of M. Froment', *The Great Exhibition and London 1851*, London, 1852.

Magazine of Useful Knowledge, a Co-operative Miscellany, London.

19. 'Radicals Debate Machinery', 30 October, 1830.

Mavor, James

48. 'The Scottish Railway Strike', *Economic Journal*, 1891.

McCormac, Henry

20. 'On the Best Means of Improving the Moral and Physical Condition of the Working Classes. An Address to the Belfast Mechanics Institute', Belfast, 1830.

Montgomery, James

7. *On the Theory and Practice of Cotton Spinning*, Glasgow, 1836.

Nasmyth, James

34. 'Testimony on Machine Tools and Engineering' *Royal Commission on Trade Unions*, Parliamentary Papers, vol. 29, 1867-8.

ERRATA

Table of Illustrations, Cover source is Oxfordshire County Libraries; p. 72, should be 'Thrashing'; p. 100, should be 'Breaking'.
Contents, Document 4 and page 40, date should be 1869.
Contents, Document 11, page 74 and 244, date confirmed as 1831.
Page 7, line 6, 'Printmaking' should be 'Pinmaking'.
Page 7, line 14, should read 'constituted an exercise'.
Page 14, line 3, should be 'linotype'.
Page 16, note 15, should be 'Parsinnen'.
Page 17, note 17, should by 'Bythall'.
Page 18, line 17, should read 'new standardized'.
Bibliography, Zola, date should be 1876, not 1870.